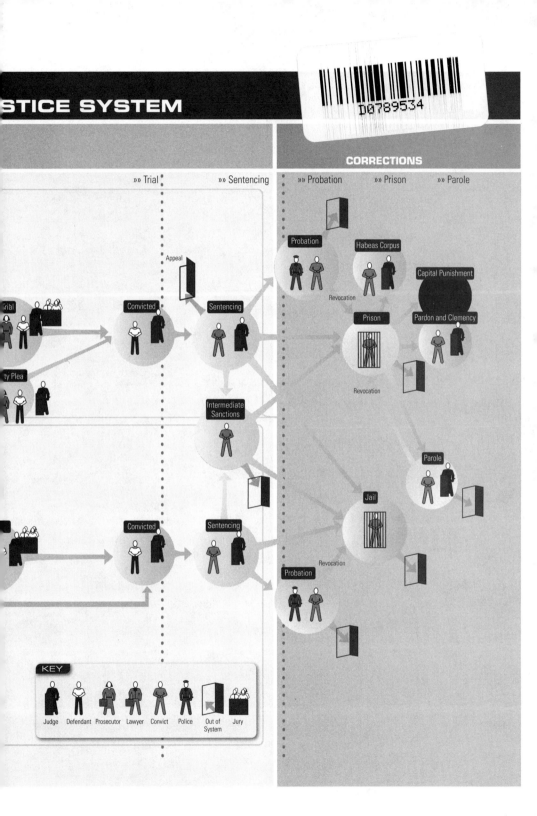

STICE SYSTEM

D0789534

CORRECTIONS

»» Trial »» Sentencing »» Probation »» Prison »» Parole

Appeal

Probation

Habeas Corpus

Capital Punishment

Convicted

Sentencing

Revocation

Prison

Pardon and Clemency

rial

ty Plea

Intermediate
Sanctions

Revocation

Parole

Convicted

Sentencing

Jail

Revocation

Probation

Revocation

CRIMINAL PROCEDURE LAW

Police Issues and the Supreme Court

Frances P. Bernat

Emeritus Faculty
Arizona State University
Tempe, AZ
Chair of the Behavioral Sciences Department
Texas A&M International University
Laredo, TX

Nicholas Godlove, JD

U.S. District Court, District of Alaska
Anchorage, AK

JONES & BARTLETT
LEARNING

World Headquarters
Jones & Bartlett Learning
5 Wall Street
Burlington, MA 01803
978-443-5000
info@jblearning.com
www.jblearning.com

Jones & Bartlett Learning books and products are available through most bookstores and
online booksellers. To contact Jones & Bartlett Learning directly, call 800-832-0034,
fax 978-443-8000, or visit our website, www.jblearning.com.

Substantial discounts on bulk quantities of Jones & Bartlett Learning publications are
available to corporations, professional associations, and other qualified organizations. For
details and specific discount information, contact the special sales department at Jones &
Bartlett Learning via the above contact information or send an email to specialsales@
jblearning.com.

This publication is designed to provide accurate and authoritative information in regard
to the Subject Matter covered. It is sold with the understanding that the publisher is not
engaged in rendering legal, accounting, or other professional service. If legal advice or other
expert assistance is required, the service of a competent professional person should be sought.

Production Credits

Publisher: Cathleen Sether
Acquisitions Editor: Sean Connelly
Editorial Assistant: Caitlin Murphy
Director of Production: Amy Rose
Production Assistant: Alyssa Lawrence
Marketing Manager: Lindsay White
Manufacturing and Inventory Control
   Supervisor: Amy Bacus

Composition: Laserwords Private Limited,
   Chennai, India
Cover Design: Kristin E. Parker
Cover Image: Scales: © Gunnar Pippel/
   ShutterStock, Inc. Handcuffs:
   © AriuszNawrocki/ShutterStock, Inc.
Printing and Binding: Malloy, Inc
Cover Printing: Malloy, Inc

Library of Congress Cataloging-in-Publication Data
Bernat, Frances P.
  Criminal procedure law : police issues and the Supreme Court / Frances P. Bernat, Nicholas
Godlove.
       p. cm.
  Includes index.
  ISBN-13: 978-0-7637-9311-1 (pbk.)
  ISBN-10: 0-7637-9311-6 (pbk.)
1. Criminal procedure—United States. 2. Searches and seizures—United States.
3. Police—United States. I. Godlove, Nicholas. II Title.
  KF9619.B47 2012
  345.73'05—dc23
                                                                    2011026665
6048

Printed in the United States of America
15 14 13 12 11   10 9 8 7 6 5 4 3 2 1

To our families and loved ones.

Contents

Preface

Criminal Procedure Law: Police Issues and the Supreme Court aims to address contemporary issues and the Supreme Court's rulings affecting contemporary police work. This text will be useful to anyone who wants to understand the criminal procedural process, from the initial investigation through the arrest and charging. Every step of the process is important: how an officer handles an initial stop, frisk, and search; the subsequent questioning that will later be scrutinized in court; and the admissibility of evidence depending on how it was gathered by the officers. Because these first steps are magnified and later examined, it is essential to know what the rules are and why they exist.

Criminal procedure and law are changing. Throughout the 20th century, social and technological advancements led the Supreme Court to reexamine and incorporate many elements of the Constitution. As the Court laid down new precedents, law enforcement officers and lawyers across the nation had to learn and adapt to new rules of criminal procedure that directly influenced the outcomes of prosecutions. The rules continue to change.

Legal commentators and scholars have both lauded and decried the Court's activism, but the Court has some constraints it must follow. The Supreme Court is reactive—it can only respond to a live controversy relating to a critical national issue that involves the U.S. Constitution or federal statutes. When delivering a ruling, the Court must give an answer that will help guide criminal justice practitioners. This is the area where the Court comes under fire. Can the Court clearly articulate such procedural rules? Will the Court's ruling need later clarification or adjustment?

This book will explain the Supreme Court's most important cases in early criminal procedural work. Some of the cases are vague; others have been revisited and reinterpreted over time. This book will make the rules clear, explain the Court's rationale, and explore current controversies. It will prepare students and practitioners alike for a career in criminal law, and enable them to stay abreast of its future development.

Acknowledgments

We want to thank Sean Connelly and Caitlin Murphy at Jones & Bartlett Learning for their careful oversight of this text. They have carefully assisted us and helped to strengthen and shape this text. We also want to express great appreciation to Alyssa Lawrence, our production editor at Jones & Bartlett Learning, who coordinated and handled the smooth production of the text. We also wish to thank our copyeditor, Joyce Ippolito, who did a fantastic job of improving our submission and clarifying our thoughts. Any errors that remain are our own.

Thank you to the following people for reviewing the text:

Timothy R. Hart
College of the Sequoias

John R. Michaud
Husson University

Kerry Muehlenbeck
Mesa Community College

W. Jesse Weins
Dakota Wesleyan University

CHAPTER 1

Criminal Trials

KEY POINTS

- Criminal procedure law sets out the process that the courts and criminal justice system actors are to follow when handling criminal matters.

- Among the constitutional rights analyzed in criminal procedure law are those found in the Fourth, Fifth, Sixth, and Fourteenth Amendments.

- The Fourth Amendment provides for protections against unreasonable searches and seizures of persons, their houses, and personal effects.

- The Fifth Amendment provides for protections of due process and the right of a person not be to a witness against himself or herself.

- The Sixth Amendment provides for the right to counsel and a fair trial.

- The Fourteenth Amendment provides for the due process rights of persons against violations by the state.

INTRODUCTION

Criminal procedure is an essential aspect of the processing of a person accused of crime. Understanding the law in contemporary society requires attention to critical cases that have revolutionized police practices. The

U.S. Supreme Court has been continually redefining what the police can and cannot do when investigating crimes and apprehending individuals for their violation. As the new century dawns, it is time to reinvestigate the core Supreme Court cases that emerged over the past century and understand how they affect police and court processes today.

The power of the state to take action against a criminal suspect is to be balanced against the right of the people to be left alone. In order to determine how to balance these seemingly contradictory interests, our legal system gives the judiciary the responsibility of determining whether a police action has exceeded accepted practices. The focus of this book is the legal rules that restrict police action but also provide them with enough latitude to investigate crime and apprehend offenders.

THE CONSTITUTION AND ITS AMENDMENTS

The U.S. Constitution was signed in 1787 by state delegates to the Constitutional Convention, which met in Philadelphia. However, it was not ratified until the following year, when an agreement was reached to amend the document with provisions to protect individual freedoms. These amendments became known as the Bill of Rights. States realized that if a federal government was to function, they had to create one governmental system that could provide oversight on matters pertaining to national interests shared among the states. However, some states were concerned that if the federal government was too powerful, then state powers and individual liberties would be diminished. The Constitution has two main components: its body, which creates the governmental structure with three branches of government, and its amendments, which limit governmental power. The unique characteristics of the Constitution make it appear to be a living document that can respond to changing social, economic, and political issues. In the years since its ratification, the number of amendments has increased from the initial 10 (the Bill of Rights) to 27. Ratified in 1992, the last amendment places limits on congressional pay increases.

Among the amendments of primary interest to this text are those that address law enforcement and criminal procedure law. The Fourth, Fifth, Sixth, and Fourteenth Amendments provide for a variety of individual liberties to be protected from governmental action. Among the most salient features of these amendments are the following protections:

- Fourth Amendment: Provides protection for individuals against governmental intrusions in relation to searches and seizures.

- Fifth Amendment: Provides protection for individuals against self-incrimination during custodial police interrogations.

- Sixth Amendment: Supports individual liberty by providing individuals with the right to counsel.

- Fourteenth Amendment: Provides protection against state governmental actors infringing on an individual's due process rights.

CRIMINAL PROCEDURE

Criminal procedure in the United States is organized around issues of federalism and separation of powers. These issues present unique challenges for understanding and interpreting cases decided by the U.S. Supreme Court. Federalism is the division of responsibility between the federal government and the states. Separation of powers is the division of responsibility among the three branches of government: the executive, the judicial, and the legislative branches.

Federalism

The U.S. Supreme Court is empowered under the U.S. Constitution to decide cases and controversies that arise under it. Until the 20th century and the Court's interpretation of the Fourteenth Amendment, the U.S. Supreme Court's rulings applied only to issues pertaining to the federal government. In the first 10 amendments, the Bill of Rights, our Founding Fathers set out the rights held by individuals that cannot be infringed upon or denied by the federal government. They believed that our governmental structure, as set out in the Constitution, should be one where states have the right to enact and enforce their own laws. Thus, we have a system of *federalism*. Federalism means that we have a vertical system of government: state governments and a superior federal government.

The Founding Fathers initially met in Philadelphia during the Constitutional Convention to revise the Articles of Confederation. When the convention was under way, they realized that entirely separate state systems weakened the national government too much and then set out to create the federal system with powers reserved for the states. Each state that joins the union must have a compatible state constitution, but each state can vary its own laws. The U.S. Constitution forms the centralized form of government that enables the states to function cooperatively. For example, the uniform system of coinage under our constitutional government allows for easy trade between states.

After the Civil War, the Fourteenth Amendment was enacted. This amendment has three provisions:

> No state shall make or enforce any law which shall abridge the privileges or immunities of citizens of the United States; nor shall any state deprive any person of life, liberty, or property, without due process of law; nor deny to any person within its jurisdiction the equal protection of the laws.

Two provisions in this amendment impact state powers: the due process clause and the equal protection clause. Throughout the 20th century, the U.S. Supreme Court heard cases in which state citizens claimed that various state actions infringed on their due process and equal protection rights. In order to determine if the Fourteenth Amendment was violated—that is to say, deprived a person of "life, liberty, or property" without due process—the Court began to selectively incorporate the Bill of Rights. Incorporation means that the Court used the Bill of Rights as a template for understanding individual freedom as juxtaposed against the federal government's powers. On a case-by-case basis, the various interpretations of the Bill of Rights were then applied to state actions; this case-by-case approach is called "selective incorporation." Not all of the first 10 amendments apply to the states. States can, for example, determine if they wish to have a grand jury proceeding (Fifth Amendment) or if persons have a right to have bail if they are detained upon an arrest (Eighth Amendment).

When a state case comes to the U.S. Supreme Court, the appellant (person bringing the appeal) must show that there is a federal question. Most of the time when the U.S. Supreme Court is interpreting the Bill of Rights, the Court's decision applies to both federal and state actors. Due to federalism, however, states can determine that their state constitutions protect individual rights to a greater extent than does the U.S. Constitution. The U.S. Constitution provides a floor; states cannot infringe on a person's basic rights as set out in the Constitution but can provide more rights and liberties. The federal question is usually whether the Fourteenth Amendment and specific Bill of Rights provision (e.g., the privilege against self-incrimination) were violated by the state actor (e.g., the police officer) during some action taken by that state actor. As a matter of simplicity, we say we are looking at the Bill of Rights provision when analyzing a state police officer's conduct in regard to the liberty interest of a person, but in reality we are looking at both the Bill of Rights and the Fourteenth Amendment.

The main provisions of the Bill of Rights that apply to state and federal actors in regard to criminal procedure law are the Fourth, Fifth, Sixth, and Eighth Amendments. The Fourth Amendment focuses on the right of individuals to be free from unreasonable searches and seizures. The Fifth Amendment focuses on the right of an individual to have due process of law and not to be compelled to give incriminating evidence against himself or herself. The Sixth Amendment provides for fair trials and the right to counsel. The Eighth Amendment (which is not the focus of this text) provides for prohibitions against cruel and unusual punishment for persons convicted of crimes.

Separation of Powers

Separation of powers is the division among the branches of government. Each branch is given a particularized function to perform. The executive branch enforces the laws, and this branch includes not only the head of the government (e.g., the president of the United States or the governor of a state) but his or her executive offices. These offices also include law enforcement entities. The legislative branch writes the laws (statutes and codes) that the people are to obey or follow. At both the state and federal levels, the statutory codes form the primary basis for the penal law. The legislature and U.S. Congress write and pass laws that indicate what behaviors will be proscribed (prohibited) and what the punishments for their violation will be. The judicial branch interprets the law and determines if the executive or legislative action has violated the Constitution.

Understanding the role of the branches of government is important because sometimes a case decision is about the proper role of government. The Founding Fathers intended to set up a system of checks and balances so that no one branch would become too powerful. Each branch has a form of responsibility to ensure that the Constitution and, hence, our individual liberties are protected. If laws or executive actions violate the Constitution, then they must be overturned; if the laws or executive actions are within the powers assigned to them by the Constitution, then they will be upheld. Sometimes difficulty arises when one branch of government claims that its actions are constitutional; because it is the role of the Court to interpret the Constitution, it will have the "last word" on the specific matter. However, the last word does not mean that the executive or legislative branch is without any further action or recourse. For example, if a court determines that a statute violates the Constitution, the state or federal agency cannot enforce the law, and the statute is void. If the issue is important to the state, however, the legislature can go back and rewrite the statute to comply with constitutional principles.

INTERPRETING THE CONSTITUTION

The U.S. Supreme Court has the responsibility of interpreting federal law and the federal constitution. Which legal source is more important, statutes or the Constitution? In 1803, in *Marbury v. Madison*, 5 U.S. 137, the Court determined that the Constitution is superior to statutory codes. As part of the Court's legal powers, derived from the U.S. Constitution, the Court is solely responsible for "deciding cases and controversies." In this case, the Court held that any act of Congress that is contrary to the Constitution is void. This ability of a court to overturn legislation is termed the "power of judicial review." The Court also has the power to overturn acts of the executive branch (see *United States v. Nixon*, 418 U.S. 683 [1974]).

MARBURY V. MADISON, 5 U.S. 137 (1803)

Opinion by MARSHALL.

Facts: As one of his last acts in office, President John Adams named 42 persons to be justices of peace and another 16 persons to be justices on a new circuit court. Some of these commissions, though signed by the president, were not delivered prior to the end of Adams's presidency. After

President Thomas Jefferson refused to confer one of these undelivered commissions on Marbury, Marbury filed a suit against Madison in the U.S. Supreme Court. Madison, as secretary of state, was responsible for ensuring delivery of judicial appointments. The suit was based on the Judiciary Act of 1783, which granted the U.S. Supreme Court original jurisdiction to issue writs of mandamus "to any courts appointed, or persons holding office, under the authority of the United States."

Issue: Does the U.S. Supreme Court have the power to review the constitutionality of acts of Congress?

Rationale and Decision: The question, whether an act, repugnant to the constitution, can become the law of the land, is a question deeply interesting to the United States; but, happily, not of an intricacy proportioned to its interest. . . . That the people have an original right to establish, for their future government, such principles as, in their opinion, shall most conduce to their own happiness, is the basis on which the whole American fabric has been erected. The exercise of this original right is a very great exertion; nor can it nor ought it to be frequently repeated. The principles, therefore, so established are deemed fundamental. And as the authority, from which they proceed, is supreme, and can seldom act, they are designed to be permanent.

This original and supreme will organizes the government, and assigns to different departments their respective powers. It may either stop here; or establish certain limits not to be transcended by those departments. The government of the United States is of the latter description. The powers of the legislature are defined and limited; and that those limits may not be mistaken or forgotten, the constitution is written. To what purpose are powers limited, and to what purpose is that limitation committed to writing; if these limits may, at any time, be passed by those intended to be restrained? The distinction between a government with limited and unlimited powers is abolished, if those limits do not confine the persons on whom they are imposed, and if acts prohibited and acts allowed are of equal obligation. It is a proposition too plain to be contested, that the constitution controls any legislative act repugnant to it; or, that the legislature may alter the constitution by an ordinary act.

Between these alternatives there is no middle ground. The constitution is either a superior, paramount law, unchangeable by ordinary means, or it is on a level with ordinary legislative acts, and like other acts, is alterable when the legislature shall please to alter it.

If the former part of the alternative be true, then a legislative act contrary to the constitution is not law: if the latter part be true, then written constitutions are absurd attempts, on the part of the people, to limit a power in its own nature illimitable.

Certainly all those who have framed written constitutions contemplate them as forming the fundamental and paramount law of the nation, and consequently the theory of every such government must be, that an act of the legislature repugnant to the constitution is void.

This theory is essentially attached to a written constitution, and is consequently to be considered by this court as one of the fundamental principles of our society. It is not therefore to be lost sight of in the further consideration of this subject.

If an act of the legislature, repugnant to the constitution, is void, does it, notwithstanding its invalidity, bind the courts and oblige them to give it effect? Or, in other words, though it be not law, does it constitute a rule as operative as if it was a law? This would be to overthrow in fact what was established in theory; and would seem, at first view, an absurdity too gross to be insisted on. It shall, however, receive a more attentive consideration.

It is emphatically the province and duty of the judicial department to say what the law is. Those who apply the rule to particular cases, must of necessity expound and interpret that rule. If two laws conflict with each other, the courts must decide on the operation of each. So if a law be in opposition to the constitution: if both the law and the constitution apply to a particular case, so that the court must either decide that case conformably to the law, disregarding the constitution; or conformably to the constitution, disregarding the law: the court must determine which of these conflicting rules governs the case. This is of the very essence of judicial duty.

If then the courts are to regard the constitution; and the constitution is superior to any ordinary act of the legislature; the constitution, and not such ordinary act, must govern the case to which they both apply. Those then who controvert the principle that the constitution is to be considered, in court, as a paramount law, are reduced to the necessity of maintaining that courts must close their eyes on the constitution, and see only the law. This doctrine would subvert the very foundation of all written constitutions. It would declare that an act, which, according to the principles and theory of our government, is entirely void, is yet, in practice, completely obligatory. It would declare, that if the legislature shall do what is expressly forbidden, such act, notwithstanding the express prohibition, is in reality effectual. It would be giving to the legislature a practical and real omnipotence with the same breath which professes to restrict their powers within narrow limits. It is prescribing limits, and declaring that those limits may be passed at pleasure.

That it thus reduces to nothing what we have deemed the greatest improvement on political institutions—a written constitution, would of itself be sufficient, in America where written constitutions have been viewed with so much reverence, for rejecting the construction. But the peculiar expressions of the constitution of the United States furnish additional arguments in favour of its rejection.

The judicial power of the United States is extended to all cases arising under the constitution. It is also not entirely unworthy of observation, that in declaring what shall be the supreme law of the land, the constitution itself is first mentioned; and not the laws of the United States generally, but those only which shall be made in pursuance of the constitution, have that rank.

Thus, the particular phraseology of the constitution of the United States confirms and strengthens the principle, supposed to be essential to all written constitutions, that a law repugnant to the constitution is void, and that courts, as well as other departments, are bound by that instrument.

The rule must be discharged.

Activism and Restraint

An important part of understanding judicial decision making is the degree to which a court views its role in making or interpreting law. Judicial activism is the willingness of a court to create a new rule or law, and judicial restraint is the unwillingness of a court to create new policy or law. An activist court is willing to interpret the Constitution so that the court has the power to enact a new policy or legal practice without a statutory rule. A restraintist court believes that it must not impose new policy and instead defers to the executive and legislative branches to make policy and law.

Activism and restraint are sometimes viewed interchangeably with liberal and conservative decision making. A liberal outcome is one where a court decides in favor of the accused; a conservative outcome is one where a court decides in favor of the state. But activism and restraint provide a different measure than whether a court is more likely to favor the accused or the state. Activism and restraint are about how the court views its role in regard to making law. Some U.S. Supreme Courts have been liberal and activist, and others have been conservative and activist. The Warren Court, 1953–1969, is viewed as one that issued many liberal decisions and created new laws and is thus both activist and liberal. The Rehnquist Court, 1985–2005, is viewed as one that issued many conservative decisions (favoring the state). Yet it also is viewed as activist because it made new laws or policies by overturning prior established legal practices.

The question is the proper role of the court. Should a court be able to broadly interpret the Constitution beyond its "plain" words? If the legislature is empowered to create law, then some argue that the court should refrain from usurping legislative power by interpreting the Constitution beyond its plain meaning. Activist courts are viewed as ones that take on too much power and, as such, overshadow the proper role of the other branches of government. If the courts have the power of judicial review that enables them to overturn statutes, then what is the check on judicial power when the court creates its own laws? In short, what is to restrain the U.S. Supreme Court from dictating what laws can be written, what laws can be enforced, and what laws will be interpreted in favor of an accused or in favor of the state at any given time?

The short answer to these questions is that our system of federalism does put some checks on the judiciary. The executive branch appoints judges to the federal bench, and judges who do not fulfill their judicial function in accordance with high ethical and legal standards can be impeached. Also, it might be argued that some of the decisions from the Rehnquist Court are a self-correcting measure in response to decisions from the Warren Court. The ability of a court to decide "cases and controversies" enables it to either broadly interpret law or view it as a narrow response to the facts and law as it currently exists.

When the constitutional rights of an accused are juxtaposed against the power of the state to enact laws and enforce them, then the ideals of a democratic state are placed into conflict. How the court handles the juxtaposition, narrowly or broadly, may determine whether the decision will be viewed with disdain or accepted. Sometimes, a court will narrow its decision so as to limit the impact that might occur from its implementation. But if a decision is not clearly articulated, then following the court's ruling can be difficult. In the cases discussed in this text, the U.S. Supreme Court has articulated rulings on criminal procedure law that have either broadened individual liberty or restricted it in such a way as to change police practices. By looking at these decisions in terms of the legal outcome, activism or restraint, liberal or conservative, students will be better able to understand the changing constitutional demands placed upon the police in modern society.

ORGANIZATION OF THE BOOK

This criminal procedure law book will infuse major U.S. Supreme Court cases with an understanding of the contemporary social constraints that underscore the case and its impact on policing, the courts, and individuals accused of crime. The focus of the cases will follow police work from investigations, to stops, to arrests, to interrogations and searches. Each chapter will explain the social context of policing in light of the Fourth, Fifth, and Sixth Amendments. Critical cases will be integrated into the chapters with critical analysis of the dilemmas solved by subsequent court cases. The integration of the cases will resemble briefed cases so that students can readily read the Court's text and understand its impact given the legal issue and facts that gave rise to the litigation. Each chapter will end with a major social issue that remains to be resolved or that shows current trends in criminal procedure law analysis.

Criminal procedure law requires students to understand the constitutional rights of individuals under the Fourth, Fifth, Sixth, and Fourteenth Amendments. These amendments form the primary focus of this book, and the following chapters will discuss main or leading cases that have supported or changed criminal justice processing of the accused prior to trial.

The chapters are organized along the process of a police investigation: stops through preliminary pretrial processes. Each chapter will have a summary of the development of the law pertaining to police processes and end with an examination of a contemporary criminal procedure law issue facing our society.

- Chapter 1 provides a basic overview of the main issues pertaining to contemporary criminal procedure law and the police in the United States.

- Chapter 2 discusses the preliminary investigatory processes when officials either have been informed about a crime or suspect that individuals may be involved in criminal activity.

- Chapter 3 analyzes when officers may legitimately stop someone on the street and ask questions. During these stops, officers may be allowed to frisk an individual, but only if they have reason to suspect that their own safety may be threatened.

- Chapter 4 moves the police investigatory process further along and analyzes the parameters of a lawful arrest, the time period when a person is not free to leave police custody and is charged with a criminal offense.

- Chapter 5 presents one of the most controversial decisions by the U.S. Supreme Court, *Miranda v. Arizona*. Most persons know what their *Miranda* rights are, but do not understand the particular context when the rights must be asserted or what the police must do to prevent their violation.

- Chapter 6 begins the analysis of searches under the Fourth Amendment. Another controversial decision by the U.S. Supreme Court was *Mapp v. Ohio,* in which the Court articulated the exclusionary rule. The exclusionary rule has been the subject of much analysis by commentators. The Court continues to provide answers about the ability of the police to seize evidence and the rights of individuals to their privacy.

- Chapter 7 focuses the discussion of the Fourth Amendment on searches of people, and it also analyzes when the police may search a person and their immediate surroundings.

- Chapter 8 extends the Fourth Amendment discussion to residences and real property and explains when search warrants are required.

- Chapter 9 looks at the ability of the police to search other personal effects of an individual, such as their automobile.

- Chapter 10 completes the criminal justice pretrial process by analyzing other constitutional limitations for pretrial investigations, discussing, among other matters, the right to counsel and lineups.

Briefing Cases

To understand the cases highlighted and discussed in this book, students should know how to "brief" them. Briefing a case is a method for students to summarize the key parts of a court case and is useful when attempting to discern the importance of the legal decision. The main parts of a case brief are: case name, facts, legal issue, decision, rationale, and holding.

Facts

In a short paragraph, indicate what happened. It is important to note critical time periods when events occurred and what people said or did.

It may also be important to note what the lower courts decided. The court decision from the trial court might be different from that of the appellate courts, and the U.S. Supreme Court might be asked to determine whether the trial or appellate court was correct on an issue of U.S. constitutional law.

Legal Issue

In a question format, indicate what the U.S. Supreme Court is to decide. The legal issue is the particular constitutional challenge that the Court must address. For example, "Did the state violate the defendant's constitutional right to counsel under the Sixth and Fourteenth Amendments when the state refused to allow counsel to participate during the pre-indictment lineup?"

Decision

The ultimate conclusion by the Court: affirmed, reversed, remanded. Did the Court affirm the lower court, overturn the lower court, affirm the lower court in part, or overturn it in part? It is important to know what the particular decision of the immediate court below was. If the decision is coming from a state high court or the federal Court of Appeals, then it is that appellate court's decision which the U.S. Supreme Court is affirming or overturning. Some students confuse the decision by thinking that an affirmation is always a decision to uphold a conviction from a trial court; rather, an affirmation to uphold a conviction occurs if the lower appellate court also upheld the trial court's conviction decision. If the Court overturns a decision, the holding might be listed as remanded. In remanded cases, the appellate court has the case returned to it so that it may correct the constitutional errors, or to make further legal determinations. In some cases, this means that the trial court will also have the case returned to it for a retrial, which will correct errors that might have unfairly affected the trial's outcome.

Rationale

A concise summary of the main legal points that the Court used to explain or justify the decision. Understanding the legal principles, precedent, statutory language, and the constitutional law's development that the decision rests upon must be presented. The rationale explains the legal decision.

Holding

The holding is the legal outcome of the case. When affirming or rejecting the decision from the court below, the holding is the statement of law to be followed by subsequent courts. It is important to know what the immediate lower court (e.g., a state high court for the U.S. Court of Appeals) decided in order to understand what the Court is doing when issuing its holding.

SUMMARY

The criminal justice system aims to provide a systematic processing of persons charged with crimes. To determine if the methods employed by the police when investigating crimes and making arrests are acceptable, it is important to consider how the U.S. Supreme Court has interpreted important constitutional rights under the Fourth, Fifth, Sixth, and Fourteenth Amendments.

Some criminal procedure law cases have been controversial because the proper role and function of the Court have been challenged. When the U.S. Supreme Court has been activist, challenges to its legitimacy have been raised. It is not simply whether the Court favored the state action or the accused; it is whether the Court has exceeded its authority by establishing practices not literally authorized by the Constitution.

GLOSSARY

Federalism: the vertical division of power between the states and federal government. Each state and the federal government are empowered to enact and enforce their own laws.

Individual liberty: The right, privilege, or immunity of people to be free from governmental intrusion.

Judicial activism: Describes a court decision that results in the creation of new law or policy.

Judicial restraint: Describes a court decision that refrains from the creation of new law or policy.

Power of judicial review: The power of a court to declare a legislative action or statute or an executive action unconstitutional.

Separation of powers: The division of power among the three branches of government; each branch is empowered to fulfill different functions. The executive branch enforces the law, the judicial branch interprets the law, and the legislative branch creates the law.

ADDITIONAL READINGS

Bahyrch, L. R. (2009). *Legal writing in a nutshell,* 4th ed. St. Paul, MN: West Publishing.

Epps, G. (2006). *Democracy reborn: The Fourteenth Amendment and the fight for equal rights in post–Civil War America.* New York: H. Holt.

Kmiec, K. D. (2004). The origin and current meanings of "judicial activism." *California Law Review, 92,* 1441–1477.

CHAPTER 2

Police Criminal Investigations

KEY POINTS

- Police contact is an important first step in the processing of persons to be charged with a crime.

- The right of privacy is an important right that underscores criminal procedure law processes.

- The Fourteenth Amendment's due process clause selectively incorporates the various provisions of the Bill of Rights and places restrictions on state law enforcement officers.

- If evidence is seized in a manner that violates the Constitution, then it will not be admissible; this is known as the Exclusionary Rule.

- The right of privacy may apply to new areas under a person's control, such as new technological innovations.

THE CRIMINAL JUSTICE PROCESS AND POLICING

The criminal justice process depends heavily on the ability of the police to respond to calls for assistance, investigate crimes, and perform other responsibilities within the bounds of the law. The police system is usually the first point of contact that victims of crime have with the legal system. It is also the first contact that criminal suspects have with the legal system. Whether these points of police contact result in an arrest depends on the quality of information secured, the ability of the police system to connect a suspect to a particular crime, and the legality of the processes the police follow in handling a criminal investigation. Clearly the public perception of how well the police are doing relies on their perceptions of fairness in the system and whether the police are limiting their intrusions in private lives. The public want the police to respond to their needs as victims but not to intrude into their personal affairs and arrest them.

STEPS IN THE CRIMINAL JUSTICE PROCESS

Crime Occurrence

The commission of a crime is the beginning of the criminal justice system's potential involvement. Involvement is "potential" because the crime must be detected. Many crimes are not detected because they are hidden from public view or because a person might not know that they were victimized. For example, thefts are common crimes, and many people will be victims of theft in their lifetimes; however, a person who might have had property stolen might think that he or she simply lost or mislaid the object. When a victim of a crime or a witness to a crime informs the police that a crime has occurred, then the criminal justice process will begin.

Police Investigation

Once a victim or a witness contacts the police to report a crime, a case file can be opened. Usually, the police will respond to the call for assistance and take a report. The report might indicate whether the victim or witness can specifically identify the person who committed the crime, or if there is other identifying information that might lead to an arrest. The longer it has taken a person to realize that a crime occurred and to contact the police, the more difficult it will be to secure an arrest. If the police do not discover a crime in progress, it will be important for them to verify information gleaned from victims and witnesses and perform a further investigation to secure enough evidence to identify offenders, make lawful arrests, secure warrants, and secure evidence that might be used in a criminal trial against an accused.

Police investigations always involve talking with people who may be victims, witnesses, suspects, and criminal defendants. Sometimes the information received from these people can lead to the identity of a suspect, but many times such information does not immediately lead to an arrest. To gather information that could lead to an arrest, officers will engage in further investigation to obtain more evidence. This evidentiary information can be gathered through the use of warrants, interrogations, or warrantless searches of people, places, and things. Evidence is admissible in court against the accused only if the police secured the information appropriately and seized the items lawfully. Lawfulness depends on constitutional boundaries: if the police exceed their constitutional authority and infringe on individual freedom, then the police action is unconstitutional.

The Constitution places limits on the ability of the state to perform criminal investigations. The police are restricted in the ways they may approach suspects, search places and people, and secure evidence of a crime. Police investigative practices require police attention to the rights of the people when interviewing suspects, stopping and searching suspects, stopping and searching automobiles, searching homes and other places, and seizing people or their property. The fact that the police might not have found evidence of a crime or did not have enough evidence to arrest a person does not mean that the police investigation violated a person's rights. It is important to note that while the state has to ensure that police investigations are in line with constitutional rules that limit their power, the Constitution does not require that all investigations result in the arrest and detention of persons who have been the subject of a police investigation. The constitutional principles associated with limits on police practices are designed to ensure that evidence gathered through an investigation will lead to a valid arrest and, preferably, secure a conviction that will be upheld upon any appeals.

Criminal Arrests and the Right to a Fair Trial

If an arrest occurs, the individual is considered to be a criminal defendant who is afforded the right to a fair trial. The burden of proof in a criminal trial is "beyond a reasonable doubt." This burden of proof requires the state attorney (called a "prosecuting attorney" or "district attorney") to bring a quantum of evidence sufficient to show reason to believe that a crime was committed and the defendant committed it. This quantum of evidence is quite high because if the defendant is convicted, then the person's individual life, liberty, or property can be taken; a state may impose capital punishment for selected offenses, impose a term of imprisonment in a jail or prison facility, and have property seized through the imposition of fines or other approved sanctions. It is often difficult to define the reasonable doubt standard, but it helps to say that the trier of fact in a criminal trial should have no reason to disbelieve that the defendant committed the crime charged. The judge is the trier of fact in a non jury trial, and of course, the jury is the decider of fact in a jury trial.

As part of a defense to the charges, criminal defendants may make complaints about police practices that led to their arrest or the seizure of their property. Such complaints are usually tied to the level of intrusion that the arresting officer had with the defendant prior to the arrest. Defendants may allege that the police action was too aggressive or intrusive into the person's life, space, or activities. Such allegations will require the courts to review the police behavior to determine if the defendant's constitutional rights were violated. The court review may occur prior to or during trial, or upon an appeal should the defendant be convicted. A violation of a person's rights by the police could lead a court to limit the admissibility of evidence, prevent the admission of evidence, or even toss out criminal charges against an accused and overturn verdicts of guilt. Thus, the ability of the state to secure convictions can and often does depend on the appropriateness of police action that leads to arrests and the seizure of evidence. The onus is on the state to secure evidence and make arrests in accordance with constitutional principles.

NEED TO UNDERSTAND CRIMINAL PROCEDURE LAW

The law of criminal procedure provides both federal and state law enforcement actors with legal principles and procedural rules that need to be adhered to when processing criminal cases. The primary principles are found in the Bill of Rights, which was intended to place limits on federal governmental actors, and the Fourteenth Amendment, which was enacted to place limits on state governmental actors. U.S. Supreme Court decisions on criminal procedure law and police practice provide the basic foundation of rights that cannot be violated by state or federal police in their criminal investigations and apprehension of suspects.

To understand the myriad rules pertaining to arrests, and searches and seizures, the police must be informed about the latest criminal procedure cases decided by the U.S. Supreme Court and adhere to them. As a pragmatic matter, police departments use their understanding of criminal procedure law to develop internal police policies to ensure uniformity in their investigations and arrest practices. A critical consideration about a police investigative technique is whether the state infringed upon the rights of privacy of the citizen who was being investigated. The right of privacy is so paramount to the understanding of police practices that it underscores the basic principles that guide any understanding of contemporary criminal procedure law.

The Right of Privacy

Nowhere in the Constitution or its amendments is the "right of privacy" explicitly mentioned. Rather, the U.S. Supreme Court has determined in various cases that the right of privacy is a fundamental right. Fundamental rights are those that exist because people are individuals "endowed by our creator with certain inalienable rights." Inalienable rights can be neither given nor taken away by the government because the Constitution empowers the government to act in the interests of the people, but the people are not limited by it. Privacy rights are found within the meanings of various amendments, including those pertaining to criminal procedure law concerns (e.g., the Fourth, Fifth, Sixth, Eighth, and Fourteenth Amendments). For the purposes of understanding how the right of privacy pertains to police investigations, the remainder of this chapter will look at how and why there are limits on police intrusion into a person's life so as to protect the individual's right of privacy from state action.

The Fourth Amendment and the Right of Privacy

The Fourth Amendment was ratified on December 15, 1791, and is based upon the idea that any governmental official (e.g., the police) should not enter a peroson's home, search one's personal items, or search and seize a person without probable cause. During colonial times, agents of the Crown could enter a person's home and seize people and their property with a general warrant or general writ, also known as a writ of assistance. The general writ afforded the Crown broad powers to intrude into people's lives to investigate alleged acts of defiance. The Fourth Amendment sought to limit the power of the government to enter private homes and intrude into the private lives of people. It is generally assumed that the Fourth Amendment protects a person's right of privacy since the amendment states (emphasis added):

> *The right of the people to be secure in their persons, houses, papers, and effects, against unreasonable searches and seizures, shall not be violated,* and no warrants shall issue, but upon probable cause, supported by oath or affirmation, and particularly describing the place to be searched, and the persons or things to be seized.

However, as noted above, the right of privacy is not explicit in the Fourth Amendment. In U.S. Supreme Court decisions, the Court has held that the right of privacy is a fundamental right that is implicit within the meaning of various amendments, including the Fourth, to protect people, their homes, and their personal effects.

Selective Incorporation of the Bill of Rights

Many contemporary criminal procedure law cases that are heard by the U.S. Supreme Court arise in state courts, so it is important to understand how the Fourteenth Amendment places limits on state powers. The Fourteenth Amendment provides that:

> No State shall . . . deprive any person of life, liberty, or property, without due process of law.

To understand the meaning of the Fourteenth Amendment, the U.S. Supreme Court in the 20th century began to look at the Bill of Rights. On a case-by-case basis, the Court selectively incorporated (applied) the established principles that protected fundamental rights in the Bill of Rights and applied these principles to the meaning of due process found in the Fourteenth Amendment. Most provisions in the Bill of Rights were thus selected, one by one, to apply to state actors. The net effect of selective incorporation of the Bill of Rights is that both state and federal law enforcement actors must not violate individual rights protected by the federal constitution. Among the few provisions that have *not* have been selectively incorporated are the right to have a grand jury proceeding (Fifth Amendment) and the right not to have excessive bail imposed (Eighth Amendment). Almost every other provision in the first 10 amendments has been applied to the states. As a matter of discussion, it is not uncommon to talk about Fourth Amendment or Fifth Amendment police practices when discussing limits on state and local police rather than saying that the Fourteenth Amendment protects a particular right. In this way, when criminal procedure law cases are discussed in light of state or federal police powers, the Bill of Rights provisions and their meanings are usually presented. Of importance here, the Fourteenth Amendment's due process clause and the various Bill of Rights provisions are treated synonymously and provide the basic limits on both state and federal police investigations and criminal justice processes. These limits are a "floor," or the bare minimum that the government must abide by in protecting individual freedoms.

AMENDMENT	Bill of Rights Provisions that Apply to the States
First Amendment	Establishment of Religion
	Exercise of Religion
	Freedom of Speech
	Freedom of Press
	Freedom of Assembly
Second Amendment	Right to Bear Arms
Third Amendment	Right Against Quartering of Soldiers
Fourth Amendment	Right Against Unreasonable Searches and Seizures
	Warrant Requirement for Searches and Seizures
Fifth Amendment	Privilege Against Self-Incrimination
	Protection Against Double Jeopardy
	Protection Against the Taking of Property Without Just Compensation
Sixth Amendment	Right to a Speedy Trial
	Right to a Public Trial
	Right to an Impartial Jury of One's Peers
	Right to Confront Witnesses
	Right to Compulsory Process
	Right to Counsel
Seventh Amendment	Right to Trial in a Civil Law Case
Eighth Amendment	Protection Against Cruel and Unusual Punishments
	Prohibition Against Excessive Bail and Fines

FIGURE 2-1   Fourteenth Amendment and Selective Incorporation.

The Third Amendment has been incorporated in some jurisdictions and the re-examination clause of the Seventh Amendment has been incorporated by the Supreme Court.

While the U.S. Supreme Court's decisions interpreting constitutional amendments provide a floor for individual protections, states can choose to provide greater protections to their citizens. State supreme courts have the ability to interpret their own constitutions as placing more limitations on their state actors than would be required under the U.S. Constitution. States cannot fall below the level of constitutional protections afforded by the U.S. Constitution—as members of the union, the states have agreed to abide by the U.S. Constitution and provide the same protections for individual liberty as determined by the U.S. Supreme Court. Because of our system of federalism, states can determine that their state citizens have enhanced protections that might not be found at the federal level.

For example, in 1975, the Alaska State Supreme Court was asked to determine whether a person could possess marijuana in one's home. In other states, both private and public possession of marijuana is a crime, and privacy protections are not afforded within the meaning of the Fourth Amendment. The Alaska Supreme Court, in *Ravin v. State*, 537 P.2d 494 (Alaska, 1975), held that the state's constitution protects the right of privacy within a person's home so that adults could possess and consume marijuana in an individual and noncommercial capacity. The Court was careful not to infringe on the power of the state to criminalize marijuana use or possession generally. In order to prevent private marijuana possession, Alaskan voters attempted to recriminalize private possession in 1990 by a referendum vote. The Alaska Supreme Court upheld an appeals court decision that held that the state constitutional right of privacy could not be overturned by a referendum. State constitutions, like the federal constitution, are more supreme than statutory laws or public referendum processes because constitutions create the governmental system and can be modified only through constitutional amendment processes.

RAVIN V. STATE, 537 P.2D 494 (ALASKA, 1975)

Opinion by RABINOWITZ.

Facts: Ravin was arrested and charged with violating a state law that prohibited individuals from manufacturing, possessing, controlling, selling, and distributing controlled substances. Ravin was arrested when he was found to be in possession of marijuana in his home. The constitutionality of Alaska's statute was challenged under a claim by the defendant that he had a constitutional right of privacy.

Issue: Does the state constitution protect an adult individual's right of privacy to possess marijuana in one's home?

Rationale and Decision: For in our view, the right to privacy amendment to the Alaska Constitution cannot be read so as to make the possession or ingestion of marijuana itself a fundamental right. . . . In Alaska we have also recognized the distinctive nature of the home as a place where the individual's privacy receives special protection. This court has consistently recognized that the home is constitutionally protected from unreasonable searches and seizures, *reasoning that the home itself retains a protected status under the Fourth Amendment and Alaska's constitution distinct from that of the occupant's person.* The privacy amendment to the Alaska Constitution was intended to give recognition and protection to the home. Such a reading is consonant with the character of life in Alaska. Our territory and now state has traditionally been the home of people who prize their individuality and who have chosen to settle or to continue living here in order to achieve a measure of control over their own lifestyles which is now virtually unattainable in many of our sister states.

The state has a legitimate concern with avoiding the spread of marijuana use to adolescents who may not be equipped with the maturity to handle the experience prudently, as well as a legitimate concern with the problem of driving under the influence of marijuana. Yet these interests are insufficient to justify intrusions into the rights of adults in the privacy of their own homes. Further, neither the federal or Alaska constitution affords protection for the buying or selling of marijuana, nor absolute protection for its use or possession in public. Possession at home of amounts of marijuana indicative of intent to sell rather than possession for personal use is likewise unprotected.

The record does not disclose any facts as to the situs of Ravin's arrest and his alleged circumstances, we hold that the matter must be remanded to the district court for the purpose of developing the facts concerning Ravin's arrest and circumstances of his possession of marijuana. Once this is accomplished, the district court is to consider Ravin's motion to dismiss in conformity with this opinion.

Remanded for further proceedings consistent with this opinion.

PRIVACY RIGHTS AND PEOPLE, PLACES, AND THINGS

People's individual rights might apply to their bodies (themselves) and/or to their homes, to other places where they are located, and to their things. The difficulty that the police have when investigating crimes is how a person's privacy rights are to be protected when the officers are utilizing new forms of police investigative techniques. Technological advances enable the police to intrude into the lives of individuals seemingly unobtrusively. The question that the U.S. Supreme Court may have to decide is whether the Constitution supports or limits the intrusion. Among the issues that arise is whether police intrusion into the electronic communications of citizens is constitutional.

Use of Telecommunications and Other Electronic Devises

In *Katz v. United States,* 389 U.S. 347 (1967), the U.S. Supreme Court was asked to determine whether the right of privacy extended to a conversation that Katz had in a public telephone booth. Officers had a suspicion that Katz was using a public booth to engage in interstate gambling. The officers decided to place a listening device on the exterior of the booth in order to record Katz's side of the conversation. Based on these recordings, Katz was charged with and then convicted of violating 18 U.S.C.

§1084, transmitting gambling information across state lines. Justice Potter Stewart, writing for the majority, overturned the conviction because it violated the Fourth Amendment. At issue was whether a warrantless wiretap violated the Fourth Amendment's reasonableness requirement. Specifically, the Court addressed whether the police had to physically enter or intrude into the physical space of the phone booth to violate the Fourth Amendment, or whether it was enough that the police tapped private conversations without a warrant to violate the amendment. The Court held that the wiretap violated the Fourth Amendment.

KATZ V. UNITED STATES, 389 U.S. 347 (1967)

Opinion by STEWART.

Facts: Defendant Katz was charged with transporting illegal gambling information to other states by use of a telephone. Believing that Katz was using a particular public telephone booth, Federal Bureau of Investigation (FBI) agents set up a wiretap of the booth that Katz used. During his conversations, Katz would close the door of the booth. Through use of wiretaps, however, the FBI agents were able to hear his conversations. The officers did not actually enter the telephone booth when they listened in on the tapped phone. The court of appeals affirmed the conviction after finding that the entry into the phone booth did not violate the Fourth Amendment.

Issues: The Court addressed two issues: "A. Whether a public telephone booth is a constitutionally protected area so that evidence obtained by attaching an electronic listening recording device to the top of such a booth is obtained in violation of the right to privacy of the user of the booth" and "B. Whether physical penetration of a constitutionally protected area is necessary before a search and seizure can be said to be violative of the Fourth Amendment to the United States Constitution."

Rationale and Decision: [The Fourth] Amendment protects individual privacy against certain kinds of governmental intrusion, but its protections go further, and often have nothing to do with privacy at all, other provisions of the Constitution protect personal privacy from other forms of governmental invasion. But the protection of a person's *general* right to privacy—his right to be let alone by other people—is, like the protection of his property and of his very life, left largely to the law of the individual States.

Because of the misleading way the issues have been formulated, the parties have attached great significance to the characterization of the telephone booth from which the petitioner placed his calls. . . . For the Fourth Amendment protects people, not places. What a person knowingly exposes to the public, even in his own home or office, is not a subject of Fourth Amendment protection. But what he seeks to preserve as private, even in an area accessible to the public, may be constitutionally protected.

The Government stresses the fact that the telephone booth from which the petitioner made his calls was constructed partly of glass, so that he was as visible after he entered it as he would have been if he had remained outside. But what he sought to exclude when he entered the booth was not the intruding eye—it was the uninvited ear. He did not shed his right to do so simply because he made his calls from a place where he might be seen. No less than an individual in a business office, in a friend's apartment, or in a taxicab, a person in a telephone booth may rely upon the protection of the Fourth Amendment. One who occupies it, shuts the door behind him, and pays the toll that permits him to place a call is surely entitled to assume that the words he utters into the mouthpiece will not be broadcast to the world. To read the Constitution more narrowly is to ignore the vital role that the public telephone has come to play in private communication. . . . Once this much is acknowledged, and once it is recognized that the Fourth Amendment protects people—and not simply "areas"— against unreasonable searches and seizures, it becomes clear that the reach of that Amendment cannot turn upon the presence or absence of a physical intrusion into any given enclosure.

We conclude that . . . [t]he Government's activities in electronically listening to and recording the petitioner's words violated the privacy upon which he justifiably relied while using the telephone booth, and thus constituted a "search and seizure" within the meaning of the Fourth Amendment. The fact that the electronic device employed to achieve that end did not happen to penetrate the wall of the booth can have no constitutional significance.

It is apparent that the agents in this case acted with restraint. Yet the inescapable fact is that this restraint was imposed by the agents themselves, not by a judicial officer. They were not required, before commencing the search, to present their estimate of probable cause for detached scrutiny by a neutral magistrate. They were not compelled, during the conduct of the search itself, to observe precise limits established in advance by a specific court order. Nor were they directed, after the search had been completed, to notify the authorizing magistrate in detail of all that had been seized. In the absence of such safeguards, this Court has never sustained a search upon the sole ground that officers reasonably expected to find evidence of a particular crime and voluntarily confined their activities to the least intrusive means consistent with that end.

. . . These considerations do not vanish when the search in question is transferred from the setting of a home, an office, or a hotel room to that of a telephone booth. Wherever a man may be, he is entitled to know that he will remain free from unreasonable searches and seizures. The government agents here ignored "the procedure of antecedent justification . . . that is central to the Fourth Amendment," a procedure that we hold to be a constitutional precondition of the kind of electronic surveillance involved in this case. Because the surveillance here failed to meet that condition, and because it led to the petitioner's conviction, the judgment must be reversed.

The *Katz* decision is known for the ruling that the Fourth Amendment protects people and not places. In a concurrence by Justice John M. Harlan, the idea that the amendment provides a "reasonable expectation of privacy" was raised. It is the reasonable belief that people will not be subjected to intrusions by the government/police. Justice Harlan, in his concurring opinion, set out a two-part test for determining the reasonableness of a search. In agreeing with the majority that the Fourth Amendment protects "people and not places," Justice Harlan stated that "there is a twofold requirement, first that a person have exhibited an actual (subjective) expectation of privacy and, second, that the expectation be one that society is prepared to recognize as 'reasonable.'" Thus, because Katz had entered a booth, closed the door, and expected to have a private conversation, the Fourth Amendment applied to his conversations. Although the booth is located in a public place, Katz had a reason to expect that his conversation was not overheard and intruded upon by the state.

The lone dissent by Justice Hugo Black is based on his view of the Court's role vis-à-vis separation of powers and federalism. Justice Black argued, "If I could agree with the Court that eavesdropping carried on by electronic means (equivalent to wiretapping) constitutes a 'search' or 'seizure,' I would be happy to join the Court's opinion. . . . My basic objection is two-fold: (1) I do not believe that the words of the Amendment will bear the meaning given them by today's decision, and (2) I do not believe that it is the proper role of this Court to rewrite the Amendment in order 'to bring it into harmony with the times,' and thus reach a result that many people believe to be desirable." He argued that the amendment did not protect personal privacy and that the wiretap is akin to the police overhearing a conversation by other eavesdropping methods known to the Founding Fathers, thus the use of modern devices to listen into criminal conversations should be allowed.

The extent to which *Katz*'s holding applies in other contexts needs more attention. In 1979, the U.S. Supreme Court in *Smith v. Maryland*, 442 U.S. 735 (1979), held that bank customers do not have an expectation of privacy for their bank statements. In response, Congress passed legislation to require the state (police) to secure a search warrant before a bank could procure a customer's statements or account. Additionally, perhaps in the post–9/11 age, a person's right of privacy might need to bend for national security purposes.

CONTEMPORARY ISSUES: STATE ACCESS TO COMPUTER ACCOUNTS, CELL PHONES, AND TEXT MESSAGES

Justice Black's admonitions are still of concern today as the question of privacy in other scenarios involving new technologies arises. Are modern technological devices used in the daily lives of people going about their ordinary business subject to police scrutiny? Should the police forgo judicial oversight so that they can detect people engaged in the commission of crimes that reach across physical space into cyberspace? In a modern technological world in which electronic communications are easily breached without an individual knowing that he or she is being observed by officers looking for criminal activities, concerns arise about when and how a state can gain access to electronic files and communications that are intended to be kept private. The USA PATRIOT Act of 2001 (commonly known as the Patriot Act) allows federal law enforcement officers to search Internet sites and use electronic search engines to detect crime.

In today's society, people use cell phones and computers regularly. Newer communication devices allow persons to communicate via text, Skype, and Web logs (blogs) and conduct private business via electronic scans and transfers. These technological advances allow persons to call and respond to personal and business messages instantly, to organize their lives, and to actively engage in the world around them. The ability of the police to intrude into a person's life by accessing his or her cell phone calls, text messages, computer files, and email is still to be decided by the U.S. Supreme Court. It is unclear if a cell phone seized at the time a person is arrested can be searched later or without a warrant (see http://www.policelink.com/training/articles/4921-cellular-phones-digital-devices-and-search-incident-to-arrest and http://news-briefs.ew.com/2009/07/28/police-search-home-of-michael-jacksons-doctor/). The Patriot Act enables the police to quickly look at or scan a person's electronic transmissions to look for criminal activities such as terrorism, organized crime, drug smuggling, and other types of domestic and international crime activities. The ability of the federal (or state) police to access various electronic sites that save or store an individual's communications or property will require the Court to determine whether people have an expectation of privacy in their communications that will prohibit governmental intrusion. The allowance for federal authorities to take a quick look at a file before closing it might be enough to justify limited intrusions. If some evidence of a crime is detected, then the officers will most likely need to get a warrant to complete their investigations and secure evidence that will lead to arrests. If the data is extracted without a warrant due to the government's need to act quickly to respond to a public danger (terrorist threats, human trafficking, or child sex predators), then the legality of the governmental action might depend on the reasonableness of governmental action in light of the magnitude of the threat to which they are responding. At some point, the U.S. Supreme Court will need to more fully explore the rights of privacy that individuals have with new communications and digital technology.

SUMMARY

The Constitution provides for the protection of people and their homes and possessions through constitutional amendments. The Bill of Rights consists of amendments to the Constitution that underscore an essential constitutional value that inherent rights must be protected against federal governmental intrusions. This essential value is the right of privacy and exists within many of the amendments' provisions. The extension of these essential rights is made applicable to the states through selective incorporation of the Fourteenth Amendment. Mere innuendo or suspicion will not be enough to justify state action that infringes upon the fundamental rights of an individual. Criminal justice processes are evaluated against the inherent right of privacy individuals have; if the right is violated, then the state action is invalid. With new communications and digital technologies, how the right of privacy might limit or nullify governmental actions remains to be decided.

GLOSSARY

Arrest warrant: A written order issued only on probable cause and signed by a magistrate that directs a law enforcement officer to arrest the person named in the paper and who is accused of committing an offense.

Individual liberty: The right, privilege, or immunity bestowed upon a person that is safeguarded against abridgement.

Right of privacy: The right of a person to be left alone or free from unwarranted intrusion into his or her life or personal effects.

Search (and seizure) warrant: A written order issued and signed by a magistrate that directs a police or peace officer to search a place particularly named in the paper and to seize items associated with an offense.

Selective incorporation: The application of select provisions of the Bill of Rights to the states through the Fourteenth Amendment.

ADDITIONAL READINGS

Ackerman, M. S., Cranor, L. F., & Reagle, J. (1999). Privacy in e-commerce: Examining user scenarios and privacy preferences. *Proceedings of the 1st ACM Conference on Electronic Commerce,* 1–8.

LaFave, W. R. (1986). The forgotten motto of obesta principiis in Fourth Amendment jurisprudence. *Arizona Law Review, 28*, 291–310.

Stops and Frisks

KEY POINTS

- The standard of reasonable suspicion must be met in order for a state actor to lawfully stop someone.

- The amount of time for a police stop depends on the circumstances of each case but should be reasonably "short."

- Stops of automobiles follow the reasonable suspicion rules for the stops of individuals.

- A lawful stop does not automatically enable the state to frisk a person; an officer must have reasonable suspicion that the person stopped might have a weapon.

- A frisk is the pat-down of the outer clothing of a lawfully stopped person for weapons.

THE RIGHT OF PRIVACY AND POLICE STOPS

Criminal procedure law distinguishes between stops and arrests. A police stop is a detention for a limited time, while an arrest deprives a person of his or her liberty. During police investigations, the police may need to detain someone for a short time to ask questions in order to determine if a crime occurred or if a person committed a crime. Understanding if a person has a right of privacy during a police stop is important. Do individuals have a right of privacy during a police stop? If so, can the police engage in other "intrusive" actions during a stop?

According to the U.S. Supreme Court, the right of privacy requires that magistrates determine that probable cause exists. The probable cause standard within the Fourth Amendment is associated with arrests and searches and seizures of homes and property. In *Mallory v. United States,* 354 U.S. 449 (1957), the Court clearly stated that an arrest is valid only if probable cause exists; suspicion does not justify an arrest. The Court in *Johnson v. United States,* 333 U.S. 10 (1948), held that a police officer cannot gain entry into a person's home under the color of his or her office in order to place a person under arrest just to perform a search for drugs. In *Johnson,* an informant and a hotel manager told the police that they could smell opiates from a particular room. Without a warrant, the police entered the room, placed the occupant under arrest, searched the room, and seized opiates and other drug paraphernalia. Without exigency or a particular reason for not securing a warrant, the arrest and subsequent search violated the Fourth Amendment. The Court was concerned that the officer entered a private dwelling without proper judicial oversight. The Court stated, "When the right of privacy must reasonably yield to the right of search is, as a rule, to be decided by a judicial officer, not by a policeman or Government enforcement agent." Police stops, unlike arrests and searches, usually occur when there is little or no time to obtain judicial oversight and review. If the Fourth Amendment places restrictions on police intrusions into a person's privacy, it might place restrictions on other police investigative actions.

Proactive police practice, however, requires officers to patrol the community in order to ensure its safety by detecting crime and apprehending offenders. As part of their police investigative and protective functions, officers will patrol communities known for certain types of criminal activities and seek to investigate suspicious persons and their behaviors. When officers can stop individuals and conduct limited searches has been the subject of court analysis since *Terry v. Ohio,* 392 U.S. 1 (1968). The Court in *Terry* created a new Fourth Amendment rule that permits, under specified conditions, limited governmental intrusions into a person's privacy. The legitimacy of a stop may impact the legality of further police intrusions and arrests without warrants; consequently, it is important to understand the constitutional rules that govern police stops.

REASONABLE SUSPICION TO STOP A PERSON

Prior to 1968, the U.S. Supreme Court's analysis of the Fourth Amendment focused on arrests and searches by officers based on probable cause. It was not known if officers could engage in practices that enabled them to detain persons who may commit or had committed a crime, nor was it known if the officers could conduct limited searches of such persons or places where they were stopped. A watershed case, *Terry v. Ohio*, 392 U.S. 1 (1968), addressed a limited intrusion into a person's privacy right and ability to go about his or her business without being briefly detained by the police. Prior to *Terry*, the Court had not announced the legal basis for lawful stops. After *Terry*, the legal basis for a stop is reasonable suspicion. The Court's ruling enables the police to investigate suspicious activities. If an officer wishes to stop and question a person to allay the officer's suspicions, the officer has to establish that the suspicions are reasonable.

TERRY V. OHIO, 392 U.S. 1 (1968)

Opinion by WARREN.

Facts: A plain-clothed Cleveland police officer was on patrol in the downtown area when he observed two men. Because he had been an officer for 39 years and a detective for 35 years, his training and experience heightened his concern about their activity. The officer began to watch the men and observed what appeared to him to be the men casing a store in which they might commit an armed robbery. The men were then joined by a third man, who appeared to be associated with them. The officer approached the three men and identified himself as a police officer. When the men mumbled something, the officer spun around the defendant, Terry, and patted down his outer clothing. He felt what appeared to him to be a pistol. The officer then had Terry take off his coat and removed a revolver from Terry's coat pocket and placed him under arrest. When the officer patted down a second man, the officer felt what appeared to him to be a gun. The officer then removed the gun from the second person's pocket. The officer limited his reach into the suspect's pockets to remove weapons. The Ohio Supreme Court dismissed the defendant's appeal on the grounds that no constitutional question was raised that would justify a suppression of the evidence.

Issue: Does the Fourth Amendment protect citizens from police stops and frisks when a police officer lacks probable cause?

Rationale and Decision: We affirm the conviction. The Fourth Amendment provides that "the right of the people to be secure in their persons, houses, papers, and effects, against unreasonable searches and seizures, shall not be violated. . . ." This inestimable right of personal security belongs as much to the citizen on the streets of our cities as to the homeowner closeted in his study to dispose of his secret affairs. For as this Court has always recognized, "No right is held more sacred, or is more carefully guarded, by the common law than the right of every individual to the possession and control of his own person, free from all restraint or interference of others, unless by clear and unquestionable authority of law." . . . We would be less than candid if we did not acknowledge that this question thrusts to the fore difficult and troublesome issues regarding a sensitive area of police activity—issues which have never before been squarely presented to this Court. Reflective of the tensions involved are the practical and constitutional arguments pressed with great vigor on both sides of the public debate over the power of the police to "stop and frisk"—as it is sometimes euphemistically termed—suspicious persons.

On the one hand, it is frequently argued that, in dealing with the rapidly unfolding and often dangerous situations on city streets, the police are in need of an escalating set of flexible responses, graduated in relation to the amount of information they possess. For this purpose, it is urged that distinctions should be made between a "stop" and an "arrest" (or a "seizure" of a person), and between a "frisk" and a "search." Thus, it is argued, the police should be allowed to "stop" a person and detain him briefly for questioning upon suspicion that he may be connected with criminal activity. Upon suspicion that the person may be armed, the police should have the power to "frisk" him for weapons. If the "stop" and the "frisk" give rise to probable cause to believe that the suspect has committed a crime, then the police should be empowered to make a formal "arrest," and a full incident "search" of the person. This scheme is justified in part upon the notion that a "stop" and a "frisk" amount to a mere "minor inconvenience and petty indignity," which can properly be imposed upon the citizen in the interest of effective law enforcement on the basis of a police officer's suspicion.

On the other side, the argument is made that the authority of the police must be strictly circumscribed by the law of arrest and search as it has developed to date in the traditional jurisprudence of the Fourth Amendment. It is contended with some force that there is not—and cannot be—a variety of police activity which does not depend solely upon the voluntary cooperation of the citizen, and yet which stops short of an arrest based upon probable cause to make such an arrest.

. . . The State has characterized the issue here as "the right of a police officer . . . to make an on-the-street stop, interrogate and pat down for weapons (known in street vernacular as 'stop and frisk')." But this is only partly accurate. . . . Courts which sit under our Constitution cannot and will not be made party to lawless invasions of the constitutional rights of citizens by permitting unhindered governmental use of the fruits of such invasions. Thus, in our system, evidentiary rulings provide the context in which the judicial process of inclusion and exclusion approves some conduct as comporting with constitutional guarantees and disapproves other actions by state agents. A ruling admitting evidence in a criminal trial, we recognize, has the necessary effect of legitimizing the conduct which produced the evidence. . . . Nothing we say today is to be taken as indicating approval of police conduct outside the legitimate investigative sphere. Under our decision, courts still retain their traditional responsibility to guard against police conduct which is overbearing or harassing, or which trenches upon personal security without the objective evidentiary justification which the Constitution requires. When such conduct is identified, it must be condemned by the judiciary, and its fruits must be excluded from evidence in criminal trials. And, of course, our approval of legitimate and restrained investigative conduct undertaken on the basis of ample factual justification should in no way discourage the employment of other remedies than the exclusionary rule to curtail abuses for which that sanction may prove inappropriate.

Having thus roughly sketched the perimeters of the constitutional debate over the limits on police investigative conduct in general and the background against which this case presents itself, we turn our attention to the quite narrow question posed by the facts before us: whether it is always unreasonable for a policeman to seize a person and subject him to a limited search for weapons unless there is probable cause for an arrest.

The distinctions of classical "stop-and-frisk" theory thus serve to divert attention from the central inquiry under the Fourth Amendment—the reasonableness in all the circumstances of the particular governmental invasion of a citizen's personal security. "Search" and "seizure" are not talismans. We therefore reject the notions that the Fourth Amendment does not come into play at all as a limitation upon police conduct if the officers stop short of something called a "technical arrest" or a "full-blown search." . . . We must decide whether . . . it was reasonable for Officer McFadden to have interfered with petitioner's personal security as he did. And, in determining whether the seizure and search were "unreasonable," our inquiry is a dual one—whether the officer's action was justified at its inception, and whether it was reasonably related in scope to the circumstances which justified the interference in the first place. . . .

[W]e consider first the nature and extent of the governmental interests involved. One general interest is, of course, that of effective crime prevention and detection; it is this interest which underlies the recognition that a police officer may, in appropriate circumstances and in an appropriate manner, approach a person for purposes of investigating possibly criminal behavior even though there is no probable cause to make an arrest. It was this legitimate investigative function. . . . The crux of this case, however, is not the propriety of Officer McFadden's taking steps to investigate petitioner's suspicious behavior, but, rather, whether there was justification for McFadden's invasion of Terry's personal security by searching him for weapons in the course of that investigation. We are now concerned with more than the governmental interest in investigating crime; in addition, there is the more immediate interest of the police officer in taking steps to assure himself that the person with whom he is dealing is not armed with a weapon that could unexpectedly and fatally be used against him. Certainly it would be unreasonable to require that police officers take unnecessary risks in the performance of their duties.

In view of these facts, we cannot blind ourselves to the need for law enforcement officers to protect themselves and other prospective victims of violence in situations where they may lack probable cause for an arrest. When an officer is justified in believing that the individual whose suspicious behavior he is investigating at close range is armed and presently dangerous to the officer or to others, it would appear to be clearly unreasonable to deny the officer the power to take necessary measures to determine whether the person is, in fact, carrying a weapon and to neutralize the threat of physical harm.

We must still consider, however, the nature and quality of the intrusion on individual rights which must be accepted if police officers are to be conceded the right to search for weapons in situations where probable cause to arrest for crime is lacking. Even a limited search of the outer clothing for weapons constitutes a severe, though brief, intrusion upon cherished personal security, and it must surely be an annoying, frightening, and perhaps humiliating experience. . . . Our evaluation of the proper balance that has to be struck in this type of case leads us to conclude that there must be a narrowly drawn authority to permit a reasonable search for weapons for the protection of the police officer, where he has reason to believe that he is dealing with an armed and dangerous individual, regardless of whether he has probable cause to arrest the individual for a crime. The officer need not be absolutely certain that the individual is armed; the issue is whether a reasonably prudent man, in the circumstances, would be warranted in the belief that his safety or that of others was in danger.

We must now examine the conduct of Officer McFadden in this case to determine whether his search and seizure of petitioner were reasonable, both at their inception and as conducted. . . . We cannot say his decision at that point to seize Terry and pat his clothing for weapons was the product of a volatile or inventive imagination, or was undertaken simply as an act of harassment; the record evidences the tempered act of a policeman who, in the course of an investigation, had to make a quick decision as to how to protect himself and others from possible danger, and took limited steps to do so.

The manner in which the seizure and search were conducted is, of course, as vital a part of the inquiry as whether they were warranted at all. The Fourth Amendment proceeds as much by limitations upon scope of governmental action as by imposing preconditions upon its initiation. . . . The sole justification of the search in the present situation is the protection of the police officer and others nearby, and it must therefore be confined in scope to an intrusion reasonably designed to discover guns, knives, clubs, or other hidden instruments for the assault of the police officer.

The scope of the search in this case presents no serious problem in light of these standards. Officer McFadden patted down the outer clothing of petitioner and his two companions. He did not place his hands in their pockets or under the outer surface of their garments until he had felt weapons, and then he merely reached for and removed the guns. He never did invade Katz' person beyond the outer surfaces of his clothes, since he discovered nothing in his pat-down which might have been a weapon. Officer McFadden confined his search strictly to what was minimally necessary to learn whether the men were armed and to disarm them once he discovered the weapons. He did not conduct a general exploratory search for whatever evidence of criminal activity he might find.

. . . We merely hold today that, where a police officer observes unusual conduct which leads him reasonably to conclude in light of his experience that criminal activity may be afoot and that the persons with whom he is dealing may be armed and presently dangerous, where, in the course of investigating this behavior, he identifies himself as a policeman and makes reasonable inquiries, and where nothing in the initial stages of the encounter serves to dispel his reasonable fear for his own or others' safety, he is entitled for the protection of himself and others in the area to conduct a carefully limited search of the outer clothing of such persons in an attempt to discover weapons which might be used to assault him. Such a search is a reasonable search under the Fourth Amendment, and any weapons seized may properly be introduced in evidence against the person from whom they were taken.

Affirmed.

Reasonable suspicion is more than a mere hunch or suspicion. An officer can stop an individual *if* the officer can articulate a reason for the belief that a person is about to commit a crime or just committed a crime. The officer's experience, knowledge, and training can form the basis of an articulable reason to suspect that criminal activity might be afoot. The intent of the officer in conducting a stop is to investigate potential criminal activity or to determine if someone committed a criminal offense.

If a stop is reasonable, the person can be prevented from leaving the location until the officer's reasonable suspicions are allayed. The time that is necessary to conduct a stop can vary depending upon the circumstances of the case. In many circumstances, the time might be a matter of minutes, but the time might be extended depending on the actions of the suspect. An officer can request that lawfully stopped individuals identify themselves and indicate what they are doing. If the individual refuses to answer the officer's questions, then the officer's suspicions may be increased to a degree justifying a longer stop, or the officer might gather more information that could lead to a lawful arrest.

The police cannot use a stop to harass an individual or detain persons after the reason for the stop is satisfied. That is, if the individual addresses the officer's suspicions and the officer has no other legitimate reason to continue an investigation, the person is free to leave. The question as to whether a person has been unlawfully "seized" during an investigation in which the officers did not have reasonable suspicion and the defendant chose to remain where he was (on a bus) was addressed in *Florida v. Bostick*, 501 U.S. 429 (1991). In *Bostick*, the Court determined that even if the officers did not have reasonable suspicion, they could conduct an investigation in a public place. If the individual wishes to not answer the officer's questions, then it is incumbent upon that individual to refuse the inquiries. The Court did not view the close quarters of a bus as sufficiently intimidating that would prevent uniformed officers from boarding a bus just prior to its departure and questioning passengers to determine if drugs were being transported in someone's luggage.

FLORIDA V. BOSTICK, 501 U.S. 429 (1991)

Opinion by O'CONNOR.

Facts: Two uniformed officers boarded a public bus that was traveling from Miami to Atlanta and asked the defendant Bostick if they could search his luggage. The officers did not have any reason to suspect the defendant, but they immediately picked him out and asked to see his ticket and identification. The officers then indicated that they wanted to search his luggage for drugs. There is a conflict as to whether the defendant gave consent or was intimidated by the officer's gun and presence. The search of the luggage produced cocaine, and the defendant was convicted of a trafficking offense. The Florida Supreme Court adopted a *per se* rule that reasonable passengers would believe that they were seized by the police on a bus because they would not feel free to leave; such seizures were unconstitutional.

Issue: Can police officers under the Fourth Amendment "seize" individuals on a bus at random, without articulable suspicion, and question them so as to obtain consent to search their luggage?

Rationale and Decision: Since *Terry,* we have held repeatedly that mere police questioning does not constitute a seizure. . . . There is no doubt that, if this same encounter had taken place before Bostick boarded the bus or in the lobby of the bus terminal, it would not rise to the level of a seizure. . . .

Bostick insists that this case is different because it took place in the cramped confines of a bus. A police encounter is much more intimidating in this setting, he argues, because police tower over a seated passenger and there is little room to move around. . . . Bostick maintains that a reasonable bus passenger would not have felt free to leave under the circumstances of this case because there is nowhere to go on a bus. Also, the bus was about to depart.

Had Bostick disembarked, he would have risked being stranded and losing whatever baggage he had locked away in the luggage compartment. . . . [T]he appropriate inquiry is whether a reasonable person would feel free to decline the officers' requests or otherwise terminate the encounter. . . .

[W]e . . . do reject, however, Bostick's argument that he must have been seized because no reasonable person would freely consent to a search of luggage that he or she knows contains drugs. . . . [T]his Court is not empowered to forbid law enforcement practices simply because it considers them distasteful. The Fourth Amendment proscribes unreasonable searches and seizures; it does not proscribe voluntary cooperation. The cramped confines of a bus are one relevant factor that should be considered in evaluating whether a passenger's consent is voluntary. . . . We adhere to the rule that, in order to determine whether a particular encounter constitutes a seizure, a court must consider all the circumstances surrounding the encounter to determine whether the police conduct would have communicated to a reasonable person that the person was not free to decline the officers' requests or otherwise terminate the encounter. That rule applies to encounters that take place on a city street or in an airport lobby, and it applies equally to encounters on a bus. . . . The judgment of the Florida Supreme Court is reversed, and the case remanded for further proceedings not inconsistent with this opinion.

It is so ordered.

To conduct an investigation that initially may lack reasonable suspicion is one part of police practice to prevent crime and protect the community. While the lack of reasonable suspicion prevents a legal stop, it does not prevent an officer from attempting to satisfy any suspicions about crime and individuals. If an officer receives an anonymous tip about crime, the officers can use that tip to engage in further investigation. If the officer's experience and training then lead to reasonable suspicion that crime is afoot, the officer can then engage in stops.

In addition, if officers briefly detain persons who are not engaged in crime and make the persons feel uncomfortable, such brief encounters are lawful if they are limited in nature. In *Los Angeles County v. Retelle,* 127 S. Ct. 1989 (2007), the police executed a search warrant on a home where there was a change of tenants. The previous occupants of the home were African American, but the current occupants were Caucasian. Though the current occupants were not involved in any of the previous tenants' activities, the police nonetheless ordered them out of bed and forced them to stand naked for a few minutes while the police search was carried out and the room secured. The U.S. Supreme Court held that the individual's Fourth Amendment rights were not violated. The *per curiam* court stated:

> When the deputies ordered respondents from their bed, they had no way of knowing whether the African-American suspects were elsewhere in the house. The presence of some Caucasians in the residence did not eliminate the possibility that the suspects lived there as well. . . . The deputies, who were searching a house where they believed a suspect might be armed, possessed authority to secure the premises before deciding whether to continue with the search.

Concern for officer safety is a legitimate reason to prevent persons from moving around in their home while the officers, armed with a warrant, secure the room.

CAR STOPS

Automobile intrusions add an interesting problem for police officers who wish to stop a vehicle. In *Terry*, the officer stopped and frisked individuals who were in a public place and who seemed to be reconnoitering a store. Automobiles, driven by individuals, may also provide officers on patrol with an opportunity to observe and suspect that criminal activity might have occurred or is under way. As with stops of persons, a car can be stopped if an officer has a reason to suspect that criminal activity is about to occur or has just occurred. In *United States v. Cortez,* 449 U.S. 411 (1981), the U.S. Supreme Court applied the Fourth Amendment's provisions to the temporary investigatory stop of a vehicle. If all of the circumstances known to the officer provide that officer with a reasonable belief that the car is involved in criminal activity, then the vehicle can be constitutionally stopped.

UNITED STATES V. CORTEZ, 449 U.S. 411 (1981)

Opinion by BURGER.

Facts: In 1976 and 1977, Border Patrol officers discovered numerous footprints, one set of which had a distinctive chevron imprint, in southern Arizona. The officers believed that these footprints indicated that there had been illegal border crossings from Mexico into the United States. Their investigation also led them to believe that illegal smuggling was likely to occur on a particular night. During their stakeout on that night, they observed a vehicle—a pickup truck with an attached camper—which they believed to be of the right size and driving in a likely manner to denote that it was transporting illegal immigrants. At that point, they flashed their police lights and intercepted the vehicle. One person, Jesus Cortez, was the driver and owner of the pickup; another person, Hernandez-Loera, was sitting in the passenger's seat. Hernandez-Loera was wearing shoes that matched the "chevron" shoeprint. The officers identified themselves and told Cortez they were conducting an immigration check. They asked if he was carrying any passengers in the camper, and when Cortez told them he had picked up some hitchhikers, the officers proceeded to open the back of the camper. In the back of the truck were six illegal aliens. The officers then arrested the both Cortez and Hernandez-Lorera. The Court of Appeals held that the officers did not have a sufficient legal basis to stop the vehicle.

Issue: Did the facts of the investigation provide a sufficient basis for the officers to stop a vehicle on a public highway?

Rationale and Decision: The Fourth Amendment applies to seizures of the person, including brief investigatory stops such as the stop of the vehicle here. . . . Courts have used a variety of terms to capture the elusive concept of what cause is sufficient to authorize police to stop a person. Terms like "articulable reasons" and "founded suspicion" are not self-defining; they fall short of providing clear guidance dispositive of the myriad factual situations that arise. But the essence of all that has been written is that the totality of the circumstances—the whole picture—must be taken into account. Based upon that whole picture the detaining officers must have a particularized and objective basis for suspecting the particular person stopped of criminal activity.

The idea that an assessment of the whole picture must yield a particularized suspicion contains two elements, each of which must be present before a stop is permissible. First, the assessment must be based upon all of the circumstances. The analysis proceeds with various objective observations, information from police reports, if such are available, and consideration of the modes or patterns of operation of certain kinds of lawbreakers. From these data, a trained officer draws inferences and makes deductions—inferences and deductions that might well elude an untrained person. . . . The process does not deal with hard certainties, but with probabilities. . . .

The second element contained in the idea that an assessment of the whole picture must yield a particularized suspicion is the concept that the process just described must raise a suspicion that the particular individual being stopped is engaged in wrongdoing.

This case portrays at once both the enormous difficulties of patrolling a 2,000-mile open border and the patient skills needed by those charged with halting illegal entry into this country. . . . Here, fact on fact and clue on clue afforded a basis for the deductions and inferences that brought the officers to focus on "Chevron." Of critical importance, the officers knew that the area was a crossing point for illegal aliens. They knew that it was common practice for persons to lead aliens through the desert from the border to Highway 86, where they could—by prearrangement—be picked up by a vehicle. Moreover, based upon clues they had discovered in the 2-month period prior to the events at issue here, they believed that one such guide, whom they designated "Chevron," had a particular pattern of operations. By piecing together the information at their disposal, the officers tentatively concluded that there was a reasonable likelihood that "Chevron" would attempt to lead a group of aliens on the night of Sunday, January 30–31. Someone with chevron-soled shoes had led several groups of aliens in the previous two months, yet it had been two weeks since the latest crossing. "Chevron," they deduced, was therefore due reasonably soon. "Chevron" tended to travel on clear weekend nights. Because it had rained on the Friday and Saturday nights of the weekend involved here, Sunday was the only clear night of that weekend; the officers surmised it was therefore a likely night for a trip.

Once they had focused on that night, the officers drew upon other objective facts known to them to deduce a timeframe within which "Chevron" and the aliens were likely to arrive. From what they knew of the practice of those who smuggle aliens, including what they knew of "Chevron's" previous activities, they deduced that the border crossing and journey through the desert would probably be at night. They knew the time when sunset would occur at the point of the border crossing; they knew about how long the trip would take. They were thus able to deduce that "Chevron" would likely arrive at the pickup point on Highway 86 in the timeframe between 2 a.m. and 6 a.m. From objective facts, the officers also deduced the probable point on the highway—milepost 122—at which "Chevron" would likely rendezvous with a pickup vehicle. They deduced from the direction taken by the sets of "Chevron" footprints they had earlier discovered that the pickup vehicle would approach the aliens from, and return with them to, a point east of milepost 122. They therefore staked out a position east of milepost 122 (at milepost 149) and watched for vehicles that passed them going west and then, approximately one and a half hours later, passed them again, this time going east. From what they had observed about the previous groups guided by the person with "chevron" shoes, they deduced that "Chevron" would lead a group of 8 to 20 aliens. They therefore focused their attention on enclosed vehicles of that passenger capacity. . . .

The limited purpose of the stop in this case was to question the occupants of the vehicle about their citizenship and immigration status and the reasons for the round trip in a short timespan in a virtually deserted area. No search of the camper or any of its occupants occurred until after respondent Cortez voluntarily opened the back door of the camper; thus, only the stop, not the search, is at issue here. The intrusion upon privacy associated with this stop was limited, and was "reasonably related in scope to the justification for [its] initiation. . . ."

We have recently held that stops by the Border Patrol may be justified under circumstances less than those constituting probable cause for arrest or search. . . . Thus, the test is not whether Officers Gray and Evans had probable cause to conclude that the vehicle they stopped would contain "Chevron" and a group of illegal aliens. Rather, the question is whether, based upon the whole picture, they, as experienced Border Patrol officers, could reasonably surmise that the particular vehicle they stopped was engaged in criminal activity. On this record, they could so conclude.

Reversed.

As with a police stop of an individual, if an officer receives an anonymous tip about a crime, the officer needs to engage in further investigation before a car stop will be allowed under *Terry*. In 2009, the U.S. Supreme Court denied certiorari in a case originating in Virginia that addressed the issue of anonymous tips and police stops. In *Virginia v. Harris,* 558 U.S. ___, 130 S. Ct. 10 (2009), in his dissent from the denial of certiorari, Chief Justice Roberts, joined by Justice Scalia, stated that (1) the United States Supreme Court has not answered whether anonymous tips reporting drunk driving are sufficient in and of themselves to support a *Terry* stop in the DWI context, (2) it is unclear whether *Florida v. J. L.,* 529 U.S. 266, applies in the DWI context, and (3) courts encountering this issue are divided. See *Harris,* 130 S. Ct. at 10–11, 175 L. Ed. 2d at 322. However, the dissent recognized that most courts have decided that a face-to-face tip can be sufficient in and of itself to support an investigatory detention in a DWI case, and that the Commonwealth of Virginia's stance is a minority view. The Virginia State Supreme Court overturned a person's conviction for drunk driving. The officer stopped Harris on a tip that he was driving while under the influence; however, the officer stopped Harris's car without independently observing any indicia that Harris was driving erratically or under the influence. The automobile was stopped despite the fact that the driver did not swerve while driving and did not drive in any particularly dangerous manner.

VIRGINIA V. HARRIS, 558 U.S. ____, 130 S. CT. 10 (2009)

Dissenting opinion by ROBERTS.

Facts: The U.S. Supreme Court denied certiorari to hear an appeal from the State of Virginia in which the Virginia State Supreme Court overturned a conviction. The defendant's conviction for driving under the influence was overturned by the state high court because the police officer stopped the vehicle before independently verifying an anonymous tip that the defendant was driving while intoxicated. Justice Roberts, with whom Justice Scalia joined, wrote a dissenting opinion from the denial of certiori.

Issue: Should the U.S. Supreme Court hear the appeal on anonymous tips and lawful automobile stops?

Dissenting Opinion: Every year, close to 13,000 people die in alcohol-related car crashes—roughly one death every 40 minutes. Ordinary citizens are well aware of the dangers posed by drunk driving, and they frequently report such conduct to the police. By a 4-to-3 vote, the Virginia Supreme Court below adopted a rule that will undermine such efforts to get drunk drivers off the road. The decision below commands that police officers following a driver reported to be drunk *do nothing* until they see the driver actually do something unsafe on the road—by which time it may be too late.

I am not sure that the Fourth Amendment requires such independent corroboration before the police can act, at least in the special context of anonymous tips reporting drunk driving. This is an important question that is not answered by our past decisions, and that has deeply divided federal and state courts. The Court should grant the petition for certiorari to answer the question and resolve the conflict.

On the one hand, our cases allow police to conduct investigative stops based on reasonable suspicion, viewed under the totality of the circumstances. *Terry* v. *Ohio*, 392 U.S. 1, 22 (1968); *Alabama* v. *White*, 496 U.S. 325, 328–331 (1990). In *Florida* v. *J. L.*, 529 U.S. 266, 270 (2000), however, we explained that anonymous tips, in the absence of additional corroboration, typically lack the "indicia of reliability" needed to justify a stop under the reasonable suspicion standard. But it is not clear that *J. L.* applies to anonymous tips reporting drunk or erratic driving.

There is no question that drunk driving is a serious and potentially deadly crime, as our cases have repeatedly emphasized. . . . The imminence of the danger posed by drunk drivers exceeds that at issue in other types of cases. . . . The conflict is clear and the stakes are high. The effect of the rule below will be to grant drunk drivers "one free swerve" before they can legally be pulled over by police. It will be difficult for an officer to explain to the family of a motorist killed by that swerve that the police had a tip that the driver of the other car was drunk, but that they were powerless to pull him over, even for a quick check.

Maybe the decision of the Virginia Supreme Court below was correct, and the Fourth Amendment bars police from acting on anonymous tips of drunk driving unless they can verify each tip. If so, then the dangerous consequences of this rule are unavoidable. But the police should have every

legitimate tool at their disposal for getting drunk drivers
off the road. I would grant certiorari to determine if this is
one of them.

FRISKS AND PLAIN FEEL RULE

The ability to stop a person to ascertain if a crime had been or is about
to be committed does not immediately justify a limited search of that
person. A "frisk" is a limited search allowed under *Terry* if the officer
reasonably fears for his or her safety. Stops of individuals may pose a risk
to the officer from the unknown individuals who have been stopped.
Officers should be able to protect themselves from harm by patting down
the outer clothing of the person who was stopped, if the officer reasonably suspects that the individual could hurt the officer. If the officer feels
something that appears to be a weapon during this limited intrusion, then
the officer can reach into the person's clothing to retrieve the item.

Finding items other than a weapon may pose additional Fourth
Amendment concerns, as was noted in *Minnesota v. Dickerson*, 508 U.S.
366 (1993). If an officer can immediately recognize contraband during a
protective pat-down of a stopped individual, then the officer can retrieve
it from a person's pockets. However, if the officer has to conduct further
evaluation before determining what an item felt during a frisk could be,
then the officer cannot remove the item to justify its seizure; the officer in
such a situation would have conducted a search that exceeded the reasonable basis for the officer's knowledge and suspicions.

MINNESOTA V. DICKERSON, 508 U.S. 366 (1993)

Opinion by WHITE.

Facts: While on patrol in an area known for drug sales
and use, officers observed a person leave a building known

to be a site for cocaine trafficking. Because the person, Dickerson, seemed to engage in evasive actions, the officers decided to stop him and investigate further. The officers pulled their squad car into the alley and ordered Dickerson to stop and submit to a pat-down search. The search revealed no weapons, but the officer conducting the search did take an interest in a small lump in Dickerson's nylon jacket. After squeezing the object, the officer's experience led him to believe the item was illegal contraband. The officer removed the package and then placed Dickerson under arrest for possession. The Minnesota Supreme Court affirmed his conviction on the ground that the stop and frisk were valid under *Terry*.

Issue: Does the Fourth Amendment permit officers to seize contraband detected through a police officer's sense of touch during a protective pat-down search?

Rationale and Decision: We granted certiorari . . . to resolve a conflict among the state and federal courts over whether contraband detected through the sense of touch during a pat down search may be admitted into evidence. . . . Most state and federal courts have recognized a so-called "plain-feel" or "plain-touch" corollary to the plain-view doctrine. . . . *Terry v Ohio* . . . held that . . . the officer may conduct a patdown search "to determine whether the person is in fact carrying a weapon." . . . If the protective search goes beyond what is necessary to determine if the suspect is armed, it is no longer valid under *Terry* and its fruits will be suppressed. . . . The question presented today is whether police officers may seize nonthreatening contraband detected during a protective patdown search of the sort permitted by *Terry*. We think the answer is clearly that they may, so long as the officers' search stays within the bounds marked by *Terry*.

[T]he dispositive question before this Court is whether the officer who conducted the search was acting within the lawful bounds marked by *Terry* at the time he gained probable cause to believe that the lump in respondent's jacket was contraband. . . . The Minnesota Supreme Court, after "a close examination of the record," held that the officer's own testimony "belies any notion that he 'immediately'" recognized the lump as crack cocaine. . . . Rather, the court concluded, the officer determined that the lump was contraband only after "squeezing, sliding and otherwise manipulating the contents of the defendant's pocket"—a pocket which the officer already knew contained no weapon.

Under the State Supreme Court's interpretation of the record before it, it is clear that the court was correct in holding that the police officer in this case overstepped the bounds of the "strictly circumscribed" search for weapons allowed under *Terry*. . . . Here, the officer's continued exploration of respondent's pocket after having concluded that it contained no weapon was unrelated to "[t]he sole justification of the search. . . . It therefore amounted to the sort of evidentiary search that *Terry* expressly refused to authorize, . . . and that we have condemned in subsequent cases.

For these reasons, the judgment of the Minnesota Supreme Court is *Affirmed*.

Automobiles: Frisks of People and Their Cars

Once an automobile has been stopped, an officer can order individuals out of the vehicle. If the officer wants to have an individual remain in the car or step outside of it in order to better observe the person and protect the officer's safety, such a limited intrusion is acceptable. The court in *Pennsylvania v. Mimms,* 434 U.S. 106 (1977), indicated that in addition to the need to protect officers from assaults during a traffic stop, officers may need to have individuals step out of a vehicle for their protection from potential roadside accidents. Once exited from the vehicle, officers may remove what they believe to be hidden weapons from a person's pockets. The rules governing reasonable suspicion that a person has a hidden weapon remain intact; the officer can only frisk a person or remove an item from a person that the officer reasonably suspects to be a weapon.

PENNSYLVANIA V. MIMMS, 434 U.S. 106 (1977)

PER CURIAM Opinion.

Facts: Two officers observed a person driving with an expired license plate and pulled him over. The officers asked the driver, Mimms, to step out of the vehicle. As Mimms stepped out of the car, an officer observed a bulge in his coat that seemed to the officer to be a weapon. The officer reached into the coat pocket and removed a .38-caliber revolver loaded with five rounds of ammunition. Mimms was immediately arrested for carrying a concealed deadly weapon and for unlawfully carrying a firearm without a license. The Pennsylvania Supreme Court reversed his conviction on the grounds that the officer's request for Mimms to exit the vehicle was unlawful under the Fourth Amendment.

Issue: Did the seizure of the weapon violate the Fourth Amendment?

Rationale and Decision: The touchstone of our analysis under the Fourth Amendment is always "the reasonableness in all the circumstances of the particular governmental invasion of a citizen's personal security." . . . Reasonableness, of course, depends "on a balance between the public interest and the individual's right to personal security free from arbitrary interference by law officers." . . . In this case, unlike *Terry v. Ohio,* there is no question about the propriety of the initial restrictions on respondent's freedom of movement. . . . This inquiry must therefore focus not on the intrusion resulting from the request to stop the vehicle or from the later "pat down," but on the incremental intrusion resulting from the request to get out of the car once the vehicle was lawfully stopped.

Placing the question in this narrowed frame, we look first to that side of the balance which bears the officer's interest in taking the action that he did. . . . It was his practice to order all drivers out of their vehicles as a matter of course whenever they had been stopped for a traffic violation. . . . We think it too plain for argument that the State's proffered justification—the safety of the officer—is both legitimate and weighty. . . . According to one study, approximately 30% of police shootings occurred when a police officer approached a suspect seated in an automobile. . . . We are aware that not all these assaults occur when issuing traffic summons, but we have before expressly declined to accept the argument that traffic violations necessarily involve less danger to officers than other types of confrontations. . . . The hazard of accidental injury from passing traffic to an officer standing on the driver's side of the vehicle may also be appreciable in some situations. Rather than conversing while standing exposed to moving traffic, the officer prudently may prefer to ask the driver of the vehicle to step out of the car and off onto the shoulder of the road where the inquiry may be pursued with greater safety to both.

Against this important interest, we are asked to weigh the intrusion into the driver's personal liberty occasioned not by the initial stop of the vehicle, which was admittedly justified, but by the order to get out of the car. We think this additional intrusion can only be described as *de minimis.* The driver is being asked to expose to view very little more of his person than is already exposed. The police have already lawfully decided that the driver shall be briefly detained; the only question is whether he shall spend that period sitting in the driver's seat of his car or standing alongside it. Not only is the insistence of the police on the latter choice not a "serious intrusion upon the sanctity of the person," but it hardly rises to the level of a *'petty indignity.'* . . . *What is, at most, a mere inconvenience cannot prevail when balanced against legitimate concerns for the officer's safety.* . . .

There remains the second question of the propriety of the search once the bulge in the jacket was observed. We have as little doubt on this point as on the first; the answer is controlled by *Terry v. Ohio*. . . .—there is little question the officer was justified. The bulge in the jacket permitted the officer to conclude that Mimms was armed, and thus posed a serious and present danger to the safety of the officer. In these circumstances, any man of "reasonable caution" would likely have conducted the "pat down." The . . . case is remanded for further proceedings not inconsistent with this opinion.

It is so ordered.

Both the driver and passengers in an automobile can be ordered to exit the vehicle. In *Arizona v. Johnson*, 555 U.S. ___, 129 S. Ct. 781 (2009), police officers stopped a vehicle for a civil traffic infraction. They did not suspect the driver or its passengers of any criminal activity at the time of the stop. Nonetheless, in questioning one passenger, he was ordered out of the car. The officer then noticed that the individual was wearing a gang color (bandana), acted suspiciously when he was approached and when exiting the vehicle, was carrying a police scanner, and volunteered that he was from a place known to the officer to be a gang area. The officer immediately frisked the individual and found a weapon. An officer effectively seizes "everyone in the vehicle" during a traffic stop, and the Court accordingly stated that during a stop, the officers do not have to have any particular reason to believe that the occupants are engaged in criminal activity, but if the officers fear for their safety, they can engage in pat-downs. The Court held:

> Accordingly, we hold that, in a traffic-stop setting, the first *Terry* condition—a lawful investigatory stop—is met whenever it is lawful for police to detain an automobile and its occupants pending inquiry into a vehicular violation. . . . To justify a patdown of the driver or a passenger during a traffic stop, however, just as in the case of a pedestrian reasonably suspected of criminal activity, the police must harbor reasonable suspicion that the person subjected to the frisk is armed and dangerous.

An automobile, the car itself, may additionally be frisked for weapons if an officer reasonably fears for his safety when a vehicle has been lawfully stopped. A stop does not automatically justify a frisk; there must be reasonable suspicion to believe that the officer's safety is compromised. Officers can rely on their experience and their training to determine if there is a risk to their safety from unknown individuals when they engage in roadside stops. The Court in *Michigan v. Long*, 463 U.S. 1032 (1983), ruled that officers could "frisk" a car if they had reasonable suspicion to believe that there is a weapon inside. The scope of the frisk allowed in *Long* was the interior passenger compartment of a car because the suspect might have been able to retrieve weapons and threaten an officer or others.

MICHIGAN V. LONG, 463 U.S. 1032 (1983)

Opinion by O'CONNOR.

Facts: Police found contraband in the passenger compartment and trunk of the automobile that was driven by Long. The police searched the passenger compartment because they had reason to believe that the vehicle contained weapons potentially dangerous to the officers. The Michigan Supreme Court held that the search of the vehicle violated the Fourth Amendment.

Issue: To what extent can an officer conduct a protective frisk of the area around a suspect during a stop?

Rationale and Decision: In *Terry v. Ohio*, . . . we did not . . . expressly address whether . . . a protective search for weapons could extend to an area beyond the person in the absence of probable cause to arrest. The Court below held, and respondent Long contends, that Deputy Howell's entry into the vehicle cannot be justified under the principles set forth in *Terry*, because "*Terry* authorized only a limited pat-down search of a *person* suspected of criminal activity," rather than a search of an area. . . . Contrary to Long's view, *Terry* need not be read as restricting the preventative search to the person of the detained suspect. . . .

We also held that the police may examine the contents of any open or closed container found within the passenger compartment, "for if the passenger compartment is within the reach of the arrestee, so will containers in it be within his reach." . . . [The] protection of police and others can justify protective searches when police have a reasonable belief that the suspect poses a danger, that roadside encounters between police and suspects are especially hazardous, and that danger may arise from the possible presence of weapons in the area surrounding a suspect. These principles compel our conclusion that the search of the passenger compartment of an automobile, limited to those areas in which a weapon may be placed or hidden, is permissible if the police officer possesses a reasonable belief based on "specific and articulable facts which, taken together with the rational inferences from those facts, reasonably warrant" the officer in believing that the suspect is dangerous and the suspect may gain immediate control of weapons.

The circumstances of this case clearly justified Deputies Howell and Lewis in their reasonable belief that Long posed a danger if he were permitted to reenter his vehicle. The hour was late, and the area rural. Long was driving his automobile at excessive speed, and his car swerved into a ditch. The officers had to repeat their questions to Long, who appeared to be "under the influence" of some intoxicant. Long was not frisked until the officers observed that there was a large knife in the interior of the car into which Long was about to reenter. The subsequent search of the car was restricted to those areas to which Long would generally have immediate control, and that could contain a weapon. The trial court determined that the leather pouch containing marihuana could have contained a weapon. . . . It is clear that the intrusion was "strictly circumscribed by the exigencies which justifi[ed] its initiation."

. . . During any investigative detention, the suspect is "in the control" of the officers in the sense that he "may be briefly detained against his will. . . ." . . . Just as a *Terry* suspect on the street may, despite being under the brief control of a police officer, reach into his clothing and retrieve a weapon, so might a *Terry* suspect in Long's position break away from police control and retrieve a weapon from his automobile. . . . In addition, if the suspect is not placed under arrest, he will be permitted to reenter his automobile, and he will then have access to any weapons inside. . . . Or, as here, the suspect may be permitted to reenter the vehicle before the *Terry* investigation is over, and again, may have access to weapons. In any event, we stress that a *Terry* investigation, such as the one that occurred here, involves a police investigation "at close range," . . . when the officer remains particularly vulnerable in part because a full custodial arrest has not been effected, and the officer must make a "quick decision as to how to protect himself and others from possible danger. . . ." . . . In such circumstances, we have not required that officers adopt alternative means to ensure their safety in order to avoid the intrusion involved in a *Terry* encounter.

. . . We remand this issue to the court below, to enable it to determine whether the trunk search was permissible. . . . The judgment of the Michigan Supreme Court is reversed, and the case is remanded for further proceedings not inconsistent with this opinion.

It is so ordered.

CONTEMPORARY ISSUES: CRIMINAL AND RACIAL PROFILING

Good police practice involves the ability to assess whether a person may be involved in criminal activity. Police often engage in criminal profiling, in which they are aware of certain characteristics of individuals who are likely to be associated with particular types of crimes. Criminal profiling is a relatively new tool available to law enforcement, but its efficacy has been debated. The goals of profiling are to provide law enforcement with a social and psychological assessment of the offender, and belongings that may be in the offender's possession, and to suggest possible strategies for interviewing the offender.

Controversy arises when the police are accused of unlawfully racially profiling persons—in other words, suspecting a person of a crime based solely on his or her race. Although police may lawfully consider a suspect's race in the totality of the circumstances, an officer may not lawfully stop or detain a person based solely on their race. It has been estimated that about 1 in 10 African American men will be incarcerated and about half of the incarcerated population is composed of African Americans, although African Americans comprise about 13 percent of the U.S. population. Questions arise whether the minority persons arrested and punished are discriminatorily singled out for arrest or whether the police are effectively and legitimately targeting criminals in their communities. Studies show that police focus more on the inner cities than in suburbs, and that minorities are more likely to be arrested for drug offenses on the city streets than Caucasians using drugs within their homes. In addition, studies have shown that African American motorists are more likely than Caucasian motorists to have their cars *searched* when stopped. However, it is hard to determine from the research to date whether initial stops of minority motorists tends to be because of their race as opposed to legitimate traffic violations. In a recent study by Vera Sanchez and Rosenbaum (2011), the authors found that officers' perceptions about offenders are affected by the types of neighborhoods they patrol, the attitudes of the community toward officers, and the work that the police perform and the age of the suspects they stop. Vera Sanchez and Rosenbaum found that officers were more likely to hold negative views of youth regardless of race or ethnicity; rather, the officers were concerned about gangs, drugs, violence, and other offenses that occur within inner-city communities.

Complicating matters, states may want to enact laws that empower the police to stop and detain persons who are suspected of being in the United States illegally. The debate hinges on whether the stop is based upon reasonable beliefs that the immigration laws are violated or if the stop and subsequent detention are racially based. In 2010, the Arizona legislature passed SB 1070 in order to provide local and state police the power to question and detain persons who might be in the United States illegally. The law also created new crimes associated with illegal immigration.

The U.S. Justice Department sought to prevent the law from going into effect by filing suit in federal court and arguing that the law conflicts with the power of the national government to regulate immigration. Some police agencies within the state also did not want the law effectuated because of their belief that it would divert limited police resources to minor crimes rather than serious offenses. At present, the federal district court's preliminary injunction prohibits the state from enforcing the following provisions that would:

- Require state and local police officers to investigate the immigration status of all individuals upon reasonable suspicion that the person is an illegal immigrant;

- Allow the warrantless arrest of individuals whom the state or local police believe to be "removable" from the United States;

- Detain all arrested individuals in jail facilities, even for minor offenses that might ordinarily result in a ticket, if they cannot verify that they are authorized to be in the United States;

- Punish criminally noncitizens who either fail to register with the Department of Homeland Security or fail to carry their registration documents; and

- Punish alleged undocumented immigrants who apply for, solicit, or perform work.

In granting the preliminary injunction blocking the controversial provisions of SB 1070, the federal district court focused on the burden to law enforcement and citizens alike. Judge Bolton in *United States v. Arizona*, 703 F. Supp. 2d 980 (2010), stated:

> Requiring Arizona law enforcement officials and agencies to determine the immigration status of every person who is arrested burdens lawfully-present aliens because their liberty will be restricted while their status is checked. Given the large number of people who are technically "arrested" but never booked into jail or perhaps even transported to a law enforcement facility, detention time for this category of arrestee will certainly be extended during an immigration status verification.

The case is now on appeal to the Ninth Circuit Court of Appeals and may ultimately reach the U.S. Supreme Court.

SUMMARY

Police officers need to stop persons to inquire about unlawful activity. Whether the police have the ability to detain a person to ask questions depends on whether an officer has reasonable suspicion to believe that a person has committed a crime or is about to commit a crime. If an officer fears for his or her safety or if the officer has a reasonable suspicion that an individual who has been stopped has a weapon, then the officer may frisk the person. During a frisk, if an officer feels what he or she believes to be a weapon, then the officer may take the item from the offender's person or pockets. Such frisks might then turn into an arrest if the item seized from the lawful frisk is unlawful for the individual to possess. Contemporary concerns arise when the police are charged with stopping people solely because of their race or ethnicity. Racial profiling is not legal, but the police may use information on a suspect's race or ethnicity within the basis of knowledge they have to form reasonable suspicion or probable cause to arrest someone. Profiling a person for involvement of a crime is lawful when the profile is reasonably related to the offense the police are investigating. Criminal profiling, which involves the use of specific characteristics of individuals most closely associated with particular crimes, does not violate the Constitution.

GLOSSARY

Automobile frisk: Inspection of the passenger compartment of a vehicle based on the officer's reasonable fear for his or her safety.

Automobile stop: The police detention of a vehicle on a public highway, based on reasonable suspicion.

Criminal profiling: The practice of using characteristics of individuals who are most closely associated with particular crimes.

Frisk: The pat-down of the outer clothing of a person stopped by the police to determine if he or she is carrying a weapon.

Plain feel: The principle that a police officer may seize an item that can be clearly and immediately identified by touch as an unlawful item or weapon during the course of a lawful pat-down.

Racial profiling: Unlawful targeting of persons of color for investigation and arrests by the police.

Stop: The detaining of a person by police for a short time in order to ascertain if the person has committed or is about to commit a crime, based on reasonable suspicion. May include a frisk for concealed weapons.

ADDITIONAL READINGS

Gladwell, M. (2007, November 12). Dangerous minds: Criminal profiling made easy. *The New Yorker*. Retrieved January 1, 2008, from http://www.newyorker.com/reporting/2007/11/12/071112fa_fact_gladwell

Harris, D. (1999). *Driving while black: Racial profiling on our nation's highways* (National Criminal Justice Data Base, NCJ 182825). Washington, DC: U.S. Department of Justice.

Muffler, S. J. (Ed.). (2006). *Racial profiling: Issues, data and analyses*. New York: Nova Sciences.

Vera Sanchez, C. G., & Rosenbaum, D. P. (2011). Racialized policing: Officers' voices on policing Latino and African American neighborhoods. *Journal of Ethnicity in Criminal Justice, 9*, 152–178.

Weitzer, R., & Tuch, S. A. (2002.) Perceptions of racial profiling: Race, class, and personal experience. *Criminology, 20*, 435–456.

CHAPTER 4

Arrests

KEY POINTS

- Arrests involve the detention by the government of a person for a crime; the person is not free to leave.

- An arrest must be based upon probable cause to believe that a crime was committed and the person detained committed the offense.

- An arrested person does not have to be booked for a crime for the arrest to be valid; rather, a person may be given an appearance ticket to show up in court for the alleged charges.

- Arrestees have basic constitutional rights even if they are detained because they are considered to be enemy combatants.

- Juveniles who are detained also retain basic constitutional rights that cannot be violated merely because they are detained by public school officials.

THE FOURTH AMENDMENT AND ARRESTS

An arrest is the detention of a person for a crime that the person is reasonably believed to have committed. It may also involve the custodial holding of a person for the purpose of interrogation or prosecution for a crime. An arrest deprives a person of his or her liberty, and a person is said to be "held" in a jail, at a police station, or at the scene if the person is not free to leave of his or her own volition. Arrests may occur with or without a warrant to arrest.

If arrested for an offense, a person may be taken to jail and criminally processed or booked for a crime. Jail detention is aimed at ensuring that a person will be held until a trial can determine whether the charges are to be sustained (the person is found guilty or not guilty). Because jail facilities are crowded and courts may not worry if a person will answer to the charges, arrestees may be released pending trial. A number of methods have been developed to enable an arrestee to get out of a jail facility pending trial and disposition of the charges. Persons may post cash bail or have a bond posted. Others may be released on their own recognizance or other conditions of release. The Eighth Amendment requires that bail for federal charges not be excessive. In some states, an arrestee has a right to bail release (remember that the Eighth Amendment is one of the few amendments *not* incorporated under the Fourteenth Amendment, and thus not applicable to states). Whether released on bail, bond, or his or her own recognizance, an arrestee must show up for a particular court date and appear in court. Failure to do so may result in a court-issued warrant for his or her arrest for failure to appear in court.

Whether the arrest will result in a formal booking and jail detention for a charge may depend on state laws, the individual's demeanor at the time of the arrest, the seriousness of the charge (felony, misdemeanor, or violation), potential harm to victims or others, and other factors known to the police (e.g., departmental policy). Sometimes, a person may be arrested but not subsequently booked and jailed at the time of the police encounter. Such a person may be given or mailed an appearance ticket that will require him or her to appear in court for the stated charge or charges. Many persons erroneously believe that they are not arrested if they are not brought down to the stationhouse at the time of their police contact. If a person is stopped by an officer for an offense, the officer may use discretion to determine whether to issue a citation or appearance ticket for a criminal offense or to take the person into custody and book him or her into jail. This detention, although brief, is tantamount to an arrest. Such arrests may trigger further intrusions by the police as lawful police actions subsequent to the arrest. As with release on bail, bond, or other approved court release provisions, if a person fails to respond to the citation and show up at the assigned court date, a judge may issue a warrant for that person's arrest for failure to appear in court.

Probable Cause

The main requirement for an arrest to be lawful is probable cause. Probable cause is a higher standard than reasonable suspicion, which is required for a stop. The Fourth Amendment states (emphasis added):

> The *right of the people to be secure in their persons,* houses, papers, and effects, *against unreasonable searches and seizures,* shall not be violated, and no Warrants shall issue, but upon *probable cause,* supported by Oath or affirmation, and *particularly describing* the place to be searched, and *the persons* or things *to be seized.*

Most arrests occur without a warrant. At common law, a police officer could arrest a person if a misdemeanor was committed in his or her presence, or if a felony was committed and there were reasonable grounds to believe that the person to be arrested committed the felony. Reasonable grounds to believe that a felony was committed can be based on witness and victim information given to the officer, police investigation at the scene, a suspect's demeanor and behavior, and so on. Under these situations, the police have developed probable cause to believe that a crime was committed and that the person arrested committed it. A warrantless arrest is justified under the above-noted situations so long as the officer can articulate clearly the reason for the arrest.

Type of Intrusion	Level of Proof Required
Arrest of a Person	Probable cause to believe a person committed a crime
Stop of a Person	Reasonable suspicion that a crime might occur or that the individual committed a crime
Search of a Person Incident to Arrest	Probable cause to arrest a person
Frisk of a Person	Reasonable suspicion that the person might have a weapon
Search of an Area Where a Person Was Arrested	Probable cause to arrest a person
Frisk of an Area Where a Person is Detained	Reasonable suspicion that the area might have a weapon

FIGURE 4-1   Levels of Proof Needed under the Fourth Amendment

The major Supreme Court cases establishing the standard required by the Fourth Amendment for various state intrusions.

States may modify the basic common-law rules on when a person should be formally booked and processed for a crime, but the requirement of probable cause remains. It is generally believed that officer training, knowledge, departmental policy, and state laws will govern how and when persons arrested will be criminally processed. Texas, for example, requires officers who arrest a person at a scene to swear out an affidavit and complaint that will be given to the local magistrate. The judge will then determine if probable cause exists to hold the individual.

A warrantless arrest is reasonable if there is a probable cause to believe (1) that a crime was committed and (2) that the person held is responsible for committing the offense.

Recently, the U.S. Supreme Court held that even if an arrest was not permitted under state statutes, the arrest is valid if it comports with the "reasonable" requirement. Arrests based on Fourth Amendment principles of probable cause do not, according to the Court, incorporate state laws and rules because doing so would encumber the application of the Constitution. In *Virginia v. Moore*, 553 U.S. 164 (2008), the Court did not wish to make the Fourth Amendment dependent on state rules. Rather, the Court held that so long as arrests are based on probable cause, the seizures of individuals, even if in violation of more restrictive state laws, are lawful. In *Moore,* the State of Virginia required officers not to book a person into a jail facility for traffic violations. However, when officers learned that Moore had been driving on a suspended license, they went to his room to formally arrest him and take him into police custody. The Court declined to read the Fourth Amendment as bending to every state's laws; rather, while states can enact and enforce their own rules in accordance with rules that provide greater protections to their citizenry, the basic floor of the Constitution does not require it to bend to state requirements.

VIRGINIA V. MOORE, 553 U.S. 164 (2008)

Opinion by SCALIA.

Facts: Two officers heard over the patrol's radio that "Chubs" was driving with a suspended license. One of the officers knew that the person who went by that nickname was

Moore. After checking to ascertain if the license was in fact suspended, the officers arrested him for the misdemeanor of driving on a suspended license. In a subsequent search, they found that Moore was carrying 16 grams of crack cocaine and $516 in cash. However, under state law, the officers should have issued Moore a summons instead of arresting him for driving on a suspended license. The Virginia Supreme Court held that the evidence should have been suppressed at trial.

Issue: Is an arrest prohibited under state law also a violation of the Fourth Amendment?

Rationale and Decision: . . . We are aware of no historical indication that those who ratified the Fourth Amendment understood it as a redundant guarantee of whatever limits on search and seizure legislatures might have enacted. The immediate object of the Fourth Amendment was to prohibit the general warrants and writs of assistance that English judges had employed against the colonists. . . . That suggests, if anything, that founding-era citizens were skeptical of using the rules for search and seizure set by government actors as the index of reasonableness.

When history has not provided a conclusive answer, we have analyzed a search or seizure in light of traditional standards of reasonableness "by assessing, on the one hand, the degree to which it intrudes upon an individual's privacy and, on the other, the degree to which it is needed for the promotion of legitimate governmental interests." . . . In a long line of cases, we have said that when an officer has probable cause to believe a person committed even a minor crime in his presence, the balancing of private and public interests is not in doubt. The arrest is constitutionally reasonable. . . . We concluded that whether state law authorized the search was irrelevant. States, we said, remained free "to impose higher standards on searches and seizures than required by the Federal Constitution," . . . but regardless of state rules, police could search a lawfully seized vehicle as a matter of federal constitutional law. . . .

[A]n arrest based on probable cause serves interests that have long been seen as sufficient to justify the seizure. . . . Arrest ensures that a suspect appears to answer charges and does not continue a crime, and it safeguards evidence and enables officers to conduct an in-custody investigation. . . .

Moore argues that a State has no interest in arrest when it has a policy against arresting for certain crimes. That is not so, because arrest will still ensure a suspect's appearance at trial, prevent him from continuing his offense, and enable officers to investigate the incident more thoroughly. . . . A State is free to prefer one search-and-seizure policy among the range of constitutionally permissible options, but its choice of a more restrictive option does not render the less restrictive ones unreasonable, and hence unconstitutional. . . . We conclude that warrantless arrests for crimes committed in the presence of an arresting officer are reasonable under the Constitution, and that while States are free to regulate such arrests however they desire, state restrictions do not alter the Fourth Amendment's protections.

Moore argues that even if the Constitution allowed his arrest, it did not allow the arresting officers to search him. . . . The state officers *arrested* Moore, and therefore faced the risks that are "an adequate basis for treating all custodial arrests alike for purposes of search justification." . . . This argument might have force if the Constitution forbade Moore's arrest, because we have sometimes excluded evidence obtained through unconstitutional methods in order to deter constitutional violations. . . . But the arrest rules that the officers violated were those of state law alone, and as we have just concluded, it is not the province of the Fourth Amendment to enforce state law. That Amendment does not require the exclusion of evidence obtained from a constitutionally permissible arrest.

We reaffirm against a novel challenge what we have signaled for more than half a century. When officers have probable cause to believe that a person has committed a

crime in their presence, the Fourth Amendment permits
them to make an arrest, and to search the suspect in order
to safeguard evidence and ensure their own safety. The
judgment of the Supreme Court of Virginia is reversed, and
the case is remanded for further proceedings not inconsistent with this opinion.

It is so ordered.

The Fourth Amendment would also enable officers to make an arrest
and book a person into a jail facility if the offense would not impose any
jail time and require only a small fine upon a conviction. In *Atwater v.
City of Lago Vista*, 532 U.S. 318 (2001), the U.S. Supreme Court found
no Fourth Amendment violation when the person was arrested for not
wearing a seatbelt, in which the only punishment is a fine of not more
than $50. After reviewing the history of warrantless arrests in the common law and reviewing the rules that informed our Founding Fathers in
the drafting of the Fourth Amendment, the Court reasoned that there are
no clear guidelines that would prohibit an officer from arresting a person
for an offense that is neither violent nor a breach of the public peace.
Thus, if an officer determines in his or her discretion that a person should
be booked into a jail facility even if the punishment for the offense would
not require jail time, then the officer is acting within the requirements of
the Fourth Amendment so long as the officer has probable cause to charge
the individual with the offense.

ATWATER V. CITY OF LAGO VISTA, 532 U.S. 318 (2001).

Opinion by SOUTER.

Facts: Defendant Atwater was convicted under a State of
Texas law that requires all persons to wear a seat belt and to
have all children buckled, if their vehicle is equipped with

them, while vehicles are operated on the public highways. The punishment for a violation of this law is a nominal fine of not more than $50. The officer noticed that Atwater was not wearing her seatbelt and pulled her over; her young children were also unbuckled. Instead of issuing a citation and releasing her, the officer placed her under arrest and booked her into jail. She was released on bond within the hour. The Court of Appeals ruled that the arrest was lawful under the Fourth Amendment.

Issue: Does the Fourth Amendment prohibit a warrantless arrest for a minor criminal offense, such as a misdemeanor seatbelt violation, punishable by only a fine?

Rationale and Decision: The Fourth Amendment safeguards "[t]he right of the people to be secure in their persons, houses, papers, and effects, against unreasonable searches and seizures." In reading the Amendment, we are guided by "the traditional protections against unreasonable searches and seizures afforded by the common law at the time of the framing," since "[a]n examination of the common-law understanding of an officer's authority to arrest sheds light on the obviously relevant, if not entirely dispositive, consideration of what the Framers of the Amendment might have thought to be reasonable, . . ." As will be seen later, the view of warrantless arrest authority as extending to at least "some misdemeanors" beyond breaches of the peace was undoubtedly informed by statutory provisions authorizing such arrests, but it reflected common law in the strict, judge-made sense as well. . . .

We need not, and thus do not, speculate whether the Fourth Amendment entails an "in the presence" requirement for purposes of misdemeanor arrests. . . . To be sure, Atwater has cited several 19th-century decisions that, at least at first glance, might seem to support her contention that "warrantless misdemeanor arrest was unlawful when not [for] a breach of the peace." . . . But none is ultimately availing. . . . Our attention has been called to no case, nor have we in our research found one, in which the contrary doctrine has been asserted. . . . Small wonder, then, that today statutes in all 50 States and the District of Columbia permit warrantless misdemeanor arrests by at least some (if not all) peace officers without requiring any breach of the peace. . . .

This, therefore, simply is not a case in which the claimant can point to "a clear answer [that] existed in 1791 and has been generally adhered to by the traditions of our society ever since."

While it is true here that history, if not unequivocal, has expressed a decided, majority view that the police need not obtain an arrest warrant merely because a misdemeanor stopped short of violence or a threat of it, Atwater does not wager all on history. Instead, she asks us to mint a new rule of constitutional law on the understanding that when historical practice fails to speak conclusively to a claim grounded on the Fourth Amendment, courts are left to strike a current balance between individual and societal interests by subjecting particular contemporary circumstances to traditional standards of reasonableness. . . . Atwater accordingly argues for a modern arrest rule, one not necessarily requiring violent breach of the peace, but nonetheless forbidding custodial arrest, even upon probable cause, when conviction could not ultimately carry any jail time and when the government shows no compelling need for immediate detention.

If we were to derive a rule exclusively to address the uncontested facts of this case, Atwater might well prevail. She was a known and established resident of Lago Vista with no place to hide and no incentive to flee, and common sense says she would almost certainly have buckled up as a condition of driving off with a citation. In her case, the physical incidents of arrest were merely gratuitous humiliations imposed by a police officer who was (at best) exercising be "reluctant . . . to conclude that the Fourth Amendment proscribes a practice that was accepted at the time of adoption of the Bill of Rights and has continued to receive the support of many state legislatures," . . . as the practice of making warrantless misdemeanor arrests surely was and has. . . .

Often enough, the Fourth Amendment has to be applied on the spur (and in the heat) of the moment, and the object in implementing its command of reasonableness is to draw standards sufficiently clear and simple to be applied with a fair prospect of surviving judicial second-guessing months and years after an arrest or search is made. Courts attempting to strike a reasonable Fourth Amendment balance thus credit the government's side with an essential interest in readily administrable rules. . . . But the claim is not ultimately so simple, nor could it be, for complications arise the moment we begin to think about the possible applications of the several criteria Atwater proposes for drawing a line between minor crimes with limited arrest authority and others not so restricted. . . . Atwater's rule therefore would not only place police in an almost impossible spot but would guarantee increased litigation over many of the arrests that would occur. For all these reasons, Atwater's various distinctions between permissible and impermissible arrests for minor crimes strike us as "very unsatisfactory line[s]" to require police officers to draw on a moment's notice. . . .

The upshot of all these influences, combined with the good sense (and, failing that, the political accountability) of most local lawmakers and law-enforcement officials, is a dearth of horribles demanding redress. Indeed, when Atwater's counsel was asked at oral argument for any indications of comparably foolish, warrantless misdemeanor arrests, he could offer only one. . . . He referred to a newspaper account of a girl taken into custody for eating french fries in a Washington, D.C., subway station. . . . Not surprisingly, given the practical and political considerations discussed in text, the Washington Metro Transit Police recently revised their "zero-tolerance" policy to provide for citation in lieu of custodial arrest of subway snackers.

. . . In fact, as we have pointed out in text, there simply is no evidence of widespread abuse of minor-offense arrest authority.

Accordingly, we confirm today what our prior cases have intimated: the standard of probable cause "applie[s] to all arrests, without the need to 'balance' the interests and circumstances involved in particular situations." . . . If an officer has probable cause to believe that an individual has committed even a very minor criminal offense in his presence, he may, without violating the Fourth Amendment, arrest the offender.

Atwater's arrest satisfied constitutional requirements. There is no dispute that Officer Turek had probable cause to believe that Atwater had committed a crime in his presence. She admits that neither she nor her children were wearing seatbelts, as required by Tex. Transp. Code Ann. § 545.413 (1999). Turek was accordingly authorized (not required, but authorized) to make a custodial arrest without balancing costs and benefits or determining whether or not Atwater's arrest was in some sense necessary. Nor was the arrest made in an "extraordinary manner, unusually harmful to [her] privacy or . . . physical interests." . . . Atwater's arrest was surely "humiliating," as she says in her brief, but it was no more "harmful to . . . privacy or . . . physical interests" than the normal custodial arrest. She was handcuffed, placed in a squad car, and taken to the local police station, where officers asked her to remove her shoes, jewelry, and glasses, and to empty her pockets. They then took her photograph and placed her in a cell, alone, for about an hour, after which she was taken before a magistrate, and released on $310 bond. The arrest and booking were inconvenient and embarrassing to Atwater, but not so extraordinary as to violate the Fourth Amendment.

The Court of Appeals's en banc judgment is affirmed.

It is so ordered.

Sometimes minor encounters with the police may appear to be contentious. People do not like to be stopped by officers even if they have committed a violation of the law. When dealing with the public, officers may respond to the attitudes of a detainee and modify their response as the detainee's behavior becomes aggressive. Police officers have increasing discretion to respond to the situation as it occurrs. As noted in *Atwater,* such increasing authoritative responses by officers are lawful so long as they have behaved within the bounds of the Fourth Amendment. An arrest can upset individuals who do not wish to go to jail, but an individual's embarrassments, inconveniences, or annoyances do not invalidate arrests based on probable cause.

THE FOURTH AMENDMENT REQUIREMENT FOR A WARRANT

When officers need to secure more information about a person and crimes that the individual may have committed, the police will engage in investigations. As was seen in *United States v. Cortez,* 449 U.S. 411 (1981), a two-month investigation into illegal human smuggling led the officers to engage in a stakeout operation that resulted in a lawful stop and then a lawful warrantless arrest of persons engaging in smuggling activity at the time of the stop. If an investigation then leads an officer to develop probable cause during an investigatory stop, then an arrest without a warrant is lawful. But when the investigation produces enough evidence to give an officer probable cause to believe that a particular person committed a particular crime, the Fourth Amendment may require the officer to secure an arrest warrant in order to seek out and apprehend the individual. The arrest warrant helps to protect a person's right of privacy to his or her home but enables officers to enter the home when there is a strong likelihood of apprehending the person there.

An arrest warrant requires probable cause. To secure the warrant, officers must affirm to a neutral and detached magistrate that they have specific information that a crime occurred and a particular individual committed the offense. If the officers do not have the offender's name, other indicia of identification can be used, such as the person's nicknames and physical description. An arrest warrant can be executed at any place where the officers are likely to find a person, including the person's home or workplace.

A person may also be detained if he or she is expected to be a material witness in a criminal proceeding. While it is rare for a state to arrest and place material witnesses in a jail facility to ensure their appearance as witnesses, it can occur. The state power to detain is based on the need to ensure a conviction of a person and the expectation that the witness is critical to the state's case against some other individual. In *Ashcroft v. al-Kidd*, 563 U.S. ___, 131 S. Ct. 2074 (2011), decided on May 31, 2011, the Court held that if the state has probable cause to detain a person needed as a material witness in a criminal case, then a magistrate can issue a search warrant. Al-Kidd was about to board an airplane bound for Saudi Arabia when he was held pursuant to the warrant. Federal prosecutors were trying Sami Omar al-Hussayen in a criminal case of terrorism. The government had obtained a warrant two days before al-Kidd's departure indicating that if he boarded a plane to leave the United States, they believed important information would be lost in their case against al-Hussayen. At al-Hussayen's trial, the prosecution never called al-Kidd to the stand, but al-Kidd was held in detention for 16 days. In his claim against the federal government for unlawful detention, al-Kidd claims that his arrest was a pretext to keep him in the United States as a suspected criminal. Al-Kidd argued that the government detained him not as a material witness but as someone that they might later charge with terrorism. The Court rejected al-Kidd's claim. Writing for the majority, Justice Scalia stated:

> Needless to say, warrantless, "suspicionless intrusions pursuant to a general scheme," are far removed from the facts of this case. A warrant issued by a neutral Magistrate Judge authorized al-Kidd's arrest. The affidavit accompanying the warrant application (as al-Kidd concedes) gave individualized reasons to believe that he was a material witness and that he would soon disappear. The existence of a judicial warrant based on individualized suspicion takes this case outside the domain of not only our special-needs and administrative-search cases, but of *Edmond* as well.

The Court was not troubled that al-Kidd was not called as a witness in the case against al-Hussayen. The Court noted that it was not concerned with any subjective reasons by which the government wished to detain him. Rather, what is needed are articulable, objective facts that are reviewed by a detached and neutral magistrate issuing a warrant. Satisfied that the magistrate was given sufficient basis upon which to issue warrant for al-Kidd's removal from an airplane and subsequent jailing, the Court held that the material witness warrant was valid and his detention lawful.

DNA AND OTHER ITEMS IDENTIFYING A PERSON

Many times, a person may be identified by witnesses who recognize his or her face, body features, voice, or other external visual and audio clues. As technology progresses, such identifying clues can be more invasive of personal privacy. The question of whether a person can request or refuse to have his or her DNA used as a method of identifying the offender of a crime is controversial. Almost every state, and the federal government, has rules that allow offenders who have been convicted of a crime to have DNA evidence tested to determine if they should be exonerated for the crime for which they are serving a prison sentence. According to the Koshland Science Museum of the National Academy of Sciences (retrieved September 17, 2009, from http://www.koshland-science-museum.org/exhibitdna/crim02.jsp): "When two DNA samples match completely in a large number of regions, such as the 13 used in the FBI's CODIS system, the probability that they could have come from two unrelated people is virtually zero. This fact makes DNA identification extremely reliable." Federal courts have held that, so long as reasonable suspicion exists, DNA evidence can be taken by the use of a buccal swab as it is not an intrusive invasion of a person.

Despite the widespread scientific recognition that DNA is relevant and can accurately identify persons who committed crimes, the U.S. Supreme Court has held that a prisoner does not have the constitutional right to have access to DNA evidence. In *District Attorney's Office v. Osborne*, 557 U.S. ___, 128 S. Ct. 2308 (2009), Osborne sought both postconviction direct appeals as well as a *habeas corpus* relief, claiming he should be given access to a DNA test that produced more reliable results than those used by the state in his criminal trial. Prosecutors, the Court held, can use whichever test they have available even if another scientific test exists that is more accurate in identifying persons from samples taken at a crime scene. A conviction for a crime does not hinge just on DNA evidence; other evidence of responsibility can sustain convictions such as victim testimony, tangible evidence found on suspects or in their possession, and testimony by codefendants.

DISTRICT ATTORNEY'S OFFICE V. OSBORNE, 557 U.S. ___, 129 S. CT. 2308 (2009)

Opinion by ROBERTS.

Facts: In 1993, two men raped, choked, and beat a woman and left her for dead in the state of Alaska. The victim survived the attack and gave a description of the men and their vehicle to the police. At the crime scene, the police recovered a spent shell casing, the axe handle used in the beating, some of the victim's clothing stained with blood, and a blue condom. Six days later, one defendant, Jackson, was stopped for a traffic violation. In the car, which matched the victim's description, police found a gun that matched the shell casing and other items the victim had been carrying the night of the attack. Jackson admitted that he had been the driver during the rape and assault, and told the police that Osborne had been with him. The state performed DQ alpha testing on sperm found in the blue condom. This form of testing is a somewhat inexact form of DNA testing. The semen found on the condom had a genotype that matched Osborne's blood sample. Osborne is black, and approximately 16% of black individuals have such a genotype. The state also examined some pubic hairs found at the crime scene that were found to be similar to Osborne's. Osborne and Jackson were convicted by an Alaska jury of kidnapping, assault, and sexual assault. Osborne's conviction and sentence were affirmed on appeal, and Osborne then sought postconviction relief. Osborne, in his appeal, wanted to have the state perform a more exact form of DNA testing available to the state at the time of his trial. The Court of Appeals held that the defendant had a limited due process right to evidence for DNA testing purposes.

Issue: Does a criminal defendant have a due process right to obtain postconviction access to the state's evidence for DNA testing?

Rationale and Decision: Modern DNA testing can provide powerful new evidence unlike anything known before. Since its first use in criminal investigations in the mid-1980s, there have been several major advances in DNA technology, culminating in STR technology. It is now often possible to determine whether a biological tissue matches a suspect with near certainty. While of course many criminal trials proceed without any forensic and scientific testing at all, there is no technology comparable to DNA testing for matching tissues when such evidence is at issue. . . . DNA testing has exonerated wrongly convicted people, and has confirmed the convictions of many others. . . .

At the same time, DNA testing alone does not always resolve a case. Where there is enough other incriminating evidence and an explanation for the DNA result, science alone cannot prove a prisoner innocent. . . . The dilemma is how to harness DNA's power to prove innocence without unnecessarily overthrowing the established system of criminal justice.

That task belongs primarily to the legislature. . . . Alaska is one of a handful of States yet to enact legislation specifically addressing the issue of evidence requested for DNA testing. But that does not mean that such evidence is unavailable for those seeking to prove their innocence. Instead, Alaska courts are addressing how to apply existing laws for discovery and postconviction relief to this novel technology. First, access to evidence is available under Alaska law for those who seek to subject it to newly available DNA testing that will prove them to be actually innocent. Under the State's general postconviction relief statute, a prisoner may challenge his conviction when "there exists evidence of material facts, not previously presented and heard by the court, that requires vacation of the conviction or sentence in the interest of justice." . . . In addition to this statutory procedure, the Alaska Court of Appeals has invoked a widely accepted three-part test to govern additional rights to DNA access under the State Constitution. . . . [A] defendant who seeks post-conviction DNA testing . . . must show (1) that the conviction rested primarily on eyewitness identification evidence, (2) that there was a demonstrable doubt concerning the defendant's identification as the perpetrator, and (3) that scientific testing would likely be conclusive on this issue.

. . . Osborne argues that access to the State's evidence is a "process" needed to vindicate his right to prove himself innocent and get out of jail. . . . [However,] a criminal defendant proved guilty after a fair trial does not have the same liberty interests as a free man. . . . Osborne seeks access to state evidence so that he can apply new DNA-testing technology that might prove him innocent. There is no long history of such a right, and "[t]he mere novelty of such a claim is reason enough to doubt that 'substantive due process' sustains it." . . .

Establishing a freestanding right to access DNA evidence for testing would force us to act as policymakers, and our substantive-due-process rulemaking authority would not only have to cover the right of access but a myriad of other issues. We would soon have to decide if there is a constitutional obligation to preserve forensic evidence that might later be tested. . . . If so, for how long? Would it be different for different types of evidence? Would the State also have some obligation to gather such evidence in the first place? How much, and when? No doubt there would be a miscellany of other minor directives. . . . At the end of the day, there is no reason to suppose that their answers to these questions would be any better than those of state courts and legislatures, and good reason to suspect the opposite. . . .

DNA evidence will undoubtedly lead to changes in the criminal justice system. It has done so already. The question is whether further change will primarily be made by legislative revision and judicial interpretation of the existing system, or whether the Federal Judiciary must leap ahead—revising (or even discarding) the system by creating a new constitutional right and taking over responsibility for refining it.

Federal courts should not presume that state criminal procedures will be inadequate to deal with technological change. The criminal justice system has historically accommodated new types of evidence, and is a time-tested means of carrying out society's interest in convicting the guilty while respecting individual rights. That system, like any human endeavor, cannot be perfect. DNA evidence shows that it has not been. But there is no basis for Osborne's approach of assuming that because DNA has shown that these procedures are not flawless, DNA evidence must be treated as categorically outside the process, rather than within it. That is precisely what his [postconviction] suit seeks to do, and that is the contention we reject.

The judgment of the Court of Appeals is reversed, and the case is remanded for further proceedings consistent with this opinion.

It is so ordered.

PUBLIC SCHOOLS AND YOUTH

The Fourth Amendment pertains to actions by governmental officers, not private citizens. Whether school officials can legally detain or arrest youth depends on the situation in which the seizure occurred. In *New Jersey v. T.L.O.,* 469 U.S. 325 (1985), and *Vernonia School Dist. 47J v. Acton,* 515 U.S. 646 (1995), the U.S. Supreme Court found that because school officials are entrusted with minor students, they have authority to detain them under the Fourth Amendment. The Court has reasoned that the minors have a lesser expectation of privacy when they are on school grounds and the school officials have a duty of care to protect the youth through their *parens patrie* responsibility. In validating a school drug test policy for all student athletes in a public high school, the Court in *Vernonia* reasoned that even if the school officials did not have any suspicion, let alone reasonable suspicion, to determine that the youth were engaged in illegal drug usage, the officials must act in the protection of minors by determining if they are taking drugs. Because the school officials are not police officers, the youth do not have the same Fourth Amendment interests that might protect their right of privacy from intrusion by law enforcement officers.

VERNONIA SCHOOL DIST. 47J V. ACTON, 515 U.S. 646 (1995)

Opinion by SCALIA.

Facts: Drugs were considered to be a problem in the Vernonia School District. Consequently, the high school administration determined that it would perform random drug tests on all students participating in interscholastic athletics. Students wishing to play sports must sign a form consenting to the testing and must obtain the written consent of their parents. The samples are sent to an independent laboratory, which routinely tests them for amphetamines, cocaine, and marijuana. Only the superintendent, principals, vice principals, and athletic directors have access to test results, and the results are not kept for more than one year. If a sample tests positive, a second test is administered as soon as possible to confirm the result. If the second test is negative, no further action is taken. If the second test is positive, the athlete's parents are notified, and the school principal convenes a meeting with the student and his or her parents, at which time the student is given the option of (1) participating for six weeks in an assistance program that includes weekly urinalysis, or (2) suffering suspension from athletics for the remainder of the current season and the next athletic season. The student is then retested prior to the start of the next athletic season for which he or she is eligible. The policy states that a second offense results in automatic imposition of option 2; a third offense results in suspension for the remainder of the current season and the next two athletic seasons.

In the fall of 1991, Acton, then a seventh grader, signed up to play football at one of the district's grade schools. He was denied participation, however, because he and his parents refused to sign the testing consent forms. The Actons filed suit, claiming that the high school policy violated the Fourth and Fourteenth Amendments as well as their state constitution. The Court of Appeals agreed and determined that the policy was unconstitutional.

Issue: Do school officials have the right under the Fourth Amendment to engage in school procedures that will detain youth and secure urine samples without reasonable suspicion or probable cause to believe that a particular student is using illegal substances?

Rationale and Decision: The Fourth Amendment to the United States Constitution provides that the Federal Government shall not violate "[t]he right of the people to be secure in their persons, houses, papers, and effects, against unreasonable searches and seizures, ..." We have held that the Fourteenth Amendment extends this constitutional guarantee to searches and seizures by state officers, . . . including public school officials, in *New Jersey* v. *T. L. O.,* 469 U.S. 325, 336–337 (1985). . . . But a warrant is not required to establish the reasonableness of *all* government searches; and when a warrant is not required (and the Warrant Clause therefore not applicable), probable cause is not invariably required either. A search unsupported by probable cause can be constitutional, we have said, "when special needs, beyond the normal need for law enforcement, make the warrant and probable cause requirement impracticable." . . . We have found such "special needs" to exist in the public school context. There, the warrant requirement "would unduly interfere with the maintenance of the swift and informal disciplinary procedures [that are] needed," and "strict adherence to the requirement that searches be based upon probable cause" would undercut "the substantial need of teachers and administrators for freedom to maintain order in the schools." . . . We have upheld suspicionless searches and seizures to conduct drug testing of railroad personnel involved in train accidents . . . ; to conduct random drug testing of federal customs officers who carry arms or are involved in drug interdiction . . . ; and to maintain automobile checkpoints looking for illegal immigrants and contraband. . . .

The first factor to be considered is the nature of the privacy interest upon which the search here at issue intrudes. The Fourth Amendment does not protect all subjective expectations of privacy, but only those that society recognizes as "legitimate." . . . Traditionally at common law, and still today, unemancipated minors lack some of the most fundamental rights of self determination—including even the right of liberty in its narrow sense, *i.e.*, the right to come and go at will. They are subject, even as to their physical freedom, to the control of their parents or guardians. . . . When parents place minor children in private schools for their education, the teachers and administrators of those schools stand *in loco parentis* over the children. . . .

Legitimate privacy expectations are even less with regard to student athletes. School sports are not for the bashful. They require "suiting up" before each practice or event, and showering and changing afterwards. Public school locker rooms, the usual sites for these activities, are not notable for the privacy they afford. The locker rooms in Vernonia are typical: no individual dressing rooms are provided; shower heads are lined up along a wall, unseparated by any sort of partition or curtain; not even all the toilet stalls have doors. . . . There is an additional respect in which school athletes have a reduced expectation of privacy. By choosing to "go out for the team," they voluntarily subject themselves to a degree of regulation even higher than that imposed on students generally. . . .

That the nature of the concern is important—indeed, perhaps compelling—can hardly be doubted. Deterring drug use by our Nation's schoolchildren is at least as important as enhancing efficient enforcement of the Nation's laws against the importation of drugs. . . . In the present case, moreover, the necessity for the State to act is magnified by the fact that this evil is being visited not just upon individuals at large, but upon children for whom it has undertaken a special responsibility of care and direction. Finally, it must not be lost sight of that this program is directed more narrowly to drug use by school athletes, where the risk of immediate physical harm to the drug user or those with whom he is playing his sport is particularly high. Apart from psychological effects, which include impairment of judgment, slow reaction time, and a lessening of the perception of pain, the particular drugs screened by the District's Policy have been demonstrated to pose substantial physical risks to athletes. . . .

Taking into account all the factors we have considered above—the decreased expectation of privacy, the relative unobtrusiveness of the search, and the severity of the need met by the search—we conclude Vernonia's Policy is reasonable and hence constitutional. We caution against the assumption that suspicionless drug testing will readily pass constitutional muster in other contexts. . . .

We therefore vacate the judgment, and remand the case to the Court of Appeals for further proceedings consistent with this opinion.

It is so ordered.

The ability of school officials to perform an action under the guise of their *parens patriae* responsibilities is not unrestricted. School officials, while usually operating under a less severe review standard under the Fourth and Fourteenth Amendments—e.g., reasonable suspicion—must still act reasonably. In *Vernonia*, the officials tested all student athletes, regardless of whether they thought the students used drugs. In *T.L.O.*, the officials searched a student's purse after she was found smoking in the bathroom; the individual was held and her purse searched upon a reasonable expectation that the youth, who had previously been found smoking on school grounds, would have a pack of cigarettes in her bag.

USE OF FORCE

Arrests by definition involve force. An officer has the right to hold a person and keep him or her from leaving. The degree of lawful force that can be used is based on a continuum. Limited amounts of force may be exhibited by a simple order or request to remain where the individual is located. Increasing use of force may be exhibited by the use of the officer's hand to secure a person or the handcuffing of a person. More serious levels of force may be exhibited by the use of a Taser (an electroshock weapon that disrupts voluntary control of muscles) or other weapon to stop a person from leaving the scene. The degree to which an officer can use physical or deadly force varies with the situation as it is unfolding.

The U.S. Supreme Court has provided some guidelines for the use of deadly force in the apprehension of unarmed, nondangerous fleeing misdemeanants. Until *Tennessee v. Garner,* 471 U.S. 1 (1985), it was difficult for individuals to seek redress against the police if excessive force was used to arrest a suspect. In *Garner,* the police under state law had the right to use deadly force to apprehend fleeing suspects. The Court stated that a Fourth Amendment violation occurs if the police use deadly force to apprehend a fleeing, nondangerous suspect. Officers may use deadly force only if the officers or others are reasonably threatened by deadly force. If the reason for the arrest of an individual is reasonable suspicion that the person has committed a nondangerous misdemeanor or felony, an officer may use a weapon only if responding to deadly threats by the arrestee. The amount of force that officers can use is reasonably related to the amount of force used by individuals who are approached by the police.

TENNESSEE V. GARNER, 471 U.S. 1 (1985)

Opinion by WHITE.

Facts: Officers responded to a call about a prowler at a home. When they arrived at the address, a woman indicated that someone was breaking into the home next door. The officers saw someone running from the home. The fleeing suspect was observed with a flashlight and was unarmed. When the suspect, Garner, attempted to climb a fence, the officer called for him to stop. Convinced that the suspect was going to elude capture, the officer shot him. The bullet killed the suspect. State of Tennessee law allows officers to use "all necessary means to effect the arrest" if officers announce their intention to arrest the defendant and the defendant flees or forcibly resists arrest. The suspect's father sued under 42 U.S.C. §1983 for asserted violations of Garner's constitutional rights. The complaint alleged that the shooting violated the Fourth, Fifth, Sixth, Eighth, and Fourteenth Amendments of the U.S. Constitution. The Court of Appeals held that the officer's actions were a seizure and that killing a fleeing suspect was lawful only if the officer was justified in using deadly force.

Issue: Can officers use deadly force to prevent the escape of an apparently unarmed suspected felon?

Rationale and Decision: Whenever an officer restrains the freedom of a person to walk away, he has seized that person. . . . While it is not always clear just when minimal police interference becomes a seizure, . . . there can be no question that apprehension by the use of deadly force is a seizure subject to the reasonableness requirement of the Fourth Amendment. A police officer may arrest a person if he has probable cause to believe that person committed a crime. . . .

[N]otwithstanding probable cause to seize a suspect, an officer may not always do so by killing him. The intrusiveness of a seizure by means of deadly force is unmatched. The suspect's fundamental interest in his own life need not be elaborated upon. The use of deadly force also frustrates the interest of the individual, and of society, in judicial determination of guilt and punishment. Against these interests are ranged governmental interests in effective law enforcement. . . . Effectiveness in making arrests requires the resort to deadly force, or at least the meaningful threat thereof. . . .

The fact is that a majority of police departments . . . in this country have forbidden the use of deadly force against non-violent suspects. . . . The use of deadly force to prevent the escape of all felony suspects, whatever the circumstances, is constitutionally unreasonable. It is not better that all felony suspects die than that they escape. Where the suspect poses no immediate threat to the officer and no threat to others, the harm resulting from failing to apprehend him does not justify the use of deadly force to do so. It is no doubt unfortunate when a suspect who is in sight escapes, but the fact that the police arrive a little late or are a little slower afoot does not always justify killing the suspect. A police officer may not seize an unarmed, nondangerous suspect by shooting him dead. The Tennessee statute is unconstitutional insofar as it authorizes the use of deadly force against such fleeing suspects. . . .

The judgment of the Court of Appeals is affirmed, and the case is remanded for further proceedings consistent with this opinion.

So ordered.

Use of Taser

Police departments use Tasers to apprehend suspects who are resisting arrest, excessively disruptive, or engaged in dangerous behaviors when stopped. Departments consider Taser gun use to be nonlethal and may characterize it as exerting less physical force than closed fists, chemical sprays, and baton usage. Police officers may need to use physical methods during an arrest if there is a reasonable belief that they or other persons will be harmed during an arrest or a stop. However, some suspects and arrestees have died when Tasered—some due to complications on a preexisting heart condition, and some because they were on drugs at the time.

In early 2009, the U.S. Supreme Court was asked to consider if it was a violation of the Fourth Amendment to use a Taser on a person in order to apprehend him. The ACLU in Florida asked the Court to consider

> [w]hether a reasonable police officer had fair notice in 2004 suffi-
> cient to deprive him of qualified immunity that it violated the Fourth
> Amendment to administer three separate five-second-long direct contact
> "drive stun" taser shocks, over a two minute period, to a handcuffed
> nonviolent misdemeanor traffic arrestee who had already collapsed
> to the ground sobbing, who never actively resisted arrest or attempted
> to flee, and who never posed any danger to himself, the officer or the
> public, when the sole purpose of the Taser shocks was to administer
> pain to prompt the arrestee to stand up. (Retrieved September 17,
> 2009, from http://www.aclufl.org/pdfs/BuckleyCert-final.pdf).

In May 2009, the high court denied certiorari in the case. In June 2009, a New York judge ruled that a Taser could be used on a person to com- pel him to give DNA evidence. The defendant claimed in a suppression hearing that the police apprehended him on the street, took him to police headquarters, and asked him to give a DNA sample; when he refused, the officer used the Taser on him, and while he was unconscious a swab of his DNA was taken (*State of New York v. Smith*, retrieved September 17, 2009, from http://blog.simplejustice.us/files/66432-58232/TaserDecision1.pdf). In 2011, the Ninth Circuit, in *Bryan v. McPherson,* 590 F.3d. 767 (9th Cir. 2009), held that a defendant who was wearing underwear and shout- ing expletives at the officers did not pose a sufficient threat to the officer's safety to justify the use of Taser. Additionally, the Court held that if the officer thought the person posed a danger because of mental illness, then the officer should have exercised greater restraint before using the Taser. More analysis of Taser's effects on suspects and their use by police officers must be completed before its lawful usage can be ensured.

CONTEMPORARY ISSUES: DETENTIONS AND ENEMY COMBATANTS

After September 11, 2001, the United States heightened national security measures to thwart any future terrorist attacks on U.S. soil and engaged in a "War on Terror" by pursuing Taliban fighters in Afghanistan and al-Qaeda combat forces in Iran. Part of the Bush administration's strat- egy included indefinitely detaining enemy combatants who were believed to pose a threat to U.S. national security because they were members of the Taliban or part of al-Qaeda's insurgency forces. In 2002, Yaser Eser Hamdi was captured on a battlefield in Afghanistan. Although he was detained in Guantanamo Bay with other persons who were presumably engaged in warfare against the United States, he was later transferred to a military prison in Virginia. At issue before the U.S. Supreme Court is whether American citizens detained as enemy combatants in the United States are entitled to the due process protections of the Constitution. The Court ruled 8 to 1 in favor of Hamdi, holding that if the government wishes to continually hold enemy combatants, initially secured under the pressures of a battlefield, then an opportunity for the detained person to challenge his or her indefinite confinement must be allowed to appear before a neutral magistrate.

HAMDI ET AL. V. RUMSFELD, SECRETARY OF DEFENSE, ET AL., 542 U.S. 507 (2004)

Opinion by O'CONNOR.

Facts: On September 11, 2001, the al-Qaeda terrorist network used hijacked commercial airliners to attack prominent targets in the United States. Approximately 3,000 people were killed in those attacks. One week later, in response to these "acts of treacherous violence," Congress passed a resolution authorizing the President to "use all necessary and appropriate force against those nations, organizations, or persons he determines planned, authorized, committed, or aided the terrorist attacks" or "harbored such organizations or persons, in order to prevent any future acts of international terrorism against the United States by such nations, organizations or persons." Soon thereafter, the President ordered U.S. Armed Forces to Afghanistan, with a mission to subdue al-Qaeda and quell the Taliban regime that was known to support it.

This case arises out of the detention of a man whom the government alleges took up arms with the Taliban during this conflict. His name is Yaser Esam Hamdi. Born an

American citizen in Louisiana in 1980, Hamdi moved with his family to Saudi Arabia as a child. By 2001, the parties agree, he resided in Afghanistan. At some point that year, he was seized by members of the Northern Alliance, a coalition of military groups opposed to the Taliban government, and eventually was turned over to the U.S. military. The government asserts that it initially detained and interrogated Hamdi in Afghanistan before transferring him to the U.S. Naval Base in Guantanamo Bay in January 2002. In April 2002, upon learning that Hamdi is an American citizen, authorities transferred him to a naval brig in Norfolk, Virginia, where he remained until a subsequent transfer to a brig in Charleston, South Carolina. The government contends that Hamdi is an "enemy combatant" and that this status justifies holding him in the United States indefinitely—without formal charges or proceedings—unless and until it makes the determination that access to counsel or further process is warranted.

In June 2002, Hamdi's father, Esam Fouad Hamdi, filed the present petition for a writ of habeas corpus under 28 U.S.C. §2241 in the Eastern District of Virginia, naming as petitioners his son and himself as next friend. The elder Hamdi alleges in the petition that he has had no contact with his son since the government took custody of him in 2001 and that the government has held his son "without access to legal counsel or notice of any charges pending against him." The petition contends that Hamdi's detention was not legally authorized. It argues that "[a]s an American citizen, . . . Hamdi enjoys the full protections of the Constitution," and that Hamdi's detention in the United States without charges, access to an impartial tribunal, or assistance of counsel "violated and continue[s] to violate the Fifth and Fourteenth Amendments to the United States Constitution." The habeas petition asks that the Court, among other things, declare that he is being held in violation of the Fifth and Fourteenth Amendments [and] order that Hamdi be released from his "unlawful custody."

The Court of Appeals held that separation of powers requires the Court to defer to the authority of executive branch during wartime.

Issue: Does the president of the United States have the authority to detain citizens who qualify as "enemy combatants"?

Rationale and Decision: At this difficult time in our Nation's history, we are called upon to consider the legality of the government's detention of a United States citizen on United States soil as an "enemy combatant" and to address the process that is constitutionally owed to one who seeks to challenge his classification as such. The United States Court of Appeals for the Fourth Circuit held that petitioner's detention was legally authorized and that he was entitled to no further opportunity to challenge his enemy-combatant label. We now vacate and remand. We hold that although Congress authorized the detention of combatants in the narrow circumstances alleged here, due process demands that a citizen held in the United States as an enemy combatant be given a meaningful opportunity to contest the factual basis for that detention before a neutral decisionmaker.

There is some debate as to the proper scope of [the] term [enemy combatant], and the government has never provided any court with the full criteria that it uses in classifying individuals as such. It has made clear, however, that, for purposes of this case, the "enemy combatant" that it is seeking to detain is an individual who, it alleges, was "part of or supporting forces hostile to the United States or coalition partners" in Afghanistan and who "engaged in an armed conflict against the United States" there. . . . We therefore answer only the narrow question before us: whether the detention of citizens falling within that definition is authorized.

. . . There is no bar to this Nation's holding one of its own citizens as an enemy combatant. . . . It is a clearly established principle of the law of war that detention may last no longer than active hostilities. . . . Hamdi contends that the AUMF does not authorize indefinite or perpetual detention. Certainly, we agree that indefinite detention for the purpose of interrogation is not authorized. Further, we understand Congress' grant of authority for the use of "necessary and appropriate force" to include the authority to detain for the duration of the relevant conflict, and our understanding is based on longstanding law-of-war principles. If the practical circumstances of a given conflict are entirely unlike those of the conflicts that informed the development of the law of war, that understanding may unravel. But that is not the situation we face as of this date. Active combat operations against Taliban fighters apparently are ongoing in Afghanistan. . . . The United States may detain, for the duration of these hostilities, individuals legitimately determined to be Taliban combatants who "engaged in an armed conflict against the United States." If the record establishes that United States troops are still involved in active combat in Afghanistan, those detentions are part of the exercise of "necessary and appropriate force," and therefore are authorized by the AUMF.

Even in cases in which the detention of enemy combatants is legally authorized, there remains the question of what process is constitutionally due to a citizen who disputes his enemy-combatant status. Hamdi argues that he is owed a meaningful and timely hearing and that "extra-judicial detention [that] begins and ends with the submission of an affidavit based on third-hand hearsay" does not comport with the Fifth and Fourteenth Amendments. . . .

Though they reach radically different conclusions on the process that ought to attend the present proceeding, the parties begin on common ground. All agree that, absent suspension, the writ of habeas corpus remains available to every individual detained within the United States. . . .

The government's second argument requires closer consideration. This is the argument that further factual exploration is unwarranted and inappropriate in light of the extraordinary constitutional interests at stake. Under the government's most extreme rendition of this argument, "[r]espect for separation of powers and the limited institutional capabilities of courts in matters of military decision-making in connection with an ongoing conflict" ought to eliminate entirely any individual process, restricting the courts to investigating only whether legal authorization exists for the broader detention scheme. . . . At most, the government argues, courts should review its determination that a citizen is an enemy combatant under a very deferential "some evidence" standard. . . . Under this review, a court would assume the accuracy of the government's articulated basis for Hamdi's detention, . . . and assess only whether that articulated basis was a legitimate one. . . .

In response, Hamdi emphasizes that this Court consistently has recognized that an individual challenging his detention may not be held at the will of the Executive without recourse to some proceeding before a neutral tribunal to determine whether the Executive's asserted justifications for that detention have basis in fact and warrant in law. . . . Anything less, it concluded, would not be "meaningful judicial review." . . .

Both of these positions highlight legitimate concerns. And both emphasize the tension that often exists between the autonomy that the government asserts is necessary in order to pursue effectively a particular goal and the process that a citizen contends he is due before he is deprived of a constitutional right. The ordinary mechanism that we use for balancing such serious competing interests, . . . is the test that . . . the process due in any given instance is determined by weighing "the private interest that will be affected by the official action" against the government's asserted interest, "including the function involved" and the burdens the government would face in providing greater process. . . .

1. . . . We reaffirm today the fundamental nature of a citizen's right to be free from involuntary confinement

by his own government without due process of law, and we weigh the opposing governmental interests against the curtailment of liberty that such confinement entails.

2. On the other side of the scale are the weighty and sensitive governmental interests in ensuring that those who have in fact fought with the enemy during a war do not return to battle against the United States. . . . To the extent that these burdens are triggered by heightened procedures, they are properly taken into account in our due process analysis.

3. Striking the proper constitutional balance here is of great importance to the Nation during this period of ongoing combat. But it is equally vital that our calculus not give short shrift to the values that this country holds dear or to the privilege that is American citizenship. It is during our most challenging and uncertain moments that our Nation's commitment to due process is most severely tested; and it is in those times that we must preserve our commitment at home to the principles for which we fight abroad.

We therefore hold that a citizen-detainee seeking to challenge his classification as an enemy combatant must receive notice of the factual basis for his classification, and a fair opportunity to rebut the government's factual assertions before a neutral decisionmaker. . . . These essential constitutional promises may not be eroded. At the same time, the exigencies of the circumstances may demand that, aside from these core elements, enemy combatant proceedings may be tailored to alleviate their uncommon potential to burden the Executive at a time of ongoing military conflict. Hearsay, for example, may need to be accepted as the most reliable available evidence from the government in such a proceeding. Likewise, the Constitution would not be offended by a presumption in favor of the government's evidence, so long as that presumption remained a rebuttable one and fair opportunity for rebuttal were provided. . . .

In sum, while the full protections that accompany challenges to detentions in other settings may prove unworkable and inappropriate in the enemy-combatant setting, the threats to military operations posed by a basic system of independent review are not so weighty as to trump a citizen's core rights to challenge meaningfully the government's case and to be heard by an impartial adjudicator.

In so holding, we necessarily reject the government's assertion that separation of powers principles mandate a heavily circumscribed role for the courts in such circumstances. . . .

Because we conclude that due process demands some system for a citizen detainee to refute his classification, the proposed "some evidence" standard is inadequate. . . . Today we are faced only with such a case. Aside from unspecified "screening" processes, . . . and military interrogations in which the government suggests Hamdi could have contested his classification, . . . Hamdi has received no process. An interrogation by one's captor, however effective an intelligence-gathering tool, hardly constitutes a constitutionally adequate factfinding before a neutral decisionmaker. . . . In the absence of such process, however, a court that receives a petition for a writ of habeas corpus from an alleged enemy combatant must itself ensure that the minimum requirements of due process are achieved. Both courts below recognized as much, focusing their energies on the question of whether Hamdi was due an opportunity to rebut the government's case against him. . . . We have no reason to doubt that courts faced with these sensitive matters will pay proper heed both to the matters of national security that might arise in an individual case and to the constitutional limitations safeguarding essential liberties that remain vibrant even in times of security concerns.

The . . . case is remanded for further proceedings.

Justice Thomas was the lone dissenter, finding that the executive branch, when acting under explicit congressional approval, was virtually unreviewable by the judiciary in exercise of his war powers.

Immediately after the *Hamdi* decision, Congress passed the United States Military Commission Act of 2006, which authorized military tribunals to try enemy combatants. The Act sought, among other things, to limit the ability of U.S. courts to hear cases in which enemy combatants were detained:

> 10 U.S.C. sec. 949(e)(1) No court, justice, or judge shall have jurisdiction to hear or consider an application for a writ of habeas corpus filed by or on behalf of an alien detained by the United States who has been determined by the United States to have been properly detained as an enemy combatant or is awaiting such determination.

In *Boumediene v. Bush,* 553 U.S. 723 (2008), the U.S. Supreme Court again looked at the issue of whether enemy combatants could be held without due process. In a 5-to-4 decision by Justice Anthony Kennedy, the Court held that alien nationals held as enemy combatants outside the United States at Guantanamo Bay were entitled to constitutional protections because the base was under U.S. control. Justice John Paul Stevens stated "to hold that the political branches may switch the constitution on or off at will would lead to a regime in which they, not this court, 'say what the law is.'" The dissent, written by Chief Justice Roberts, decried that the majority struck down the "most generous set of procedural protections" granted enemy combatants in American history. In 2009, the act was amended so as to limit the use of hearsay evidence to justify detentions of enemy combatants and enhance the right to counsel of arrested persons.

SUMMARY

An arrest is the detention of a person for a period of time; the person is not free to leave. The detention is based on probable cause to believe that the detainee committed a crime. An arrest also implicates other police processes, such as a search. Persons who resist arrest may be subject to increased force in order that the police can arrest them. No person has a right to resist an arrest; the lawfulness of an arrest will be determined later in court. If a fleeing person resorts to deadly force to abscond, then the police may use deadly force to apprehend the person, even if the initial encounter was for a minor offense. The arrest process may be fluid and changing as the events of the police–arrestee encounter change. Once a person has been arrested, then other constitutional provisions might be implicated. Additionally, the state cannot hold individuals indefinably without charging them with a particular crime. This procedural requirement is heightened in situations when enemy combatants are held. The U.S. Supreme Court has continually asserted in recent years that the detention of enemy combatants implicates the Constitution, and arrested persons, alien and citizen alike, are entitled to its protections. Among these rights are habeas corpus protections that enable a person to know of the charges against them and to have an attorney help them ascertain the reasonableness of their detention and the right to be heard before a neutral magistrate.

GLOSSARY

Arrest: The taking of a person into custody or detaining someone for a period of time during which they are not free to leave.

Arrest warrant: A judicial order to place a person under arrest for a crime, made after review of a neutral statement sufficient to demonstrate probable cause. Permits entrance into the home or place of business of the suspect in order to effectuate the arrest.

Deadly force: An amount of force that could cause death.

Enemy combatant: A person who is considered an enemy of the state during an armed conflict.

Fleeing felon: A person who is believed by the police to have committed a felony and who is attempting to evade arrest.

Probable cause: The Fourth Amendment requirement that police have sufficient reasonable grounds to believe that a crime occurred and that a person has committed that crime.

Warrantless arrest: A legal arrest that occurs without an arrest warrant, based on probable cause of a felony or for a misdemeanor committed in the presence of a police officer.

ADDITIONAL READINGS

Lerner, C. S. (2002). The reasonableness of probable cause. *Texas Law Review, 81,* 952–1029.

Yin, T. (2006). Coercion and terrorism prosecutions in the shadow of military detention. *Brigham Young University Law Review,* 1261–1327.

CHAPTER 5

Confessions and Interrogations

KEY POINTS

- *Miranda v. Arizona* sets out the basic principles for protecting a person's Fifth and Sixth Amendment rights with a set of warnings.

- Individuals have a right to remain silent and a right to counsel when they are being interrogated and are in custody.

- The right to remain silent is not the same as the right to counsel.

- There is no particular manner (oral or written) in which the rights need to be conveyed to a suspect in custody so long as they are conveyed to the suspect prior to an interrogation.

- The defendant has to be careful and vigilant in maintaining and asserting his or her *Miranda* rights.

THE FIFTH AND SIXTH AMENDMENTS

The Fifth Amendment to the U.S. Constitution provides for a privilege against self-incrimination. This privilege is more commonly referred to as the right to remain silent. This right extends to persons during the trial and during various pretrial stages in the criminal investigation process. The Fifth Amendment specifically provides that (emphasis added):

> No person shall be held to answer for a capital, or otherwise infamous crime, unless on a presentment or indictment of a Grand Jury, except in cases arising in the land or naval forces, or in the Militia, when in

actual service in time of War or public danger; nor shall any person be subject for the same offence to be twice put in jeopardy of life or limb; *nor shall be compelled in any criminal case to be a witness against himself,* nor be deprived of life, liberty, or property, without due process of law; nor shall private property be taken for public use, without just compensation.

A suspect or accused person may claim the privilege against self-incrimination during interrogations. The accused person can also refuse to take the witness stand during a trial. However, the extent to which the right protects suspects from having their own incriminating statements used against them is complicated. In general, the U.S. Supreme Court has held that the state will not be allowed to use information obtained from a Fifth Amendment violation during a trial. But the state may be able to use such information for impeachment purposes, should the defendant choose to testify. The right therefore is contextualized by when the information was obtained, how it was obtained, how the information is to be used, and at which criminal justice system process the state wishes to use the information.

The basis of the right is to ensure that the state carries the burden of proving guilt without placing an individual in a situation that could compel him or her to confess to a crime. In this regard, the Sixth Amendment right to assistance of counsel can provide persons with a measure of protection for their Fifth Amendment privilege. The right to counsel exists at particular pretrial stages, at trial, and upon direct appeal from a conviction. Whether a person has a right to counsel when the police wish to question the person depends on the circumstances surrounding the "questioning."

THE REQUIREMENTS AS ARTICULATED IN *MIRANDA V. ARIZONA*

Information obtained from a person that implicates that person in a crime is called a confession. Often, a confession is valuable evidence because it is direct evidence from a person himself or herself. The state cannot convict a person if the only evidence is a confession because some people confess to offenses that either did not occur or they did not commit. Why someone would make a false confession is the subject of many scholarly debates. Some people confess for publicity, some because they suffer from mental illness, some because they suffer from false memories. For example, John Mark Karr confessed to the December 1996 killing of a young girl—JonBenet Ramsey (see http://www.cbsnews.com/stories/2006/08/16/national/main1901342.shtml). Although there was evidence of homicide (the 5-year-old girl was found slain in her basement), there was no evidence that Karr had committed the murder. In fact, the murder had been committed in Colorado, and there was strong evidence that Kerr had been in Alabama at the time of the murder. There was also no evidence at the crime scene that corroborated the confession, and the DNA found on the victim did not match that of Karr.

A confession is inadmissible at trial as direct evidence of a defendant's culpability if it violates the tenets provided under the landmark case of *Miranda v. Arizona*. *Miranda* makes it clear that an involuntary confession is to be excluded at trial. Involuntary confessions, under *Miranda*, may occur if either the Fifth or Sixth Amendment is violated.

MIRANDA V. ARIZONA, 384 U.S. 436 (1966)

Opinion by WARREN.

Facts: The U.S. Supreme Court consolidated four cases that came before it on the issue of custodial interrogations. In the first case, a woman had been kidnapped and raped in Phoenix, Arizona. After following some investigatory leads, police asked Miranda to come to the police station to participate in a lineup. Afterward the defendant was taken to an interrogation room, where he was not advised of his right to counsel. Miranda admitted the allegations, and the police were able to secure a signed, written confession after a two-hour interrogation. Miranda's statement indicated that he knew his legal rights and that the statements made by him could be used against him. The written statement also indicated that he waived his rights. At trial, the arresting officers indicated that at the time of the interrogation, Miranda was in police custody. He was convicted of kidnapping and rape and received a 20-year sentence. In the other three cases, the state (police officers, detectives, or prosecuting attorneys) also questioned suspects without notification of their right to remain silent or their right to counsel during the questioning. Their confessions were all admitted against them at their respective trials, and they were convicted.

Issue: Is a custodial confession obtained without warnings that a person has the privilege against self-incrimination and the right to counsel as provided in the Fifth and Sixth Amendments admissible against a defendant?

Rationale and Decision: [W]e deal with the admissibility of statements obtained from an individual who is subjected to custodial police interrogation and the necessity for procedures which assure that the individual is accorded his privilege under the Fifth Amendment to the Constitution not to be compelled to incriminate himself. . . .

Our holding . . . briefly stated, it is this: the prosecution may not use statements, whether exculpatory or inculpatory, stemming from custodial interrogation of the defendant unless it demonstrates the use of procedural safeguards effective to secure the privilege against self-incrimination. By custodial interrogation, we mean questioning initiated by law enforcement officers after a person has been taken into custody or otherwise deprived of his freedom of action in any significant way.

As for the procedural safeguards to be employed, unless other fully effective means are devised to inform accused persons of their right of silence and to assure a continuous opportunity to exercise it, the following measures are required. Prior to any questioning, the person must be warned that he has a right to remain silent, that any statement he does make may be used as evidence against him, and that he has a right to the presence of an attorney, either retained or appointed. The defendant may waive effectuation of these rights, provided the waiver is made voluntarily, knowingly and intelligently. If, however, he indicates in any manner and at any stage of the process that he wishes to consult with an attorney before speaking, there can be no questioning. Likewise, if the individual is alone and indicates in any manner that he does not wish to be interrogated, the police may not question him. The mere fact that he may have answered some questions or volunteered some statements on his own does not deprive him of the right to refrain from answering any further inquiries until he has consulted with an attorney and thereafter consents to be questioned.

Interrogation still takes place in privacy. Privacy results in secrecy, and this, in turn, results in a gap in our knowledge as to what, in fact, goes on in the interrogation rooms. . . . Unless adequate protective devices are employed to dispel the compulsion inherent in custodial surroundings, no statement obtained from the defendant can truly be the product of his free choice.

An individual swept from familiar surroundings into police custody, surrounded by antagonistic forces, and subjected to the techniques of persuasion described above cannot be otherwise than under compulsion to speak. As a practical matter, the compulsion to speak in the isolated setting of the police station may well be greater than in courts or other official investigations, where there are often impartial observers to guard against intimidation or trickery. . . .

Today, then, there can be no doubt that the Fifth Amendment privilege is available outside of criminal court proceedings, and serves to protect persons in all settings in which their freedom of action is curtailed in any significant way from being compelled to incriminate themselves. We have concluded that, without proper safeguards, the process of in-custody interrogation of persons suspected or accused of crime contains inherently compelling pressures which work to undermine the individual's will to resist and to compel him to speak where he would not otherwise do so freely. In order to combat these pressures and to permit a full opportunity to exercise the privilege against self-incrimination, the accused must be adequately and effectively apprised of his rights, and the exercise of those rights must be fully honored.

. . . At the outset, if a person in custody is to be subjected to interrogation, he must first be informed in clear and unequivocal terms that he has the right to remain silent. For those unaware of the privilege, the warning is needed simply to make them aware of it—the threshold requirement for an intelligent decision as to its exercise. More important, such a warning is an absolute prerequisite in overcoming the inherent pressures of the interrogation atmosphere. It is not just the subnormal or woefully ignorant who succumb to an interrogator's imprecations, whether implied or expressly stated, that the interrogation will continue until a confession is obtained or that silence in the face of accusation is itself damning, and will bode ill when presented to a jury. Further, the warning will show the individual that his interrogators are prepared to recognize his privilege should he choose to exercise it. . . . More important, whatever the background of the person interrogated, a warning at the time of the interrogation is indispensable to overcome its pressures and to insure that the individual knows he is free to exercise the privilege at that point in time.

The warning of the right to remain silent must be accompanied by the explanation that anything said can and will be used against the individual in court. This warning is needed in order to make him aware not only of the privilege, but also of the consequences of forgoing it. It is only through an awareness of these consequences that there can be any assurance of real understanding and intelligent exercise of the privilege. . . .

The circumstances surrounding in-custody interrogation can operate very quickly to overbear the will of one merely made aware of his privilege by his interrogators. Therefore, the right to have counsel present at the interrogation is indispensable to the protection of the Fifth Amendment privilege under the system we delineate today. Our aim is to assure that the individual's right to choose between silence and speech remains unfettered throughout the interrogation process. A once-stated warning, delivered by those who will conduct the interrogation, cannot itself suffice to that end among those who most require knowledge of their rights. A mere warning given by the interrogators is not alone sufficient to accomplish that end. . . . Thus, the need for counsel to protect the Fifth Amendment privilege comprehends not merely a right to consult with counsel prior to questioning, but also to have counsel present during any questioning if the defendant so desires.

. . . Opportunity to exercise these rights must be afforded to him throughout the interrogation. After such warnings have been given, and such opportunity afforded him, the individual may knowingly and intelligently waive these rights and agree to answer questions or make a statement. But unless and until such warnings and waiver are demonstrated by the prosecution at trial, no evidence obtained as a result of interrogation can be used against him.

. . . In a government of laws, existence of the government will be imperiled if it fails to observe the law scrupulously. Our Government is the potent, the omnipresent teacher. For good or for ill, it teaches the whole people by its example. Crime is contagious. If the Government becomes a lawbreaker, it breeds contempt for law; it invites every man to become a law unto himself; it invites anarchy. To declare that, in the administration of the criminal law, the end justifies the means . . . would bring terrible retribution. Against that pernicious doctrine this Court should resolutely set its face.

Therefore, in accordance with the foregoing, the judgments of the Supreme Court of Arizona in No. 759, of the New

York Court of Appeals in No. 760, and of the Court of Appeals for the Ninth Circuit in No. 761, are reversed. The judgment of the Supreme Court of California in No. 584 is affirmed.

It is so ordered.

As a consequence of *Miranda,* a confession will be inadmissible at trial if a custodial interrogation occurs in violation of the Fifth or Sixth Amendment. *Miranda* requires that Fifth and Sixth Amendment warnings be given to a suspect or accused person prior to a custodial interrogation. The standard "*Miranda* warning" is familiar to any American with a television set, but the exact words of the *Miranda* warning are not prescribed: Any conveyance which contains the following information is sufficient. The first two lines of warning concern the Fifth Amendment privilege against self-incrimination; the last two warning lines concern the Sixth Amendment right to counsel:

You have the right to remain silent.

Anything you say can be used against you in a court of law.

You have the right to an attorney.

If you cannot afford an attorney, one will be provided for you prior to questioning.

When Is a Person in Custody?

The police can ask a person questions without the warnings so long as the person is not in custody. *Miranda* warnings apply when a person is in custody. Because the U.S. Supreme Court does not want the police to intimidate a person who is in custody and "coerce" a confession, the warnings must be given prior to custodial interrogations (questioning). In general, a person is deemed to be in custody of the police if the individual is not "free to leave" police control. There is nothing in the Fifth Amendment's privilege against self-incrimination to prevent a person from "freely" confessing to a crime, or from leaving the presence of police officers who wish to question a person. A person can walk in off the streets and confess to any particular crime. Because such a person was not in custody and was not being interrogated, the confession can be used in trial. If the officers have a reason to suspect that the person committed the crime to which he or she is confessing, any further questioning by the officers may be subject to *Miranda*'s exclusionary principles if the person has become "in custody." It is not enough that a person confesses a crime to police authorities, or that a person is being asked questions. The issue for a court is whether a custodial interrogation is taking place.

To determine if police questioning of a suspect must be preceded by *Miranda* starts with the first prong of *Miranda:* Was the suspect or accused in police custody? In *Minnesota v. Murphy,* 465 U.S. 420 (1984), the U.S. Supreme Court was asked to consider the impact of *Miranda* on confessions given to probation officers. The Court determined that even if a probationer is compelled to admit truthful information as a condition of release, he or she must assert the right against self-incrimination in a timely fashion in order to later invoke *Miranda*-based exclusion of the admissions. In *Murphy*, the probationer's incriminating admissions led to new criminal charges and a conviction that was sustained because the admissions were not coerced. The Court determined that just because a probationer must meet with a probation officer or else risk a return to incarceration does not make the setting an inherently coercive one. If a person voluntarily admits involvement in (new) criminal activities that were not the subject of his or her probation release, the statements are admissible against the person in a trial for those new offenses.

MINNESOTA V. MURPHY, 465 U.S. 420 (1984)

Opinion by WHITE.

Facts: Murphy made incriminating admissions during a meeting with his probation officer. The terms of Murphy's probation required, among other things, that he participate in a treatment program for sexual offenders, report to his probation officer, and be truthful with the probation officer "in all matters." Failure to comply with these conditions could result in his return to the sentencing court for a probation revocation hearing. During one meeting with his probation officer, Murphy made admissions that he committed a prior rape and homicide, which were later admitted at his trial. The Minnesota Supreme Court held that he did have a valid Fifth Amendment claim to protect his privilege against self-incrimination.

Issue: Do the Fifth and Fourteenth Amendments prohibit the use of a defendant's admissions if they are made to a probation officer and then used in the defendant's subsequent criminal prosecution?

Rationale and Decision: The Fifth Amendment, in relevant part, provides that no person "shall be compelled in any criminal case to be a witness against himself." . . . A defendant does not lose this protection by reason of his conviction of a crime; notwithstanding that a defendant is imprisoned or on probation at the time he makes incriminating statements, if those statements are compelled, they are inadmissible in a subsequent trial for a crime other than that for which he has been convicted. . . . The issue in this case is whether the Fifth Amendment right that Murphy enjoyed would be violated by the admission into evidence at his trial for another crime of the prior statements made by him to his probation officer.

The Minnesota Supreme Court recognized that Murphy was not "in custody" when he made his incriminating admissions. He was, to be sure, subject to a number of restrictive conditions governing various aspects of his life, and he would be regarded as "in custody" for purposes of federal habeas corpus.

. . . Because revocation of his probation was threatened if he was untruthful with his probation officer, Murphy argues that he was compelled to make incriminating disclosures instead of claiming the privilege. Although this contention is not without force, we find it unpersuasive on close examination. . . . We conclude . . . that since Murphy revealed incriminating information instead of timely asserting his Fifth Amendment privilege, his disclosures were not compelled incriminations.

The judgment of the Minnesota Supreme Court is *Reversed.*

What Is an Interrogation?

Miranda rights are in effect not only when a suspect is in custody, but also when the police are questioning a suspect or an accused person about a crime. Interrogations involve the questioning of a suspect or an accused about a crime in order for the police to receive information about the crime and the suspect's involvement in the crime. The location of questioning and the manner in which officers discuss criminal activities may denote whether the police are interrogating an accused. In *Brewer v. Williams,* 430 U.S. 387 (1977), police detectives were interested in finding and locating the body of a young girl who had been kidnapped, raped, and killed. They were able to quickly locate the car and the suspect who may have committed the Christmastime offenses but did not find the girl's body. The defendant had been admonished by officers who detained him and by a judge who arraigned him about his *Miranda* rights, and he asserted his right to remain silent until his attorney was present. However, while transporting the defendant back to the city where the offenses occurred, one of the detectives engaged in discussion with the defendant in order to entice him into giving information about the location of the girl's body, appealing to his religious sensibility by stating that the girl deserved a "Christian burial." Responding to the speech, the defendant then directed the detectives to the body. The Court determined that the speech made by the detective amounted to an interrogation. If police officers have a person in custody (within a patrol vehicle) and make statements that they know will appeal to a suspect's sensitivity (religious beliefs) in order to induce the person to confess to a crime, the situation is the functional equivalent of a stationhouse interrogation.

BREWER V. WILLIAMS, 430 U.S. 387 (1977)

Opinion by STEWART.

Facts: The defendant, Williams, was convicted of the murder of a 10-year-old girl. Police investigation tied him to the disappearance of the girl from a YMCA when a witness saw him carry a bundle that had legs hanging from it and place it in his vehicle. His abandoned car was found the following day near Davenport, Iowa, about 160 miles from where the girl had disappeared. After a warrant was then issued in Des Moines for his arrest, his attorney advised him to surrender to police in Davenport, which he did. Both the police who booked him and the judge at his Davenport arraignment gave the defendant his *Miranda* warnings. The defendant conferred with a local lawyer, who advised him to remain silent. Officers from Des Moines were transporting Williams without the presence of counsel in the police vehicle. The officers were told by his counsel that he was asserting his rights. At no time during the trip did Williams express a willingness to be interrogated in the absence of an attorney. Instead, he stated several times that "[w]hen I get to Des Moines and see Mr. McKnight, I am going to tell you the whole story." One of the officers who transported Williams knew that he was a former mental patient, and that he was deeply religious. The officer, a police detective, said to the defendant, "I want to give you something to think about while we're traveling down the road. . . . Number one, I want you to observe the weather conditions, it's raining, it's sleeting, it's freezing, driving is very treacherous, visibility is poor, it's going to be dark early this evening. They are predicting several inches of snow for tonight, and I feel that you yourself are the only person that knows where this little girl's body is, that you yourself have only been there once, and if you get a snow on top of it you yourself may be unable to find it. And, since we will be going right past the area on the way into Des Moines, I felt that we could stop and locate the body, that the parents of this little girl should be entitled to a Christian burial for the little girl who was snatched away from them on Christmas Eve and murdered. And I feel we should stop and locate it on the way in, rather than waiting until morning and trying to come back out after a snow storm, and possibly not being able to find it at all." The defendant then showed the officers where the girl's body was located. The Court of Appeals affirmed the District Court's finding that the defendant's constitutional rights were violated because he was denied his right to counsel.

Issue: Do the *Miranda* admonitions prevent officers from engaging in discussions with a custodial arrestee in the absence of counsel so as to elicit a confession?

Rationale and Decision: There can be no serious doubt, . . . that Detective Leaming deliberately and designedly set out to elicit information from Williams just as surely as—and perhaps more effectively than—if he had formally interrogated him. Detective Leaming was fully aware before departing for Des Moines that Williams was being represented in Davenport by Kelly and in Des Moines by McKnight. Yet he purposely sought during Williams' isolation from his lawyers to obtain as much incriminating information as possible.

. . . Moreover, the statements were obtained only after Detective Leaming's use of psychology on a person whom he knew to be deeply religious and an escapee from a mental hospital—with the specific intent to elicit incriminating statements. . . . We conclude, finally, that the Court of Appeals was correct in holding that, judged by these standards, the record in this case falls far short of sustaining petitioner's burden.

[The defendant's statements that directed the officers to the girl's body were taken in violation of his *Miranda* rights are inadmissible.]

When Is Counsel Needed?

The right to counsel is important because persons may not fully understand their rights or the criminal justice processes. In order to ensure the protection of a suspect's or an accused's constitutional rights, the U.S. Supreme Court has held that a person has the right to an attorney. During an interrogation, the right to counsel is essential to protect the accused from undue coercion when in custody. As seen in *Brewer v. Williams*, 430 U.S. 387 (1977), the detective had not only provided a coercive setting in the police vehicle when soliciting admissions from the custodial defendant, but also violated the defendant's right to counsel. The transporting officer had been told on a few occasions that the defendant wished to preserve his constitutional rights and his right to counsel. The officers specifically promised that they were not going to interrogate the accused during the trip from Davenport to Des Moines. However, the transporting officer, when soliciting the admissions in the police vehicle, did so in contradiction to the asserted right-to-counsel provisions of *Miranda*. Generally, once an accused has asked for counsel, interrogation and questioning must cease until counsel is present. However, some cases uphold the admission of a confession following interrogation during which the accused only mentions a desire to see counsel or states a desire to stop but continues answering questions, as seen in the next section.

Voluntary Statements Versus Coerced Confessions

Some difficulties arise when a person is in custody and the police do not (fully) *Mirandize* a suspect or arrestee just prior to a confession being taken. A number of reasons might account for these situations: the police may be in the process of reading a person his or her *Miranda* rights when the person says that he or she wants to speak with a lawyer, but continues to talk with the police; the police may deliberately wait to provide the warnings until they get a confession, then *Mirandize* the person and continue questioning until the person repeats the incriminating information; a person might have asserted his or her *Miranda* rights for one crime but is later questioned about another crime for which the person "waives" the right to remain silent and his or her right to have counsel. The U.S. Supreme Court has held that the right to counsel was violated in the first situation (*Smith v. Illinois*, 469 U.S. 91 [1984]), and the right against self-incrimination was violated in the second situation (*Missouri v. Seibert*,

542 U.S. 600 [2004]), but the suspect's rights were not violated in the last situation (*Michigan v. Mosley,* 423 U.S. 96 [1975]; after asserting *Miranda* rights for one crime, a person who begins to answer questions about another crime waives the right to remain silent and have counsel).

THE RIGHT TO REMAIN SILENT AND TO COUNSEL

In 2010, the Court revisited *Miranda* in a couple cases and found that if a person wants to ensure the right to remain silent, then the person has to say that they want to remain silent. In one case decided during the 2009–2010 term, the Court held that the manner of the *Miranda* warnings is immaterial so long as the warnings are given prior to any questioning of the defendant. In *Florida v. Powell,* 559 U.S. ___, 130 S. Ct. 1195 (2010), the Court stated:

> By informing Powell that he had "the right to talk to a lawyer before answering any of [their] questions," the Tampa officers communicated that he could consult with a lawyer before answering any particular question. And the statement that Powell had "the right to use any of [his] rights at any time [he] want[ed] during th[e] interview" confirmed that he could exercise his right to an attorney while the interrogation was underway. In combination, the two warnings reasonably conveyed the right to have an attorney present, not only at the outset of interrogation, but at all times. To reach the opposite conclusion, *i.e.,* that the attorney would not be present throughout the interrogation, the suspect would have to imagine the counter-intuitive and unlikely scenario that, in order to consult counsel, he would be obliged to exit and reenter the interrogation room between each query.

In another case, *Berghuis v. Thompkins,* 560 U.S. ___, 130 S. Ct. 2250 (2010), the Court was asked to consider what the silence of a suspect means. As stated in the Fifth Amendment, a person has the right to remain silent, but if a person remains silent on whether he or she has asserted the *Miranda* rights, then are the rights invoked or waived? *Miranda* could be read to mean that unless there is a formal waiver of one's rights, then any admissions given during an interrogation will be considered to be voluntary; the rights are waived when a confession has been obtained during an interrogation. The *Berghuis* decision was close (five to four), with the dissent expressing concern that the Court majority had strayed too far from *Miranda.* In *Berghuis,* the defendant did not say but a few words during the interrogation. The dissent deemed it a one-sided interrogation, in which the defendant said only a few words, such as "yes" or "no," to statements made by the police. Justice Sonia Sotomayor's dissent in *Berghuis* emphasized the distinction between a waiver of the *Miranda* rights and understanding of the rights. The state, she asserted, has a heavy burden to prove that the defendant waived the rights particularly, as here, when the defendant did not sign a *Miranda* card to even acknowledge the rights. The majority's holding, however, maintained that if the defendant wished to invoke his right to remain silent or right to counsel, then he must say so in a clear and unambiguous manner. During a three-hour interrogation in which the defendant makes admissions of guilt, it is up to the defendant to assert his rights. The police do not have to first obtain a formal written waiver to establish that a confession was procured after a voluntary waiver of rights.

BERGHUIS V. THOMPKINS, 560 U.S. ___, 130 S. CT. 2250 (2010)

Opinion by KENNEDY.

Facts: Thompkins was arrested for committing murder and other offenses associated with a shooting in Michigan. Arresting officers interrogated the defendant for about three hours and presented him with a *Miranda* form that listed his rights. He read the rights out loud but refused to sign the waiver form. During most of the interrogation, the defendant answered only with cryptic "yes" or "no" responses. Toward the end of the three hours, the defendant gave a verbal confession but refused to sign a written confession. The Court of Appeals held that Thompkins did not waive his Fifth Amendment rights when he was persistently silent during most of the interview.

Issue: Are confessions admissible in court if they are taken without a formal written waiver of a person's *Miranda* rights or a formal statement that the defendant asserts *Miranda* rights?

Rationale and Decision: The *Miranda* Court formulated a warning that must be given to suspects before they can be subjected to custodial interrogation. The substance of the warning still must be given to suspects today. . . . All concede that the warning given in this case was in full compliance with these requirements. The dispute centers on the response—or nonresponse—from the suspect.

Thompkins makes various arguments that his answers to questions from the detectives were inadmissible. He first contends that he "invoke[d] his privilege" to remain silent by not saying anything for a sufficient period of time, so the interrogation should have "cease[d]" before he made his inculpatory statements. . . .

The Court has not yet stated whether an invocation of the right to remain silent can be ambiguous or equivocal, but there is no principled reason to adopt different standards for determining when an accused has invoked the *Miranda* right to remain silent. . . . There is good reason to require an accused who wants to invoke his or her right to remain silent to do so unambiguously. A requirement of an unambiguous invocation of *Miranda* rights results in an objective inquiry that "avoid[s] difficulties of proof and . . . provide[s] guidance to officers" on how to proceed in the face of ambiguity. . . . Thompkins did not say that he wanted to remain silent or that he did not want to talk with the police. Had he made either of these simple, unambiguous statements, he would have invoked his "right to cut off questioning." . . . Here he did neither, so he did not invoke his right to remain silent.

We next consider whether Thompkins waived his right to remain silent. Even absent the accused's invocation of the right to remain silent, the accused's statement during a custodial interrogation is inadmissible at trial unless the prosecution can establish that the accused "in fact knowingly and voluntarily waived *[Miranda]* rights" when making the statement. . . .

The main purpose of *Miranda* is to ensure that an accused is advised of and understands the right to remain silent and the right to counsel. . . . The prosecution therefore does not need to show that a waiver of *Miranda* rights was express. An "implicit waiver" of the "right to remain silent" is sufficient to admit a suspect's statement into evidence. . . . Where the prosecution shows that a *Miranda* warning was given and that it was understood by the accused, an accused's uncoerced statement establishes an implied waiver of the right to remain silent.

The . . . case is remanded with instructions to deny the petition.

It is so ordered.

CONTEMPORARY ISSUES: ST. JOHNS, ARIZONA, 8-YEAR-OLD BOY INTERROGATED WITHOUT *MIRANDA*

Children also have *Miranda* rights. The burden on the state to show that a child understands his or her rights and waives them is critical to the administration of justice. Children will agree with adults who are "nice" to them in order to "get out of trouble" or to prevent an impending punishment. In such cases, it is important for investigating officers to take extra precautions when questioning youth suspects. The right to counsel is asserted when a youth asks to speak with his or her parent or guardian.

In 2008, an 8-year-old boy was charged with killing his father and a man who resided in their home. The two men were shot to death with a rifle that was a gift to the boy from his father. Initially, the boy was charged with two counts of first-degree premeditated murder. In 2009, at the age of 9, the boy pleaded guilty to one count of negligent homicide in exchange for the dropping of the murder charges. The difficulty in this case is that the boy was interrogated by two officers without counsel, without a guardian, and without having his *Miranda* rights read to him. It has been unclear as to whether the boy understood what the officers' questioning was about, because initially the boy denied shooting the men. The officers continually talked with the boy about shooting his father and the other man when the child said that he found them already shot and pulled the trigger only to put them out of their misery. After a lengthy interrogation, the boy finally admitted that he shot the men because he was repeatedly spanked and decided to do something if and when he was spanked for the thousandth time. The court handling the murder trial suppressed the confession but accepted the plea and placed him in a residential treatment facility. In the treatment facility, the boy is expected to receive intensive counseling and education.

Children are more likely to give false confessions and lack the judgment to avoid detrimental choices. *J.D.B. v. North Carolina*, No. 09-11121 (2011). In evaluating whether a child was interrogated while "in custody," courts will look at a plurality of factors, including the child's age, intelligence, education, background, and mental and physical health. If the child's age was known to the officer at the time of the interview, or if it would have been objectively apparent to a reasonable officer, the child's age will be considered as part of the custody analysis.

SUMMARY

Since *Miranda v. Arizona,* the Fifth and Sixth Amendment rights to remain silent and to counsel are considered mainstays for understanding if a confession is voluntary or not. It has meant that if either right is violated when a person is being interrogated while in police custody and confesses to a crime, then the confession will be deemed inadmissible; it is considered to have been coerced. Police officers have argued that *Miranda* hurts their ability to investigate crimes and "get the bad guys." A person's *Miranda* rights show that in-custody interrogations are inherently coercive, and if a confession is to be viewed as freely given by a court, then suspects must understand that they do not have to give evidence against themselves. Talking with a lawyer who can explain the implications that can arise when a person is interrogated enables the person to make a clear choice about whether to confess. If a person clearly understands his or her rights and waives them, then any confession will be admissible against the person in court.

Modifications to *Miranda* have occurred periodically. Some of these modifications by the U.S. Supreme Court pertain to when a person is considered to be in custody, or what defines an interrogation. Thus, a person who is stopped by a police officer for a routine traffic infraction is not considered to be in custody, and basic questioning does not have to be preceded by *Miranda* warnings. Similarly, affirmative utterances made during an interrogation may be taken as a desire to speak to the police, as long as the person in police custody has indicated an understanding of his or her rights. The person does not need to sign a *Miranda* card; what is important is whether the person has indicated to the police an under-standing of the right to remain silent and the right to counsel. While the signing of a *Miranda* card is helpful to demonstrate to a court that a person was fully informed of his or her rights, it is not the only evidence of a waiver of one's rights. Interrogations are usually videotaped, and oral declarations by a person that he or she understands these rights is enough to show that a confession is voluntary and admissible in court.

GLOSSARY

Confession: A statement of admission by a person that he or she com-mitted a criminal act.

Custodial interrogation: Questioning by the police of a person who is not free to leave. The person is usually in a jail or detention facility, but could be anywhere the person has a reasonable basis to believe that he or she cannot leave.

Custody: Holding of a person who is charged with a crime in a jail facil-ity or detaining someone accused of a crime so that they are not free to leave police presence. Routine traffic stops are not a custodial situation.

Fifth Amendment: Protection of individual rights to be free from governmental interference and, among other rights, not to be a witness against oneself.

Interrogation: Questioning of a person by the police. If the person is in custody, then his or her due process rights cannot be violated.

Involuntary confession: A confession that is not freely offered and is therefore not admissible in court.

Miranda rights: The constitutional rights of a person under the Fifth and Sixth Amendments that must be protected when a person is held in custody for questioning. These rights include the right to remain silent and the right to counsel, and a warning is given to indicate that anything the person says could be admissible in court.

Privilege against self-incrimination: The Fifth Amendment provides the right for individuals to not be compelled to testify against themselves in a criminal proceeding.

Voluntary confession: A statement of admission by a person who committed a crime, made under circumstances that indicate the person understood what he or she was saying and that the person is acknowledging involvement in a crime.

ADDITIONAL READINGS

Norton, R. (2010). Matters of public safety and the current quarrel over the Quarles Exception to *Miranda*. *Fordham Law Review, 78*, 1931–1969.

Thomas, G. C., III. (2000). The end of the road for *Miranda v. Arizona*? On the history and future of rules for police interrogation. *American Criminal Law Review, 37*, 1.

Weisselberg, C. D. (2008). Mourning *Miranda*. *California Law Review, 96*, 1519.

Zalman, M., & Smith, B. W. (2006–2007). The attitudes of police executives toward *Miranda* and interrogation policies. *Journal of Criminal Law and Criminology, 97*, 873.

CHAPTER 6

The Fourth Amendment, Search Warrants, and Warrantless Searches

KEY POINTS

- The Fourth Amendment requires warrants to be based upon probable cause.

- The Fourth Amendment's warrant requirement extends to places and things for which a person has an expectation of privacy.

- Warrants are issued by detached and neutral magistrates who determine whether probable cause exists, for example, when police rely on informant information.

- If the police violate the Fourth Amendment while seizing evidence, the evidence seized is inadmissible at trial under the exclusionary rule.

- The exclusionary rule does not apply under certain noted exceptions: good faith, independent source, inevitable discovery, attenuated taint, or a voluntary action by a defendant.

- Violations of the Fourth Amendment could result in civil liability for the police.

THE RIGHT OF PRIVACY AND THE REQUIREMENT FOR A WARRANT

The Fourth Amendment protects a person's right of privacy against governmental intrusion. The right extends to people, places, papers, and personal effects. Even during the initial stages of an investigation, when officers are simply investigating the crime and may not have a particular suspect, they may be searching for evidence that might help them identify or arrest an offender. If the officers wish to search for such evidence, then they *must* have a warrant unless a legal exception for a warrant exists. Without an exception to the warrant requirement, officers cannot enter a person's private sphere (their home, car, computer, or other closely associated items) and search it based on their own hunch or whim. As with an arrest warrant, the officers need to submit an affidavit to a detached and neutral magistrate. The magistrate should be provided enough information to make an informed decision so that the police search can be authorized. The search warrant application should demonstrate (1) why the officers believe *a crime occurred*, (2) what *evidence they have* that the crime occurred, (3) the criminal *evidence they wish to seize*, and (4) *where* the evidence is expected to be. The warrant application must be an affidavit: a sworn statement, which must be truthful and particular, indicating the place to be searched and the evidence to be seized. The warrant will be issued if the judge finds that there is probable cause to believe that evidence of the crime will be found at the particular location.

A search pursuant to the warrant that erroneously identifies the location to be searched might still be constitutional. In general, a mistake of location is acceptable if officers' actions were reasonable in light of information known to them at the time. In *Maryland v. Garrison*, 480 U.S. 79 (1987), the officers searched an apartment under the mistaken belief that only one apartment existed on the third floor of a building. When they went to the defendant's apartment and began to search it, they realized that there were two apartments on the floor and that they were supposed to have searched the other one. Because the mistake was a reasonable one, the evidence seized under the warrant, which otherwise would have been overbroad because it did not specify *which* third-floor apartment to search, was admissible against the accused. If the officers knew, or even *should have* known, that there were two locations on the third floor, then they should have specified the location. The lesson to be drawn is that officers must be as particular as possible when submitting search warrants, but factual mistakes are judged in light of the knowledge available at the time. Furthermore, the validity of the warrant is independent of the evidence discovered.

When a warrant is executed by the officers, the officers have the right to enter premises under reasonable conditions as to time and place of the entry. The validity of the search warrant will not hinge on whether the evidence sought was found and seized; whether the warrant is valid depends on whether the warrant is based on reasonable cause and whether the judge was provided with appropriate information to issue the warrant.

The type of evidence that can be searched or seized pursuant to a warrant depends on the specificity of the warrant and factors that unfold at the scene. In general, a search warrant does not allow the search of a person. Searches of people in a place may be permissible, however, depending on other factors that occur after a warrant has been executed; for example, upon a search, evidence of a crime may give officers probable cause to arrest a person and perform a search pursuant to arrest. Instrumentalities of a crime (burglary tools and drug paraphernalia), fruits of a crime (stolen goods and mounds of cash), and contraband or evidence of a crime (drugs and blood-stained clothing) can lawfully be seized if found in the place legally searched.

THE EXCLUSIONARY RULE

The Founding Fathers disliked governmental intrusions into citizens' homes and distrusted governmental officials who could who infringe on personal liberties. However, there is no express method of redress written into the Constitution, should the Fourth Amendment be violated by governmental officials. In the early 20th century, federal police officers entered a person's home and seized items without a warrant and in violation of the Fourth Amendment. In *Weeks v. United States,* 232 U.S. 383 (1914), the U.S. Supreme Court unanimously held that because federal police officers violated the Fourth Amendment, they could not use the evidence seized against the defendant in federal court. The officers entered Weeks's home without a warrant and seized many personal items that they used to charge him with a violation of the lottery law. The principle established in this case—protection from unreasonable searches and seizures—is called the "exclusionary rule."

Immediately after *Weeks,* federal and state police officers found methods to get around the Fourth Amendment's exclusionary rule. For example, state police officers who seized evidence without a warrant would turn it over to federal law enforcement officers, who could admit the evidence because the Fourth Amendment violation did not occur by federal officers. Similarly, until later court decisions, the Fourth Amendment did not apply to state actions, and federal officers used to be able to avoid the rule by turning over evidence to state police. In *Wolf v. Colorado,* 338 U.S. 25 (1949), the U.S. Supreme Court held that the Fourth Amendment does apply to the states but left it up to each state to determine the remedy for violation: whether to enforce an exclusionary rule or other method to ensure that individual liberties are protected. Over dissents that expressed frustration over the neutering of the rule's force, the *Wolf* court stated that the exclusionary rule is a judicial pronouncement and therefore not mandated by the Constitution.

The rules changed after *Mapp v. Ohio,* 367 U.S. 643 (1961), which held that the exclusionary rule applied to the states under the Fourth and Fourteenth Amendments. The U.S. Supreme Court found that states, rejecting the directive expressed in *Wolf,* did not have an effective method of curbing police misconduct when they seized evidence without warrants. Unless the exclusionary rule is applicable in both federal and state criminal trials, the right to be free from unreasonable searches and seizures has no meaning. The explicit purpose of the exclusionary rule is to prevent police misconduct. The court's rule is controversial because it arguably hinders a police officer's crime control functions in favor of letting "the guilty" go free.

MAPP V. OHIO, 367 U.S. 643 (1961)

Opinion by CLARK.

Facts: Mapp was convicted of knowingly possessing lewd and lascivious books, pictures, and photographs that were found in her home. Officers sought entry into her home because they believed that a wanted felon was hiding there. Mapp refused their entry. When the officers forcibly opened the door, Mapp demanded to see a search warrant. When an officer showed her a piece of paper, she grabbed it and placed it in her "bosom." The paper was retrieved after a struggle, and the defendant was handcuffed. A search of

Mapp's entire house ensued; officers looked in photograph albums, dresser drawers, bedrooms, the living room, the dining room, and the kitchen and basement. In the basement, in a trunk, the obscene materials were found and seized. The Ohio Supreme Court found that the search was reasonable even if there was evidence to doubt that any warrant existed at the time of the search. The court found that it was not done forcibly and therefore did not violate the defendant's rights.

Issue: Does the Fourth Amendment's exclusionary rule apply to the actions of state law enforcement officers?

Rationale and Decision: In 1949, 35 years after *Weeks* was announced, this Court, in *Wolf v. Colorado, supra,* again for the first time, discussed the effect of the Fourth Amendment upon the States through the operation of the Due Process Clause of the Fourteenth Amendment. It said:

"[W]e have no hesitation in saying that, were a State affirmatively to sanction such police incursion into privacy, it would run counter to the guaranty of the Fourteenth Amendment."

. . . It therefore plainly appears that the factual considerations supporting the failure of the *Wolf* Court to include the *Weeks* exclusionary rule when it recognized the enforceability of the right to privacy against the States in 1949, while not basically relevant to the constitutional consideration, could not, in any analysis, now be deemed controlling.

. . . Today we once again examine *Wolf's* constitutional documentation of the right to privacy free from unreasonable state intrusion, and, after its dozen years on our books, are led by it to close the only courtroom door remaining open to evidence secured by official lawlessness in flagrant abuse of that basic right, reserved to all persons as a specific guarantee against that very same unlawful conduct. We hold that all evidence obtained by searches and seizures in violation of the Constitution is, by that same authority, inadmissible in a state court.

Since the Fourth Amendment's right of privacy has been declared enforceable against the States through the Due Process Clause of the Fourteenth, it is enforceable against them by the same sanction of exclusion as is used against the Federal Government. Were it otherwise, then, just as without the *Weeks* rule the assurance against unreasonable federal searches and seizures would be "a form of words," valueless and undeserving of mention in a perpetual charter of inestimable human liberties, so too, without that rule, the freedom from state invasions of privacy would be so ephemeral and so neatly severed from its conceptual nexus with the freedom from all brutish means of coercing evidence as not to merit this Court's high regard as a freedom "implicit in the concept of ordered liberty." . . .

Moreover, our holding that the exclusionary rule is an essential part of both the Fourth and Fourteenth Amendments is not only the logical dictate of prior cases, but it also makes very good sense. There is no war between the Constitution and common sense. Presently, a federal prosecutor may make no use of evidence illegally seized, but a State's attorney across the street may, although he supposedly is operating under the enforceable prohibitions of the same Amendment. Thus, the State, by admitting evidence unlawfully seized, serves to encourage disobedience to the Federal Constitution which it is bound to uphold. Moreover, as was said in *Elkins*, "[t]he very essence of a healthy federalism depends upon the avoidance of needless conflict between state and federal courts." . . . Yet the double standard recognized until today hardly put such a thesis into practice. . . . If the fruits of an unconstitutional search had been inadmissible in both state and federal courts, this inducement to evasion would have been sooner eliminated. . . .

There are those who say, as did Justice (then Judge) Cardozo, that, under our constitutional exclusionary doctrine, "[t]he criminal is to go free because the constable has blundered." . . . In some cases, this will undoubtedly be the result. . . . The criminal goes free, if he must, but it is the law that sets him free. Nothing can destroy a government more quickly than its failure to observe its own laws, or worse, its disregard of the charter of its own existence. . . .

The ignoble shortcut to conviction left open to the State tends to destroy the entire system of constitutional restraints on which the liberties of the people rest. Having once recognized that the right to privacy embodied in the Fourth Amendment is enforceable against the States, and that the right to be secure against rude invasions of privacy by state officers is, therefore, constitutional in origin, we can no longer permit that right to remain an empty promise. . . . Our decision, founded on reason and truth, gives to the individual no more than that which the Constitution guarantees him, to the police officer no less than that to which honest law enforcement is entitled, and, to the courts, that judicial integrity so necessary in the true administration of justice.

The judgment of the Supreme Court of Ohio is reversed, and the cause remanded for further proceedings not inconsistent with this opinion.

Reversed and remanded.

USE OF KNOWN AND ANONYMOUS INFORMANTS

Police officers conduct investigations as an important part of their crime-fighting responsibility and to secure the arrests of criminal offenders. In the course of their investigation, officers may need to rely on and use statements from people who may be "known" or "unknown" to them. A "known informant" is a person who has previously worked with the police and has provided information about crime or criminals to them that turned out to be truthful. Whether officers will be able to use information from "unknown informants" will depend on the information provided and what the officer later learns from further investigation.

In the 1960s, the U.S. Supreme Court issued two opinions that formed the basis of criminal procedure law when police officers use informants to secure a warrant. First in *Aguilar v. Texas*, 378 U.S. 108 (1964), and then in *Spinelli v. United States*, 393 U.S. 410 (1969), the court held that submitted search warrants relying on informants must contain enough information about the informant to allow magistrates to conclude that the information provided to the police is "reliable" and that a "crime ha[s] been committed." In many situations, although an informant is known to the police, the police may wish to keep the identity of the individual confidential and not specifically name the informant in a warrant application. This is because warrants become public during trial, which may open informants to retaliation. In this regard, the police generally argue that they need to protect the safety of the individual or that they are using the informant in more than one covert police operation. The *Aguilar–Spinelli* test of informant reliability generally requires the police to show in their application for a warrant that an informant is known to them, has given reliable information that led to previous arrests, and in the current case has given reliable and truthful information upon which the warrant application is based. The court in *Aguilar* said: "[T]he magistrate must be informed of some of the underlying circumstances relied on by the person providing the information and some of the underlying circumstances from which the affiant concluded that the informant, whose identity was not disclosed, was creditable or his information reliable." In the ensuing years, this now-defunct legal doctrine came to be known as the "two-pronged test" of *Aguilar* and *Spinelli*. Although this test is no longer used in federal law and by many states, it retains power in a few states. The two prongs required that the police in their warrant applications:

1. affirm that the informant is reliable and credible

2. provide underlying information that forms the basis of the informant's knowledge of a crime.

If the magistrate is not assured that the informant is reliable, credible, and has specific knowledge of the crime, then a warrant based on probable cause will not be issued. A few states continue to follow the *Aguilar–Spinelli* rule: Massachusetts (*Commonwealth v. Upton*, 476 N.E.2d 548 [1985]), New York (*People v. Bigelow*, 497 N.Y.S.2d 630 [1985]; *People v. Parris*, 632 N.E.2d 870 [1994]), and Tennessee (*State v. Jacumin*, 778 S.W.2d 430 [Tenn. 1989]). The *Aguilar–Spinelli* rule is more restrictive than the current rule, which is a flexible test based on the "totality of the circumstances."

In 1983, the U.S. Supreme Court overturned the two-pronged approach when it issued its "totality of the circumstances" test in *Illinois v. Gates,* 462 U.S. 213 (1983). In *Illinois v. Gates,* the U.S. Supreme Court had to decide whether the police could secure a valid warrant when an unknown informant provided information about a crime. The police had received a letter from an anonymous source that said that Lance and Susan Gates were selling drugs from their home in Bloomington, Illinois. Because the police officers did not know who sent the letter, they decided to use the tip to investigate the situation. The tip indicated that the Gateses would be involved in a drug transaction, and the letter gave details about Gates, his wife, the car they drove, and details about a quick trip to Florida they were about to take so that illegal drugs could be loaded into their car and driven back to Illinois. The Bloomington police called their peers in Florida (West Palm Beach) and asked them to verify the tip. The information from the tip checked out: the defendants did arrive as stated, did stay in a particular hotel in Florida, and were driving back in the direction of Chicago. The Illinois officers thus procured a search warrant for the defendant's car and home. The search found marijuana in the trunk of the defendants' car, and weapons and drugs were later found in their home. It was obvious to the U.S. Supreme Court that the police would not have enough to secure a warrant if they had relied solely on the information gleaned from the anonymous letter. But when the officers investigated the tip, they gained further information about the criminal activity that the defendant was committing. At issue in the case was whether the search warrant was invalid because it did not satisfy the two-pronged test of *Aguilar* and *Spinelli*. The Court held that the lower court had misused the *Spinelli* test and that the proper test for determining the validity of a search warrant application was one based upon the "totality of the circumstances." In this manner, police officers can and should rely on tips from informants, even if the informants were previously unknown to them. But the officers must aver to a magistrate that the unknown informant information, together with the officers' investigation skills and knowledge, is enough to sustain a probable cause finding for the issuance of a warrant. Although there were some discrepancies between the informants' predictions and the facts known to the officers (a fact that the dissents in the case found should have invalidated the warrant even under the new test), the Court's new rule found that enough of the unknown informant's information was verified by independent police work to make the warrant constitutionally valid.

ILLINOIS V. GATES, 462 U.S. 213 (1983)

Opinion by REHNQUIST.

Facts: A police detective's affidavit for a warrant included the use of an anonymous letter. Officers used the anonymous tip to engage in further investigation of the Gateses, who were believed to be involved in drug trafficking. The tip indicated that the Gateses would fly from Illinois to Miami and stay at a particular hotel, then drive back to Illinois with illegal contraband. The officers, after performing their own investigation and getting assistance from law enforcement in Florida that verified the tip, went to a neutral and detached magistrate to procure a search warrant. In holding that the affidavit in fact did not contain sufficient additional information to sustain a determination of probable cause, the Illinois Supreme Court applied a "two-pronged test" derived from the U.S. Supreme Court's *Spinelli v. United States,* 393 U.S. 410 (1969), decision. The *Spinelli* decision was interpreted by lower courts to require that the anonymous informant information satisfy each of two independent requirements, veracity and reliability, before it was used to satisfy probable cause.

Issue: What is the appropriate test to determine if probable cause exists for magistrates to issue warrants that are based on tips from informants who are not known to the police and who, therefore, may not have provided reliable information?

Rationale and Decision: We agree with the Illinois Supreme Court that an informant's "veracity," "reliability," and "basis of knowledge" are all highly relevant in determining the value of his report. We do not agree, however, that these elements should be understood as entirely separate and independent requirements to be rigidly exacted in every case. . . . Rather, as detailed below, they should be understood simply as closely intertwined issues that may usefully illuminate the common sense, practical question whether there is "probable cause" to believe that contraband or evidence is located in a particular place.

This totality-of-the-circumstances approach is far more consistent with our prior treatment of probable cause than is any rigid demand that specific "tests" be satisfied by every informant's tip. Perhaps the central teaching of our decisions bearing on the probable cause standard is that it is a "practical, nontechnical conception." . . . "In dealing with probable cause, . . . as the very name implies, we deal with probabilities. These are not technical; they are the factual and practical considerations of everyday life on which reasonable and prudent men, not legal technicians, act." . . . "Long before the law of probabilities was articulated as such, practical people formulated certain common sense conclusions about human behavior; jurors as factfinders are permitted to do the same—and so are law enforcement officers. Finally, the evidence thus collected must be seen and weighed not in terms of library analysis by scholars, but as understood by those versed in the field of law enforcement." As these comments illustrate, probable cause is a fluid concept—turning on the assessment of probabilities in particular factual contexts—not readily, or even usefully, reduced to a neat set of legal rules. Informants' tips doubtless come in many shapes and sizes from many different types of persons. . . . Rigid legal rules are ill-suited to an area of such diversity.

As early as . . . (1813), Chief Justice Marshall observed, in a closely related context: "[T]he term 'probable cause,' according to its usual acceptation, means less than evidence which would justify condemnation. . . . It imports a seizure made under circumstances which warrant suspicion." More recently, we said that "the *quanta* . . . of proof" appropriate in ordinary judicial proceedings are inapplicable to the decision to issue a warrant. . . . Finely tuned standards such as proof beyond a reasonable doubt or by a preponderance of the evidence, useful in formal trials, have no place in the magistrate's decision. While an effort to fix some general, numerically precise degree of certainty corresponding to "probable cause" may not be helpful, it is clear that "only the probability, and not a *prima facie* showing, of criminal activity, is the standard of probable cause." . . .

We also have recognized that affidavits "are normally drafted by nonlawyers in the midst and haste of a criminal investigation. Technical requirements of elaborate specificity once exacted under common law pleadings have no proper place in this area." . . . Likewise, search and arrest warrants long have been issued by persons who are neither lawyers nor judges, and who certainly do not remain abreast of each judicial refinement of the nature of "probable cause." . . . The rigorous inquiry into the *Spinelli* prongs and the complex superstructure of evidentiary and analytical rules that some have seen implicit in our *Spinelli* decision, cannot be reconciled with the fact that many warrants are—quite properly, . . .—issued on the basis of nontechnical, common sense judgments of laymen applying a standard less demanding than those used in more formal legal proceedings. Likewise, given the informal, often hurried context in which it must be applied, the "built-in subtleties," . . . of the "two-pronged test" are particularly unlikely to assist magistrates in determining probable cause.

Similarly, we have repeatedly said that after-the-fact scrutiny by courts of the sufficiency of an affidavit should not take the form of *de novo* review. A magistrate's "determination of probable cause should be paid great deference by reviewing courts." . . . If the affidavits submitted by police officers are subjected to the type of scrutiny some courts have deemed appropriate, police might well resort to warrantless searches, with the hope of relying on consent or some other exception to the Warrant Clause that might develop at the time of the search. In addition, the possession of a warrant by officers conducting an arrest or search greatly reduces the perception of unlawful or intrusive police conduct, by assuring "the individual whose property is searched or seized of the lawful authority of the executing officer, his need to search, and the limits of his power to search." . . . We think reaffirmation of this standard better serves the purpose of encouraging recourse to the warrant procedure and is more consistent with our traditional deference to the probable cause determinations of magistrates than is the "two-pronged test."

Finally, the direction taken by decisions following *Spinelli* poorly serves "[t]he most basic function of any government:" is "to provide for the security of the individual and of his property." . . . The strictures that inevitably accompany the "two-pronged test" cannot avoid seriously impeding the task of law enforcement, . . . Ordinary citizens, like ordinary witnesses, . . . generally do not provide extensive recitations of the basis of their everyday observations. . . . As a result, anonymous tips seldom could survive a rigorous application of either of the *Spinelli* prongs. Yet such tips, particularly when supplemented by independent police investigation, frequently contribute to the solution of otherwise "perfect crimes." While a conscientious assessment of the basis for crediting such tips is required by the Fourth Amendment, a standard that leaves virtually no place for anonymous citizen informants is not. For all these reasons, we conclude that it is wiser to abandon the "two-pronged test" established by our decisions in *Aguilar* and *Spinelli*.

In its place, we reaffirm the totality-of-the-circumstances analysis that traditionally has informed probable cause determinations. . . . The task of the issuing magistrate is simply to make a practical, common sense decision whether, given all the circumstances set forth in the affidavit before him, including the "veracity" and "basis of knowledge" of persons supplying hearsay information, there is a fair probability that contraband or evidence of a crime will be found in a particular place. And the duty of a reviewing court is simply to ensure that the magistrate had a "substantial basis for . . . conclud[ing]" that probable cause existed. . . . We are convinced that this flexible, easily applied standard will better achieve the accommodation of public and private interests that the Fourth Amendment requires than does the approach that has developed from *Aguilar* and *Spinelli.*

Our decisions applying the totality-of-the-circumstances analysis outlined above have consistently recognized. . . . Even standing alone, the facts obtained through the independent investigation of Mader and the DEA at least suggested that the Gateses were involved in drug trafficking. In addition to being a popular vacation site, Florida is well known as a source of narcotics and other illegal drugs. . . . Lance Gates' flight to West Palm Beach, his brief, overnight stay in a motel, and apparent immediate return north to Chicago in the family car, conveniently awaiting him in West Palm Beach, is as suggestive of a prearranged drug run, as it is of an ordinary vacation trip. In addition, the judge could rely on the anonymous letter, which had been corroborated in major part by Mader's efforts. . . . The corroboration of the letter's predictions that the Gateses' car would be in Florida, that Lance Gates would fly to Florida in the next day or so, and that he would drive the car north toward Bloomingdale all indicated, albeit not with certainty, that the informant's other assertions also were true. . . . It is enough, for purposes of assessing probable cause, that "[c]orroboration through other sources of information reduced the chances of a reckless or prevaricating tale," thus providing "a substantial basis for crediting the hearsay." . . . Finally, the anonymous letter contained a range of details relating not just to easily obtained facts and conditions existing at the time of the tip, but to future actions of third parties ordinarily not easily predicted. The letter writer's accurate information as to the travel plans of each of the

Gateses was of a character likely obtained only from the Gateses themselves, or from someone familiar with their not entirely ordinary travel plans. If the informant had access to accurate information of this type a magistrate could properly conclude that it was not unlikely that he also had access to reliable information of the Gateses' alleged illegal activities. Of course, the Gateses' travel plans might have been learned from a talkative neighbor or travel agent; under the "two-pronged test" developed from *Spinelli,* the character of the details in the anonymous letter might well not permit a sufficiently clear inference regarding the letterwriter's "basis of knowledge." But, as discussed previously, . . . probable cause does not demand the certainty we associate with formal trials. It is enough that there was a fair probability that the writer of the anonymous letter had obtained his entire story either from the Gateses or someone they trusted. And corroboration of major portions of the letter's predictions provides just this probability. It is apparent, therefore, that the judge issuing the warrant had a "substantial basis for . . . conclud[ing]" that probable cause to search the Gateses' home and car existed. The judgment of the Supreme Court of Illinois therefore must be *Reversed.*

LIMITS TO THE EXCLUSIONARY RULE

The exclusionary rule has met with criticism by law enforcement agencies. They argue that the rule is not a deterrent to police misconduct when the police are doing what they believe is procedurally appropriate to apprehend law violators. The Supreme Court has struggled to find a balance between allowing police freedom to pursue evidence and incentivizing constitutional violations with insufficient remedy. The exclusionary rule has been found to be the most certain way of protecting Fourth Amendment rights, but many exceptions have been created by the U.S. Supreme Court to admit evidence seized in technical violation of the warrant requirement.

Judicial Misconduct and the Exclusionary Rule

In *United States v. Leon et al.*, 468 U.S. 897 (1984), police officers were investigating the defendant, and when they believed that they had probable cause, they secured a search warrant. The warrant was later deemed invalid because the magistrate should not have issued it on the limited facts presented. Still, according to the U.S. Supreme Court, the evidence seized during the execution of an invalid but judicially issued warrant should be admitted against the defendant because the purpose of the exclusionary rule is to deter police misconduct, not judicial misconduct. In this case, the judge should not have issued the warrant but the officers reasonably relied on the warrant because they had secured it in "good faith."

UNITED STATES V. LEON, 468 U.S. 897 (1984)

Opinion by WHITE.

Facts: In 1981, a confidential informant of unproven reliability informed an officer of the Burbank Police Department that two persons known to him as "Armando" and "Patsy" were selling large quantities of cocaine and methaqualone from their residence and that he had witnessed a sale of illegal drugs approximately five months earlier. On the basis of the informant's information, the police initiated an extensive investigation. During the course of the investigation, officers observed persons they believed were engaged in illegal drug trafficking and sought a search warrant for three residences. A facially valid search warrant was issued by a judge, and the subsequent searches produced various quantities of drugs at the residences, including Leon's. The Court of Appeals affirmed the lower court's determination that the search warrant lacked probable cause and refused to recognize a good-faith exception to the Fourth Amendment's exclusionary rule.

Issue: Does the Fourth Amendment bar the use of evidence when officers reasonably rely on a search warrant issued by a detached and neutral magistrate but later found to be invalid because it lacked probable cause?

Rationale and Decision: The Fourth Amendment contains no provision expressly precluding the use of evidence obtained in violation of its commands, and an examination of its origin and purposes makes clear that the use of fruits of a past unlawful search or seizure "work[s] no new Fourth Amendment wrong." . . . The rule thus operates as "a judicially created remedy designed to safeguard Fourth Amendment rights generally through its deterrent effect, rather than a personal constitutional right of the party aggrieved." . . . Whether the exclusionary sanction is appropriately imposed in a particular case, our decisions make clear, is "an issue separate from the question whether the Fourth Amendment rights of the party seeking to invoke the rule were violated by police conduct."

Because a search warrant "provides the detached scrutiny of a neutral magistrate, which is a more reliable safeguard against improper searches than the hurried judgment of a law enforcement officer 'engaged in the often competitive enterprise of ferreting out crime,'" . . . we have expressed a strong preference for warrants, and declared that, "in a doubtful or marginal case, a search under a warrant may be sustainable where without one it would fall." . . .

Deference to the magistrate, however, is not boundless. . . . To the extent that proponents of exclusion rely on its behavioral effects on judges and magistrates in these areas, their reliance is misplaced. First, the exclusionary rule is designed to deter police misconduct, rather than to punish the errors of judges and magistrates. Second, there exists no evidence suggesting that judges and magistrates are inclined to ignore or subvert the Fourth Amendment, or that lawlessness among these actors requires application of the extreme sanction of exclusion. Third, and most important, we discern no basis, and are offered none, for believing that exclusion of evidence seized pursuant to a warrant will have a significant deterrent effect on the issuing judge or magistrate. . . . Judges and magistrates are not adjuncts to the law enforcement team; as neutral judicial officers, they have no stake in the outcome of particular criminal prosecutions. The threat of exclusion thus cannot be expected significantly to deter them. Imposition of the exclusionary sanction is not necessary meaningfully to inform judicial officers of their errors, and we cannot conclude that admitting evidence obtained pursuant to a warrant while at the same time declaring that the warrant was somehow defective will in any way reduce judicial officers' professional incentives to comply with the Fourth Amendment, encourage them to repeat their mistakes, or lead to the granting of all colorable warrant requests.

We conclude that the marginal or nonexistent benefits produced by suppressing evidence obtained in objectively reasonable reliance on a subsequently invalidated search warrant cannot justify the substantial costs of exclusion. . . . Finally, depending on the circumstances of the particular case, a warrant may be so facially deficient—*i.e.,* in failing to particularize the place to be searched or the things to be seized—that the executing officers cannot reasonably presume it to be valid. . . . In so limiting the suppression remedy, we leave untouched the probable cause standard and the various requirements for a valid warrant. . . . The good faith exception for searches conducted pursuant to warrants is not intended to signal our unwillingness strictly to enforce the requirements of the Fourth Amendment, and we do not believe that it will have this effect. As we have already suggested, the good faith exception, turning as it does on objective reasonableness, should not be difficult to apply in practice. When officers have acted pursuant to a warrant, the prosecution should ordinarily be able to establish objective good faith without a substantial expenditure of judicial time.

Nor are we persuaded that application of a good faith exception to searches conducted pursuant to warrants will preclude review of the constitutionality of the search or seizure, deny needed guidance from the courts, or freeze Fourth Amendment law in its present state. There is no need for courts to adopt the inflexible practice of always deciding whether the officers' conduct manifested objective good faith before turning to the question whether the Fourth Amendment has been violated. Defendants seeking suppression of the fruits of allegedly unconstitutional searches or seizures undoubtedly raise live controversies which Art. III empowers federal courts to adjudicate. As cases addressing questions of good faith immunity under 42 U.S.C. § 1983 . . . and cases involving the harmless error doctrine, . . . make clear, courts have considerable discretion in conforming their decisionmaking processes to the exigencies of particular cases.

When the principles we have enunciated today are applied to the facts of this case, it is apparent that the judgment of the Court of Appeals cannot stand. The Court of Appeals applied the prevailing legal standards to Officer Rombach's warrant application, and concluded that the application could not support the magistrate's probable cause determination. In so doing, the court clearly informed the magistrate that he had erred in issuing the challenged warrant. This aspect of the court's judgment is not under attack in this proceeding.

Having determined that the warrant should not have issued, the Court of Appeals understandably declined to adopt a modification of the Fourth Amendment exclusionary rule that this Court had not previously sanctioned. Although the modification finds strong support in our previous cases, the Court of Appeals' commendable self-restraint is not to be criticized. We have now reexamined the purposes of the exclusionary rule and the propriety of its application in cases where officers have relied on a subsequently invalidated search warrant. Our conclusion is that the rule's purposes will only rarely be served by applying it in such circumstances.

In the absence of an allegation that the magistrate abandoned his detached and neutral role, suppression is appropriate only if the officers were dishonest or reckless in preparing their affidavit or could not have harbored an objectively reasonable belief in the existence of probable cause. Only respondent Leon has contended that no reasonably well trained police officer could have believed that there existed probable cause to search his house; significantly, the other respondents advance no comparable argument. Officer Rombach's application for a warrant clearly was supported by much more than a "bare bones" affidavit. The affidavit related the results of an extensive investigation and, as the opinions of the divided panel of the Court of Appeals make clear, provided evidence sufficient to create disagreement among thoughtful and competent judges as to the existence of probable cause. Under these circumstances, the officers' reliance on the magistrate's determination of probable cause was objectively reasonable, and application of the extreme sanction of exclusion is inappropriate.

Accordingly, the judgment of the Court of Appeals is *Reversed*.

The good-faith exception to the exclusionary rule does not mean that all invalid warrants will enable the police to have unlawfully seized evidence admitted at trial. The *Leon* good-faith exception does not apply if the judge who issued the warrant was given false statements by the police and relied on these falsehoods when signing the warrant. Similarly, the police cannot intentionally or recklessly engage in misconduct to get around the Fourth Amendment's warrant requirement. The *Leon* decision is premised on the officers' good-faith efforts to abide by the requirement of securing a warrant by a detached and neutral magistrate by providing enough factual basis to secure a valid warrant. In this regard, if the officers reasonably know that the warrant is facially deficient, for example, if it does not particularly describe the items to be seized or the place to be searched, then the exclusionary rule will apply. In such situations, the officers should know that the Fourth Amendment's requirements have not been met and cannot rely on the judge's signature on the deficient warrant to override the exclusionary rule. The *Leon* decision is based on the premise that the officers reasonably relied on a warrant they thought was facially sound. The error was made by the magistrate. When judicial misconduct results in the seizure of items from a deficient warrant, the exclusionary rule does not apply because the purpose of the rule is not to deter judicial misconduct.

Who Can Claim the Exclusionary Rule?

Sometimes when the police execute a warrant, other people are in the home at the time of the search. In order to determine if these guests can claim that their things were unlawfully searched during the execution of a warrant, a court must determine if those individuals have an expectation of privacy. In *Minnesota v. Carter*, 525 U.S. 83 (1998), the defendant and two other persons were in an apartment bagging cocaine. A police officer looked in the window and saw this activity. The defendant claimed that his Fourth Amendment rights were violated and sought to have the evidence excluded at trial. The U.S. Supreme Court held that since the defendant did not lease the apartment and did not stay there overnight as a guest, he did not have any expectation of privacy and the Fourth Amendment was not violated. The Court determined that the right of privacy is a personal one held by the occupant of the residence. The defendant here was using the apartment for "commercial" purposes and was neither a social guest nor a resident occupant of the place. The dissent summarized the current state of the law with consternation:

> A homedweller places her own privacy at risk . . . when she opens her home to others, uncertain whether the duration of their stay, their purpose, and their "acceptance into the household" will earn protection.
> . . . [Although s]earches and seizures inside a home without a warrant are presumptively unreasonable absent exigent circumstances.' . . . [t]he law in practice is less secure. Human frailty suggests that today's decision will tempt police to pry into private dwellings without warrant, to find evidence incriminating guests who do not rest there through the night.

FRUIT OF THE POISONOUS TREE

The exclusionary rule can have dire consequences for the state seeking to admit other evidence that is even *associated* with inadmissibly seized evidence (e.g., evidence taken in violation of the Fourth Amendment, such as evidence seized from an illegally searched car, house, or person). The dire consequences are that secondary evidence that is found and seized *as a result of the initial violation* is also excluded at trial. The exclusionary rule applies to both evidence directly seized after a Fourth Amendment violation and all secondary evidence, which is considered to be "fruit of the poisonous tree." The fruit of the poisonous tree doctrine extends the exclusionary rule to other evidence derived from the violation because the police should not benefit from violating a person's rights. In *Wong Sun v. United States*, 371 U.S. 471 (1963), the U.S. Supreme Court held:

> The exclusionary rule has traditionally barred from trial physical, tangible materials obtained either during or as a direct result of an unlawful invasion. It follows . . . that . . . evidence which derives so immediately from an unlawful entry and an unauthorized arrest as the officers' action in the present case is no less the "fruit" of official illegality than the more common tangible fruits of the unwarranted intrusion.

The fruits of the poisonous tree doctrine excludes only tainted evidence that would not have been found and seized "but for" the police officer's illegal conduct. The U.S. Supreme Court has carved out three exceptions to this doctrine: the independent discovery rule, the independent source rule, and the attenuated connection rule. In each of these exceptions, the "poisonous fruit" evidence would have been found regardless of whether the Fourth Amendment was violated.

Independent Discovery

In *Nix v. Williams*, 467 U.S. 431 (1984), the defendant directed the police to the body of a dead 10-year-old girl. The confession was found previously by the Court to be inadmissible (see *Brewer v. Williams*, 430 U.S. 387 [1977]). The defendant was retried without the inadmissible confession that helped the police locate the girl's body and once again was convicted. On appeal, the defendant claimed that the discovery of the girl's body was tainted by the confession and should have been excluded at his retrial as a fruit of the poisonous tree. The U.S. Supreme Court determined that since the police had been looking for the girl's body and would have found her anyway, the taint from the illegal confession would not prevent the admission of the evidence. The police and volunteers looking for the girl would have "inevitably discovered" her body, with or without the confession. The evidence is admissible if the prosecution can show by a preponderance of the evidence that the found evidence would have been discovered despite the violation.

NIX V. WILLIAMS, 467 U.S. 431 (1984)

Opinion by BURGER.

Facts: The defendant, Nix, was convicted of the homicide of a girl a second time. The first trial was overturned on appeal because the police violated the defendant's *Miranda* rights by engaging in a "Christian burial" speech. The defendant led the police to the victim's body. The second trial excluded the confession but admitted the evidence pertaining to the discovery and condition of the victim's body. The trial court also ruled that if the police had not located the body, "the search would clearly have been taken up again where it left off, given the extreme circumstances of this case, and the body would [have] been found *in short order*." The Court of Appeals held that the police acted in bad faith and that even if there was an inevitable discovery exception to the exclusionary rule, the state could not avail itself of it.

Issue: Should evidence found in violation of a defendant's *Miranda* rights be admissible if the police inevitably would have found it?

Rationale and Decision: The Iowa Supreme Court correctly stated that the "vast majority" of all courts, both state and federal, recognize an inevitable discovery exception to the exclusionary rule[,] . . . [t]he doctrine requiring courts to suppress evidence as the tainted "fruit" of unlawful governmental conduct. . . .

Wong Sun v. United States, 371 U.S. 471 (1963), extended the exclusionary rule to evidence that was the indirect product or "fruit" of unlawful police conduct, but there again the Court emphasized that evidence that has been illegally obtained need not always be suppressed, stating:

"We need not hold that all evidence is 'fruit of the poisonous tree' simply because it would not have come to light *but for the illegal actions of the police . . .* "

Exclusion of physical evidence that would inevitably have been discovered adds nothing to either the integrity or fairness of a criminal trial. . . . Here, however, Detective Leaming's conduct did nothing to impugn the reliability of the evidence in question—the body of the child and its condition as it was found, articles of clothing found on the body, and the autopsy. No one would seriously contend that the presence of counsel in the police car when Leaming appealed to Williams' decent human instincts would have had any bearing on the reliability of the body as evidence. Suppression, in these circumstances, would do nothing whatever to promote the integrity of the trial process, but would inflict a wholly unacceptable burden on the administration of criminal justice.

The . . . case is remanded for further proceedings consistent with this opinion.

It is so ordered.

Independent Source

The independent source exception to the exclusionary rule is similar to the independent discovery exception in that the police would have found the evidence on their own despite some constitutional violation by the police. Similar to *Nix*'s Fifth Amendment *Miranda* rights violation, evidence found from independent means despite a Fourth Amendment violation is also admissible. In *Segura v. United States*, 468 U.S. 796 (1984), the independent source used to form a search warrant was information that the police were waiting to secure. The police had applied for a warrant but entered the home in order to secure it, in this case to ensure that the drugs at issue were not destroyed, before the warrant had been judicially issued. None of the evidence they collected while "securing" the home would have been admissible because the police entered and seized it without a valid search warrant. However, the evidence was not suppressed at trial because a magistrate later approved their search warrant, which had been lawfully granted based on information entirely collected before the police entered the house.

Attenuated Connection

The Court in *Wong Sun v. United States*, 371 U.S. 471 (1963), held that any evidence discovered while violating a defendant's constitutional rights is not admissible in court. But evidence not connected to the violation is admissible, because the connection between the evidence and the rights violation is "attenuated." The exclusionary rule is designed to ensure that police do not violate the Fourth Amendment, and so it serves no purpose in attenuated circumstances. The following considerations determine whether a connection is attenuated: Was the evidence found as a result of the taint? Was the evidence found close in time to the tainted fruit? Was there an intervening event that led to the discovery of the evidence? Did the defendant's own free will lead to the discovery? The more likely the evidence was to be found, not as a result of the taint, but instead due to closeness in time, a defendant's independent and voluntary action, or other intervening acts, the more likely the evidence is to be admissible.

SUING THE POLICE FOR A VIOLATION OF THE FOURTH AMENDMENT

When police officers use a search warrant that is invalid, they may be civilly liable for damages. In *Groh v. Ramirez*, 540 U.S. 551 (2004), federal officers had a warrant signed by a judge that did not describe what items the officers wanted to search for at all. The Court stated: "The warrant was plainly invalid." The Fourth Amendment states unambiguously that "no Warrants shall issue, but upon probable cause, supported by Oath or affirmation, and *particularly describing* the place to be searched, and *the persons or things to be seized*" (emphasis added). The warrant in this case complied with the first three of these requirements: it was based on probable cause and supported by a sworn affidavit, and it described particularly the place of the search. On the fourth requirement, however, the warrant failed altogether. "[T]he warrant . . . was deficient in particularity because it provided no description of the type of evidence sought."

Although the officers themselves had a list of items they wanted to find, they did not particularly describe the items in the warrant. The Court said: "No reasonable officer could claim to be unaware of the basic rule, well established by our cases, that, absent consent or exigency, a warrant-less search of the home is presumptively unconstitutional." Because the rule was plainly laid-out, settled law and no reasonable officer could be unaware of it, the officers who violated it (absent consent or contingency) could be sued for violating the civil rights of the person illegally searched. Even though the warrant had been signed by a magistrate, it was so obviously deficient that it was objectively unreasonable. Not only was the search unconstitutional because the officer was not relying on the warrant in good faith, but the warrant was so obviously deficient that the officers could not claim qualified immunity when sued.

CONTEMPORARY ISSUES: DEADLY FORCE AND WARRANTS

Police work can be dangerous for officers who are executing warrants. If an arrest warrant is being executed at a person's home, the officers can sweep through other rooms of the house if they have a reasonable belief that another person in the home might pose a danger to them. Officers must clearly announce their presence when entering a home to minimize these dangers. Sometimes, a search warrant is issued for an apartment complex in which more than one apartment is identified as the location to be searched. Other times, officers execute a "no-knock" forced entry warrant, in which the officer avers that the circumstances of the search are so dangerous that his safety would be compromised if he were required to knock and announce his presence before entering the premise. Typically, such warrants describe the neighborhood as dangerous, known for high levels of violence and homicide, and that according to the officer's training and experience, firearms are commonly involved in the world of illicit narcotics. For this reason, the officer requests a "no-knock" warrant that permits him to force entry into the home unannounced. During these searches, the officers may be announcing their presence to a resident who does not understand why the police are bursting into the house. Both the resident and police perceive serious danger. Even without a "no-knock" warrant, officers typically force entry pursuant to *any* valid search warrant without announcing their presence. Since the Supreme Court ruled that violations of the "knock-and-announce" rule (a vague "reasonable wait time" standard before entry) do not require suppression of the evidence collected during the search, officers have been secure in the knowledge that impermissible entry will not result in suppression of evidence.

However, some residents fearing for their safety will shoot at the person breaking in their door. If an officer is shot or killed by a resident, that resident may be charged with criminal homicide. In many states, the killing of a police officer (working in the line of duty at the time of his or her death) is an aggravating factor that can warrant the death penalty or life imprisonment upon conviction. From the resident's perspective, a person might reasonably think that his or her life or the lives of their family living in the home might be threatened by forcible entry into the premises. Every state allows persons to defend themselves and others in their home with deadly force if reasonable belief exists that the person fears for his or her life or the life of another person in the home.

The question remains: Who is accountable when a no-knock or warrant entry turns deadly? Is it the officer's responsibility or the resident's responsibility to be accountable for a deadly encounter? An example of the legal difficulties posed by deadly force encounters with the police during a search warrant execution is *Maye v. State of Mississippi*, 49 So. 3d 1124 (2010) (a Mississippi State Supreme Court case). Maye was sleeping when the police entered his home to execute a search warrant. The warrant did not specify that the search was for Maye's apartment; it indicated that the police wished to search apartments on his floor of the building. The officers came to his apartment early in the morning, knocked many times on his apartment door, and announced that they were the "police" and had a "search warrant." When officers entered the apartment, Maye awoke and went into a bedroom where his toddler was sleeping on the bed. As the officers entered the back room of the apartment, Maye shot at them and hit an officer, who later died of his wounds at the hospital. When the officers announced that they were the police and that Maye had shot an officer, Maye put down his gun and slid it away from himself. He was convicted of first-degree murder for the killing of a police officer in the line of duty. Maye argued on appeal that he should have been able to raise the issue of self-defense and defense of others (his child). He claimed that the instructions given to the jury were inadequate for them to consider his reasonable fear for his safety. He was not the target of drug sale investigations, and the warrant created a situation where he was placed in fear because he did not know or have any expectation that his home would be forcibly entered. The Mississippi State Supreme Court overturned Maye's conviction and remanded the case for retrial. The court determined that Maye should be allowed to raise the claims of both self-defense and defense of others. A shooting is reasonable if a lethal force justification existed at the time of the shooting and will not be second-guessed afterward when the individual realizes that he has shot and killed an officer.

Another recent controversy in Fourth Amendment jurisprudence involves the practice of federal agents of secretly obtaining covert-entry search warrants, also known as "sneak-and-peak" or "surreptitious entry" search warrants. Although federal agents had obtained these types of warrants previously, the USA Patriot Act granted statutory authorization for agents to obtain them, igniting a firestorm of criticism from civil liberty and privacy advocates. The "sneak-and-peak" warrant allows agents to clandestinely enter private premises, such as homes or businesses, while the owners and occupants are away, and gather information. To obtain a warrant, federal agents must explain why immediate notification would have an adverse result on the investigation, such as destruction of evidence. During the search, agents may not seize anything, but may collect intangible evidence such as agents' eyewitness information, take photographs, and sometimes install wiretaps or keylogging software on computers. Agents do not need to leave a copy of the search warrant at the premises when they leave or give immediate notice to owners that a search has been performed, and may delay notification for as long as is reasonable. The intangible evidence collected during the covert search may be used later to support a traditional search warrant.

SUMMARY

The Fourth Amendment allows the state to search individuals' houses and personal effects, but people still retain an expectation of privacy in their homes and their things. The balance between the ability of the police to conduct a search and the rights of people to be protected from unwarranted intrusions can be met when the officers get a search warrant from a detached, neutral judge. Search warrants require officers to articulate clearly to a magistrate the facts that lead them to reasonably believe that particular evidence that they seek to find and seize is in a particular place. When a danger to the officers' safety may be posed by the execution of such warrants or may result in destruction of the evidence sought, officers may be able to execute the warrants with "no-knock" or "knock-and-announce" warrants.

If the police do not secure a search warrant and seize evidence from a person's home or private place, then the evidence may be excluded when a court determines that the police intentionally, or even recklessly, violated the Fourth Amendment. The exclusionary rule is a judge-made rule that aims to deter police misconduct. Over the past few decades, the U.S. Supreme Court has modified the exclusionary rule and carved out some exceptions to it. For example, evidence seized without a valid warrant may be admissible under the good-faith doctrine. The good-faith doctrine refers to cases in which a search warrant is later determined to be invalid, but the police had originally obtained the warrant in "good faith"—in other words, they reasonably believed the information the warrant was based on to be valid. Under the good-faith doctrine, the evidence seized pursuant to a defective warrant will be admissible against an accused if the misconduct was on the part of a magistrate, not the officers. In such a situation, the exclusionary rule's stated purpose (to deter police misconduct) cannot be achieved, and the exclusionary rule should not prevent the admissibility of the evidence seized. Other exceptions to the exclusionary rule involve the reasonable efforts of the police to detect crime and secure evidence. If officers are attempting to reasonably find and secure evidence so that it will not be destroyed, then even if a defendant's Fifth Amendment rights were violated and his or her confession leads directly to the item sought, the evidence can be admitted under the inevitable discovery rule. Also, if officers have independent sources for the evidence articulated in their application for a search warrant, then evidence seized without a warrant may be admissible. Finally, if officers have reasonable grounds to search and seize items that are not directly tied to some Fourth Amendment violation, then the evidence may be admissible.

GLOSSARY

Anticipatory search warrant: Search warrant based on an affidavit showing probable cause that evidence of a certain crime will take place at a certain location in the future.

Blanket search warrant: Unconstitutionally vague warrant that authorizes the seizure of any and all items found at a given location.

Covert-entry search warrant: A warrant authorizing a search of a private premises without prior notice, in the absence of the owner, to gather information and take photographs that may be used to obtain a full search warrant, but not seize any property.

Fruit of the poisonous tree doctrine: Secondary evidence derived from an illegal search, arrest, or interrogation will not be admissible in court because it is tainted from the constitutional rights violation.

Good-faith exception: An exception to the exclusionary rule. If the police have an honest belief that they have a valid warrant but the warrant is later deemed invalid due to judicial misconduct, the evidence will not be suppressed in court for this reason.

No-knock search warrant: Search warrant authorizing the police to enter premises without first knocking and announcing their presence and purpose before entering in order to preserve evidence that may be destroyed or when the officers' safety could be endangered.

Search warrant: A written order issued by a neutral and detached magistrate. It is the legal authorization for the police to look for items that have been particularly described and in a place that has been particularly identified.

Warrantless search: A search for evidence of a crime by the police without a warrant. Such a search may be lawful if it falls within an exception to a Fourth Amendments' requirement, or it could be unlawful if evidence is seized in violation of a person's constitutional rights.

ADDITIONAL READINGS

Jackson, H. A. (1996). Expanding exclusionary rule exceptions and contracting Fourth Amendment protection. *Journal of Criminal Law and Criminology, 86*(4), 1201–1277. Retrieved from http://findarticles.com/p/articles/mi_hb6700/is_n4_86/ai_n28674289/?tag=content;col1

Moran, D. A. (2006). The end of the exclusionary rule, among other things: The Roberts Court takes on the Fourth Amendment. *Cato Supreme Court Review*, 203–309.

Oklewicz, R. M. (2010). Comment: Expanding the scope of the good-faith exception to the exclusionary rule to include a law enforcement officer's reasonable reliance on well-settled case law that is subsequently overruled. *American University Law Review, 59,* 1715.

Taslitz, A. E. (2006). Programmatic purpose, subjective intent, and objective intent: What is the proper role of "purpose" analysis to measure the reasonableness of a search or seizure? Rethinking the good faith exception to the exclusionary rule. *Mississippi Law Journal, 76,* 483.

CHAPTER 7

Warrantless Searches of People and Their Immediate Area and Things

KEY POINTS

- The Fourth Amendment permits searches of people without a warrant, if reasonable.

- Probable cause does not have to be established for a personal search under certain exceptions to a warrant requirement.

- Reasonable searches of people may occur incident to a lawful arrest, during an arrestee's booking process, or even at an airport during screening of passengers.

- Searches of a youth's body may be done by school officials, but such searches are limited in scope and must be reasonable.

SEARCHES OF PEOPLE AND THE FOURTH AMENDMENT

The Fourth Amendment permits warrantless searches of people and their immediate locations without a warrant, if reasonable. These searches of people may occur incident to an arrest or may precede an arrest. Warrantless searches of persons or their immediate area may occur at the time of a lawful arrest or may be based upon the immediacy of a situation. If based on an arrest, then the arrest must be lawful and the search limited. Many officers understand that an arrest can be followed by a search, but the scope of the search, its timing, its reasonableness, and the rationale of the search need to be understood if the items seized are to be admissible. In addition, officers can search persons and the place they are located with consent, whether an arrest has occurred or not. Consent searches are limited, however, by the nature of the consent, the identity of the person giving consent, and whether the person has withdrawn consent. Law enforcement officers and judges sometimes express surprise at how often consent is freely given to perform searches that reveal some kind of illegal activity. Once consent has been given, it may not be revoked during the course of the search, although the search may also not exceed the boundaries of consent. If a person does not consent to be searched, an officer may still perform a pat-down pursuant to the *Terry* test, and may sometimes perform a warrantless search. Indeed, most searches of people are warrantless and legally operative as reasonable under the circumstances. This chapter will look at the rules governing warrantless searches of people and their immediate area.

SEARCH OF A PERSON INCIDENT TO ARREST

When an arrest has occurred, an officer may conduct a search of the arrestee without probable cause or even a reasonable suspicion that the person might have contraband or evidence of a crime. However, the arrest must be lawful. Lawful arrests can occur with arrest warrants, or without a warrant if the officer has probable cause to believe the individual committed a crime. Warrantless arrests are valid if a crime is committed in the officer's presence or if other indicia of probable cause exist to tie a person to a crime. If the underlying arrest is unlawful, then the seizure of items incident to the arrest will be deemed unlawful.

The search incident to an arrest of a person is limited in scope. The arrestee's "body" can be searched within reason. Officers can search the arrestee's pockets and other items in the arrestee's control. Officers can use their discretion in conducting the search, but it must be reasonable. An officer does not have to have probable cause to believe that the arrestee has contraband or even has a weapon in his or her possession. The purpose of the search is to protect such evidence of a crime or to protect the officer while executing an arrest. The officer might not know if an arrestee possesses a weapon or evidentiary items that the arrestee might be able to hide or destroy. To protect the evidence and the officer, a search of the arrestee incident to a lawful arrest has become an established exception to the warrant requirement of the Fourth Amendment.

To further protect evidentiary items or to prevent an arrestee from getting access to a weapon, the immediate area where an arrest occurs is subject to a search. In an early case, the U.S. Supreme Court held that an entire room in which a person is located can be searched at the time of a person's arrest. In *United States v. Rabinowitz*, 339 U.S. 56 (1950), the Court held that a search of an entire one-room office over an arrestee's objection was acceptable and the items seized admissible against him. In *Rabinowitz*, pursuant to an arrest warrant, the defendant was arrested for unlawfully possessing and selling forged or altered stamps. Then the officers began to search the one-room office, including the individual's desk, filing cabinets, and safe. The officers found and seized more than 500 forged or altered stamps. The Court reasoned that the search for items associated with the crime for which the defendant was arrested, contemporaneous with the arrest, was reasonable because several factors existed:

1. The search and seizure were incident to a valid arrest.

2. The place of the search was a business room to which the public, including the officers, was invited.

3. The room was small and under the immediate and complete control of the defendant.

4. The search did not extend beyond the room used for unlawful purposes.

5. The possession of the forged and altered stamps was a crime.

If a search is contemporaneous to an arrest, the officers do not have to procure a search warrant even if there was time to get one prior to the arrest.

The search incident to a lawful arrest exception to a warrant is most closely associated with *Chimel v. California*, 395 U.S. 752 (1969). In

Chimel, the defendant was arrested for burglary pursuant to an arrest warrant in his home. The officers then conducted a search of the entire premises, not just the room in which the arrest occurred. The Court was concerned with the broad scope of the search because the Constitution has never supported the use of general warrants. The Founding Fathers rejected the common law's use of general warrants, which would allow extensive searches without any reasonable basis. After *Rabinowitz,* some critics were concerned that the police would be given a general warrant authority and begin to arrest persons in their homes so that they could "rummage" through a person's things without a warrant. In *Chimel,* however, the court found the search to be unreasonable and distinguished itself from *Rabinowitz.*

In *Chimel,* the Court articulated the basic three-part rule for conducting a warrantless search incident to an arrest. First, the arrest must be lawful. Second, the search must be contemporaneous to the arrest. Third, the search must be limited to the area under the arrestee's immediate control. When the officers' search of Chimel's home extended to areas beyond the arrestee's control, it became an unreasonable search. It was too broad, according to the Court, because it went beyond the area where the defendant could procure a weapon or evidence of the crime. Certainly, the officers should be able to protect themselves from a defendant's ability to get a weapon or to get and destroy evidence of the crime for which he or she is arrested. But if the officers wish to search other areas, then they need another exception to the warrant requirement or to procure a search warrant. Since the search exceeded the scope of a search incident to the arrest exception, the warrantless search of the defendant's home was unreasonable and the items inadmissible. The search should be limited to the "wingspan" of the arrestee.

CHIMEL V. CALIFORNIA, 395 U.S. 752 (1969)

Opinion by STEWART.

Facts: Three police officers arrived at Chimel's home with an arrest warrant authorizing his arrest for the burglary of a coin shop. After his arrest, officers told him that "on the basis of the lawful arrest," the officers would conduct a search of his home. No search warrant had been issued. Accompanied by Chimel's wife, the officers searched through the entire three-bedroom house, including the attic, the garage, and a small workshop. In some rooms, the search was relatively cursory. In the master bedroom and sewing room, however, the officers directed the petitioner's wife to open drawers. The search produced several items and took between 45 minutes and one hour. The California Supreme Court held that the since his arrest was lawful, the subsequent search of his home was also lawful.

Issue: What is the permissible scope of a search incident to a lawful arrest under the Fourth Amendment?

Rationale and Decision: To provide the necessary security against unreasonable intrusions upon the private lives of individuals, the framers of the Fourth Amendment required adherence to judicial processes wherever possible. . . . The test . . . "is not whether it is reasonable to procure a search warrant, but whether the search was reasonable. . . . The presence of a search warrant serves a high function. Absent some grave emergency, the Fourth Amendment has interposed a magistrate between the citizen and the police. This was done not to shield criminals, nor to make the home a safe haven for illegal activities. It was done so that an objective mind might weigh the need to invade that privacy in order to enforce the law. The right of privacy was deemed too precious to entrust to the discretion of those whose job is the detection of crime and the arrest of criminals. . . .

When an arrest is made, it is reasonable for the arresting officer to search the person arrested in order to remove any weapons that the latter might seek to use in order to resist arrest or effect his escape. Otherwise, the officer's safety might well be endangered, and the arrest itself frustrated. In addition, it is entirely reasonable for the arresting officer to search for and seize any evidence on the arrestee's person in order to prevent its concealment or destruction. And the area into which an arrestee might reach in order to grab a weapon or evidentiary items must, of course, be governed by a like rule. A gun on a table or in a drawer in front of one who is arrested can be as dangerous to the arresting officer as one concealed in the clothing of the person arrested. There is ample justification, therefore, for a search of the arrestee's person and the area "within his immediate control"—construing that phrase to mean the area from within which he might gain possession of a weapon or destructible evidence.

There is no comparable justification, however, for routinely searching any room other than that in which an arrest occurs—or, for that matter, for searching through all the desk drawers or other closed or concealed areas in that room itself. Such searches, in the absence of well recognized exceptions, may be made only under the authority of a search warrant. . . .

. . . Application of sound Fourth Amendment principles to the facts of this case produces a clear result. The search here went far beyond the petitioner's person and the area from within which he might have obtained either a weapon or something that could have been used as evidence against him. There was no constitutional justification, in the absence of a search warrant, for extending the search beyond that area. The scope of the search was, therefore, "unreasonable" under the Fourth and Fourteenth Amendments, and the petitioner's conviction cannot stand.

Reversed.

Contemporaneous to an Arrest

A warrantless search incident to a lawful arrest must be contemporaneous with the arrest. A contemporaneous search is one that occurs at the "same" time as the arrest. That is, an arrest first occurs and then the search of the person or the person's wingspan occurs.

Contemporaneous searches may reasonable even if a short delay in a search of the defendant's clothing occurs. In *United States v. Edwards*, 415 U.S. 800 (1974), the U.S. Supreme Court determined that a search of a defendant's clothing the day after an arrest was lawful. In *Edwards*, the defendant was arrested late at night and was placed in a jail cell. Because the jail did not have clean jail clothing to give to the defendant at the time of his booking, they did not take his clothing when he initially was housed in a cell. After giving him clothing the following morning, the items were searched without a warrant. The court determined that even though substantial time had passed since the initial arrest, the probable cause that would have allowed the search incident to a lawful arrest did not expire. The administrative processing was valid without a warrant.

UNITED STATES V. EDWARDS, 415 U.S. 800 (1974)

Opinion by WHITE.

Facts: Edwards was arrested late at night. Because the jail facility did not have any clothing to give to Edwards until the next day, the police did not search the clothing taken from the defendant until 10 hours after his arrest. The Court of Appeals held that although probable cause to believe that evidence would be found on the defendant's clothing existed, because the seizure occurred after his administrative processing into the jail facility had been concluded, the warrantless seizure was unconstitutional.

Issue: Does the Fourth Amendment exclude evidence seized from an arrestee's clothing taken from respondent Edwards while he was in custody at the city jail approximately 10 hours after his arrest?

Rationale and Decision: Historical evidence points to the established and routine custom of permitting a jailer to search the person who is being processed for confinement under his custody and control. . . . While "[a] rule of practice must not be allowed . . . to prevail over a constitutional right," . . . little doubt has ever been expressed about the validity or reasonableness of such searches incident to incarceration.

Holding the Warrant Clause inapplicable in the circumstances present here does not leave law enforcement officials subject to no restraint. This type of police conduct "must [still] be tested by the Fourth Amendment's general proscription against unreasonable searches and seizures." . . . But the Court of Appeals here conceded that probable cause existed for the search and seizure of respondent's clothing, and respondent complains only that a warrant should have been secured. We thus have no occasion to express a view concerning those circumstances surrounding custodial searches incident to incarceration which might "violate the dictates of reason either because of their number or their manner of perpetration."

The judgment of the Court of Appeals is reversed.

So ordered.

Where Can Officers Go When an Arrest Occurs?

Officers who are making arrests may need to take precautionary measures to ensure their safety or the safety of others. While the Court in *Chimel* was concerned that officers might be in danger from weapons within the wingspan of an arrestee, officers might also be endangered by other persons who are hiding or lying in wait when the officers effectuate an arrest. In order to protect themselves, officers can perform protective sweeps of a residence or place where an arrest occurs.

The protective sweep is not a "search" of a residence, so it does not have to be based upon probable cause that other or unknown persons might be hiding and could harm an officer who is arresting a suspect. In *Maryland v. Buie*, 494 U.S. 325 (1990), the defendant was arrested in his home. Because the officer observed him coming up from a basement, the officer became concerned that other persons might be in the basement. To make sure that no one else was there, the officer went down into the basement. The entry was not based on the arrest on probable cause that the officer would find any evidence there. While sweeping the basement, the officer saw and seized a "jump suit" lying in plain view that matched the description of one used during the armed robbery. The Court stated that "The Fourth Amendment permits a properly limited protective sweep in conjunction with an in-home arrest when the searching officer possesses a reasonable belief based on specific and articulable facts that the area to be swept harbors an individual posing a danger to those on the arrest scene."

In *Mincey v. Arizona*, 437 U.S. 385 (1978), the U.S. Supreme Court stated how extensive a search may be when an in-home arrest occurs and a protective sweep has secured the scene. In *Mincey*, an undercover narcotics officer was shot when he entered the defendant's bedroom to arrest him. Because there were several gunshots fired, other officers who were at the scene entered the premises and immediately began to look for other persons who might have been shot. This search for persons in need of emergency care is valid. However, the Court found the subsequent search of the entire apartment was unconstitutional. When homicide officers arrived (10 minutes after the protective sweep, and while emergency medical care was being provided), the homicide officers began an extensive search without a warrant that lasted four days. During the warrantless search, the entire apartment was searched, including curtains, carpets, drawers, and closets, and various items (bullets, drugs, drug paraphernalia) from the scene were seized. The Court stated that the right of privacy in one's home must be secure from unreasonable searches and rejected the argument that an exigent circumstance exists merely because the arrest occurred at a place where a homicide had taken place. The subsequent search was not incident to arrest, was not part of a protective sweep, and constituted an unlawful search because it was done without a warrant. In *Mincey*, the U.S. Supreme Court was not troubled by the entrance without a warrant by the officers because such practice was tied to an undercover police investigation and was in response to a situation where one of the officers was shot.

As part of an unfolding scene, officers have a right to follow people they have placed under arrest. If an arrestee goes from a public space into a private space (a home, apartment, or dorm room), then the officer has a right to enter the dwelling without a warrant. So long as the officer is not attempting to violate the right of privacy a person has in their home, and does not use the entry as a pretext to search the home, the officer may go where the arrestee goes. In *Washington v. Chrisman*, 455 U.S. 1 (1982), the Court clarified that the rule is that an arresting officer can follow "at the arrestee's elbow." If an arrested person moves, freely and voluntarily, from one space into another, then the area of search incident to the lawful arrest can expand. In *Chrisman*, the officer arrested a college student for violating an open container law and followed the student into his dorm room because the student wanted to get his identification. While in the dorm room, the officer seized drugs and drug paraphernalia from a desk in plain sight in the room. The initial seizure of the items from the desk was lawful incident to the arrest, and the items seized were in plain view.

WASHINGTON V. CHRISMAN, 455 U.S. 1 (1982)

Opinion by BURGER.

Facts: A campus university police officer saw a student carrying a half-gallon bottle of alcohol. Because state law prohibits possession of alcohol by persons under 21 and the student appeared to be underage, the officer stopped the student and asked him to produce his identification. The student said his identification was in his dorm room, and under the circumstances, the officer said he would have to follow him there. The officer waited at the doorjamb and watched the student collect his things. In the room, the student's roommate, Chrisman, was observed moving items around. The officer then noticed what he believed to be marijuana seeds and a pipe used to smoke marijuana on one of the desks. At that point, the officer called by radio for backup and told both students that a search of the room would be necessary. Officers explained to both students that they had an absolute right to insist that the officers first obtain a search warrant, but that they could voluntarily consent to the search. Following this explanation, which was given in considerable detail, the two students gave consent and also signed written forms consenting to the search of the room. The search yielded more marijuana and LSD. The Washington State Supreme Court held that the officer had no right to enter the dorm room, and since the consent was contingent on the officer's entry, the evidence should have been suppressed.

Issue: Can a police officer accompany an arrestee into his residence and then seize contraband discovered there in plain view?

Rationale and Decision: The "plain view" exception to the Fourth Amendment warrant requirement permits a law enforcement officer to seize what clearly is incriminating evidence or contraband when it is discovered in a place where the officer has a right to be. . . . We hold . . . that it is not "unreasonable" under the Fourth Amendment for a police officer, as a matter of routine, to monitor the movements of an arrested person, as his judgment dictates, following the arrest. The officer's need to ensure his own safety— as well as the integrity of the arrest—is compelling. Such surveillance is not an impermissible invasion of the privacy or personal liberty of an individual who has been arrested. . . . Accordingly, he had the right to act as soon as he observed the seeds and pipe. This is a classic instance of incriminating evidence found in plain view when a police officer, for unrelated but entirely legitimate reasons, obtains lawful access to an individual's area of privacy. The Fourth Amendment does not prohibit seizure of evidence of criminal conduct found in these circumstances.

Since the seizure of the marihuana and pipe was lawful, we have no difficulty concluding that this evidence and the contraband subsequently taken from respondent's room were properly admitted at his trial. Respondent voluntarily produced three bags of marihuana after being informed of his rights. . . . He then consented, in writing, to a search of the room, after being advised that his consent must be voluntary and that he had an absolute right to refuse consent and demand procurement of a search warrant. The seizure of the drugs pursuant to respondent's valid consent did not violate the Fourth Amendment. . . .

> The judgment of the Supreme Court of Washington is reversed, and the case is remanded for further proceedings not inconsistent with this opinion.
>
> *So ordered.*

SEARCH OF YOUTH IN SCHOOLS

Schools act in place of parents for the youth who are entrusted to their care and education. School administrators are concerned that drugs, weapons, or other items could be brought into schools by students. In order for school administrators to be able to protect the minor students, administrators may need to search youth for contraband. Because these searches are done by public officials who are acting in lieu of parents, the searches do not require probable cause. Searches of the youth, their books, backpacks, and school lockers can be done without a warrant if the searches are based on reasonable suspicion that contraband or weapons may be hidden there. These searches must be reasonable. The extent to which such student searches are reasonable was decided by the U.S. Supreme Court in *Safford Unified School District v. Redding*, 557 U.S. ___, 129 S. Ct. 2633 (2009).

In *Safford*, school administrators heard a rumor that a 13-year-old female student was passing out prescription-strength ibuprofen 400-mg pills and over-the-counter blue naproxen to other students. After searching the student's backpack and belongings, the administrators did not find anything. They then asked her to strip to her underwear and shake out her bra and underpants. During this search, nothing was found. The Court found that the search was unreasonable because there was no reason to suspect that she had pills hiding in her underwear, even if there was some initial reason to suspect that she might have had pills in her outer clothing or backpack. The Court recognized that based on her age and gender, the intrusive search exposed part of her breast and thigh and was humiliating. To justify such a search under the Fourth Amendment, the administrators needed something more tangible to show they would find drugs in her inner clothing. It is not enough that drugs could have been hidden there; the administrators needed to be able to point out why they specifically believed the student was hiding contraband there.

SAFFORD UNITED SCHOOL DISTRICT #1, ET AL. V. REDDING, 557 U.S. ___ (2009)

Opinion by SOUTER.

Facts: The assistant principal, Wilson, of a middle school suspected that a 13-year-old female student, Savana, had been passing out prescription-strength and over-the-counter medicine at school. When a search of her bags did not result in the finding of any pills, the assistant principal instructed an administrative assistant and the school nurse to strip-search her. During the search, she was instructed to shake out her bra and panties. No pills were found, but when she moved her bra and panties, her private areas were slightly exposed. The Court of Appeals held that the student's right to be free from unreasonable search and seizure was violated.

Issue: Are a 13-year-old student's Fourth Amendment rights violated when she is subjected to a search of her bra and underpants by school officials acting on reasonable suspicion?

Rationale and Decision: In *T. L. O.*, we recognized that the school setting "requires some modification of the level of suspicion of illicit activity needed to justify a search," . . . and held that for searches by school officials "a careful balancing of governmental and private interests suggests that the public interest is best served by a Fourth Amendment standard of reasonableness that stops short of probable cause," . . . We have thus applied a standard of reasonable suspicion to determine the legality of a school administrator's search of a student, . . . and have held that a school search "will be permissible in its scope when the measures adopted are reasonably related to the objectives of the search and not excessively intrusive in light of the age and sex of the student and the nature of the infraction," . . . The lesser standard for school searches could as readily be described as a moderate chance of finding evidence of wrongdoing.

Here, the content of the suspicion failed to match the degree of intrusion. Wilson knew beforehand that the pills were prescription-strength ibuprofen and over-the-counter naproxen, common pain relievers equivalent to two Advil, or one Aleve. He must have been aware of the nature and limited threat of the specific drugs he was searching for, and while just about anything can be taken in quantities that will do real harm, Wilson had no reason to suspect that large amounts of the drugs were being passed around, or that individual students were receiving great numbers of pills. Nor could Wilson have suspected that Savana was hiding common painkillers in her underwear . . . non dangerous school contraband does not raise the specter of stashes in intimate places, and there is no evidence in the record of any general practice among Safford Middle School students of hiding that sort of thing in underwear. . . . In sum, what was missing from the suspected facts that pointed to Savana was any indication of danger to the students from the power of the drugs or their quantity, and any reason to suppose that Savana was carrying pills in her underwear. We think that the combination of these deficiencies was fatal to finding the search reasonable. . . .

We do mean, though, to make it clear that the *T. L. O.* concern to limit a school search to reasonable scope requires the support of reasonable suspicion of danger or of resort to underwear for hiding evidence of wrongdoing before a search can reasonably make the quantum leap from outer clothes and backpacks to exposure of intimate parts. The meaning of such a search, and the degradation its subject may reasonably feel, place a search that intrusive in a category of its own demanding its own specific suspicions. . . .

The strip search of Savana Redding was unreasonable and a violation of the Fourth Amendment, but petitioners Wilson, Romero, and Schwallier are nevertheless protected from liability through qualified immunity.

It is so ordered.

SEARCH UPON BOOKING AND INVENTORY SEARCHES

A person who has been arrested will be brought to a local jail for criminal processing or given an appearance ticket. An appearance ticket is a citation given at the scene by the officer; the defendant is told when to appear in court for the criminal violation or to pay fines in lieu of going to court. If the defendant is brought to the local jail, then the person is booked. The booking process records the defendant's name, address, and the criminal charges the person is being arrested for. In addition, the defendant's photograph, fingerprints, clothing, and other items are taken. The defendant's clothing and personal items are inventoried and taken into police custody. In addition, if the defendant will spend time in a jail cell, the defendant's body will be searched and, in some cases, strip-searched. If there is a reason to suspect that the defendant is hiding drugs or weapons in his or her body cavities, a body cavity search may also occur. In order to protect the jail from disease, the person can be screened for HIV or tuberculosis; if the person has been hurt or is very ill, then further medical screening may occur and the person may be transported to a hospital or mental health facility. If the person is a danger to himself or herself, the person might also be placed in secure jail administrative confinement and placed under a suicide watch.

The police cannot just take a person, without probable cause to arrest, to the stationhouse in order to procure evidence. In *Hayes v. Florida*, 470 U.S. 811 (1985), the U.S. Supreme Court determined that an investigative detention at the stationhouse intended to procure a suspect's fingerprint identity violates the Fourth and Fourteenth Amendments because the detention is "sufficiently like an arrest" to require probable cause.

HAYES V. FLORIDA, 470 U.S. 811 (1985)

Opinion by WHITE.

Facts: A series of burglary–rapes occurred in 1980. Police found latent fingerprints that they believed belonged to the assailant on the doorknob of the bedroom of one of the victims. Although the police did not have much informa-tion to tie Hayes to the crime, they decided to obtain his fingerprints. Since he refused to give the officers his prints, they told him that he would be arrested. Hayes "blurted out" that he would rather go with the officers to the station than be arrested. He was taken to the stationhouse, and his prints were taken. He was placed under formal arrest when his prints were deemed a match to the latent prints found at the scene. Before trial, petitioner moved to suppress the fingerprint evidence, claiming it was the fruit of an illegal detention. The Florida Supreme Court denied review of Florida's Second District Court of Appeal's decision that the officers could take a person to a stationhouse for fin-gerprinting because the police action was similar to a stop and frisk.

Issue: Do the Fourth and Fourteenth Amendments allow police to transport a suspect to the stationhouse for finger-printing, without his consent and without probable cause or prior judicial authorization?

Rationale and Decision: Here, . . . there was no probable cause to arrest, no consent to the journey to the police sta-tion, and no judicial authorization for such a detention for fingerprinting purposes. . . . There is no doubt that, at some point in the investigative process, police procedures can qualitatively and quantitatively be so intrusive with respect to a suspect's freedom of movement and privacy interests as to trigger the full protection of the Fourth and Fourteenth Amendments. . . . And our view continues to be that the line is crossed when the police, without probable cause or a war-rant, forcibly remove a person from his home or other place in which he is entitled to be and transport him to the police station, where he is detained, although briefly, for investiga-tive purposes. We adhere to the view that such seizures, at least where not under judicial supervision, are sufficiently like arrests to invoke the traditional rule that arrests may constitutionally be made only on probable cause.

None of the foregoing implies that a brief detention in the field for the purpose of fingerprinting, where there is only reasonable suspicion not amounting to probable cause, is necessarily impermissible under the Fourth Amendment. . . . As we have said, absent probable cause and a warrant, . . . [the law] requires the reversal of the judgment of the Florida District Court of Appeal.

It is so ordered.

CONTEMPORARY ISSUES: AIRPORT AND BORDER SCREENINGS

There has been heightened security in the United States and at its borders since September 11, 2001. The heightened security has raised some questions about the privacy rights of travelers and whether some of the security measures are reasonable. Montoya de Hernandez (*United States v. Montoya de Hernandez*, 473 U.S. 531 [1985]) was detained at the Los Angeles airport for more than 16 hours on suspicion that she was a drug courier. She was entering the United States from Colombia, and her behavior raised some suspicions. After a rectal exam, she began to expel balloons that were later determined to be filled with cocaine. The Court held that the long detention at the border was reasonable and the cocaine admissible at her trial.

UNITED STATES V. MONTOYA DE HERNANDEZ, 473 U.S. 531 (1985)

Opinion by REHNQUIST.

Facts: Montoya de Hernandez was detained by customs officials upon her arrival at the Los Angeles Airport on a flight from Bogota, Colombia. Although her passport and visa were in order, customs officials noted that she made frequent trips between Miami and Los Angeles, had no friends or family in the United States, spoke no English, had no hotel reservations, and carried $5,000 in cash. Because Colombia is a source country for narcotics smuggling, she was detained and subjected to a pat-down search by a female officer. The officer noted that her stomach seemed firm and she was wearing two pairs of underwear with a paper towel lining. Montoya de Hernandez refused to have an x-ray, claiming that she was pregnant. Officers then detained her until she had a bowel movement. Almost 16 hours after her flight had landed, she had not defecated and refused all offers of food and drink. Customs officials sought a court order authorizing a pregnancy test, an x-ray, and a rectal examination. A federal judge issued an order just before midnight that evening, and she was taken to a hospital and given a pregnancy test, which later turned out to be negative. Before the results of the pregnancy test were known, a physician conducted a rectal examination and removed from Montoya de Hernandez's rectum a balloon containing a foreign substance. She was then placed formally under arrest. Over the next three days, she passed more balloons. She was found to be smuggling 88 cocaine-filled balloons containing a total of 528 grams of 80 percent pure cocaine hydrochloride. The Court of Appeals held that the defendant's detention violated the Fourth Amendment.

Issue: What is the Fourth Amendment requirement for the detention of a person at the border? Is it reasonable suspicion or probable cause to arrest?

Rationale and Decision: The Fourth Amendment commands that searches and seizures be reasonable. What is reasonable depends upon all of the circumstances surrounding the search or seizure and the nature of the search or seizure itself. . . . Here, the seizure of respondent took place at the international border. Since the founding of our Republic, Congress has granted the Executive plenary authority to conduct routine searches and seizures at the border, without probable cause or a warrant, in order to regulate the collection of duties and to prevent the introduction of contraband into this country. . . .

Consistently, therefore, with Congress' power to protect the Nation by stopping and examining persons entering this country, the Fourth Amendment's balance of reasonableness is qualitatively different at the international border than in the interior. Routine searches of the persons and effects of entrants are not subject to any requirement of reasonable suspicion, probable cause, or warrant, . . . and first-class mail may be opened without a warrant on less than probable cause. . . . Automotive travelers may be stopped at fixed checkpoints near the border without individualized suspicion, even if the stop is based largely on ethnicity, . . . and boats on inland waters with ready access to the sea may be hailed and boarded with no suspicion whatsoever. . . . Having presented herself at the border for admission, and having subjected herself to the criminal enforcement powers of the Federal Government, . . . respondent was entitled to be free from unreasonable search and seizure. But . . . the expectation of privacy less at the border than in the interior. . . .

We have not previously decided what level of suspicion would justify a seizure of an incoming traveler for purposes other than a routine border search. We hold that the detention of a traveler at the border, beyond the scope of a routine customs search and inspection, is justified at its inception if customs agents, considering all the facts surrounding the traveler and her trip, reasonably suspect that the traveler is smuggling contraband in her alimentary canal.

The "reasonable suspicion" standard has been applied in a number of contexts, and effects a needed balance between private and public interests when law enforcement officials must make a limited intrusion on less than probable cause. It thus fits well into the situations involving alimentary canal smuggling at the border: this type of smuggling gives no external signs, and inspectors will rarely possess probable cause to arrest or search, yet governmental interests in stopping smuggling at the border are high indeed. Under this standard, officials at the border must have a "particularized and objective basis for suspecting the particular person" of alimentary canal smuggling. . . .

The final issue in this case is whether the detention of respondent was reasonably related in scope to the circumstances which justified it initially. . . . Here, respondent was detained incommunicado for almost 16 hours before inspectors sought a warrant; the warrant then took a number of hours to procure, through no apparent fault of the inspectors. This length of time undoubtedly exceeds any other detention we have approved under reasonable suspicion. . . .

The rudimentary knowledge of the human body which judges possess in common with the rest of humankind tells us that alimentary canal smuggling cannot be detected in the amount of time in which other illegal activity may be investigated through brief *Terry*-type stops. It presents few, if any, external signs; a quick frisk will not do, nor will even a strip search. In the case of respondent, the inspectors had available, as an alternative to simply awaiting her bowel movement, an x-ray. They offered her the alternative of submitting herself to that procedure. But when she refused that alternative, the customs inspectors were left with only two practical alternatives: detain her for such time as necessary to confirm their suspicions, a detention which would last much longer than the typical *Terry* stop, or turn her loose into the interior carrying the reasonably suspected contraband drugs.

The inspectors in this case followed this former procedure. They no doubt expected that respondent, having recently disembarked from a 10-hour direct flight with a full and stiff abdomen, would produce a bowel movement without extended delay. But her visible efforts to resist the call of nature, which the court below labeled "heroic," disappointed

> this expectation, and in turn caused her humiliation and discomfort. . . . Respondent alone was responsible for much of the duration and discomfort of the seizure. Under these circumstances, we conclude that the detention in this case was not unreasonably long. . . .
>
> Her detention for the period of time necessary to either verify or dispel the suspicion was not unreasonable. The judgment of the Court of Appeals is therefore *Reversed.*

The border is a place where a person can be stopped briefly at checkpoints and detained if there is reasonable suspicion that the person is smuggling contraband. Note that the Fourth Amendment's protections are lower at borders: a sixteen-hour detention would normally require probable cause. After September 11, 2001, passengers at the airport can be subjected to x-ray body scanning that can show the private parts of individuals screened. The screening is justified on the basis of protecting the public from hijackings or terroristic threats perpetrated on air travelers. The Transportation Security Administration (TSA) claims that the x-ray dosage is very low and not harmful because people have limited exposure. In order to stay ahead of security threats, the use of technology such as the x-ray machines can assist airport security personnel in determining if someone is carrying a weapon. If persons refuse to participate in the x-ray scan, then they can be subjected to a very detailed pat-down of their person and detained for a reasonable time to ascertain if they are a security threat. Passengers and pilots complained about the intrusiveness and radiation in these machines and by February 2011, the federal government started to utilize some x-ray machines that did not reveal as much of a person's body; the devices show a more blurred body image of the individual screened (see http://www.washingtonpost.com/wp-dyn/content/article/2011/02/01/AR2011020105305.html).

Baggage carried by passengers at airports can also be subjected to screenings and searches. Airport security can use dogs to sniff for explosive materials or drug contraband. X-ray screening for contraband is also constitutional. If security officials reasonably suspect that luggage contains contraband, then the items can be detained for a limited period of time. In *United States v. Place*, 462 U.S. 696 (1983), the Court held that the defendant's personal luggage could be briefly held so that a trained narcotics dog could determine if the luggage contained narcotics; the dog sniff test was not a "search" because it is intended only to reveal the presence or absence of narcotics and therefore does not implicate the Fourth Amendment.

SUMMARY

The Fourth Amendment protects a person's right of privacy, but even a person's body and personal effects can sometimes be searched. Although the Fourth Amendment in theory requires a warrant for a body search, most searches of persons occur without a warrant. A common exception to the warrant requirement is search incident to a lawful arrest. The U.S. Supreme Court has long recognized the need of officers to be able to secure an individual who is arrested and also secure any weapons or evidence of the crime. If there is probable cause to arrest a person, then at the time of the arrest (contemporaneous to the arrest) the person and their immediate area can be searched. Any fruits of the crime and weapons can be seized if they are within the "wingspan" of the arrestee. After the person has been arrested, the person and his or her personal items can be searched at the stationhouse. Inventory searches are justified to ensure that items taken from an arrestee are secured, and the arrestee's body can be searched to ensure that no contraband is brought into the jail facility. Such searches can extend to a body cavity search of the arrestee.

The ability to search a person's body also enables youth arrestees to be searched. School officials may search youth in their schools on a reasonable suspicion of belief that the youth is engaged in criminal activity or possesses contraband. If preliminary investigations do not show that the officials' suspicions are founded, then a strip search is unreasonable.

In the past decade, concerns about various forms of community threats from terrorism to drug trafficking have given rise to various forms of technological intrusions. In order to ascertain if people or their luggage are carrying weapons, explosive materials, or drugs, law enforcement or airport security personnel can perform body scans, body pat-downs, and dog sniff tests. If the search is limited in time and reasonably tied to the government's security function of protecting the traveling public, the search will be constitutional.

GLOSSARY

Appearance ticket: A citation ordering a person to appear in court at a particular time to answer for a stated offense.

Booking process search: A warrantless search that occurs when an arrested person is going to be held in a jail or detention facility.

Consent search: A warrantless search that occurs when a person voluntarily agrees to be searched.

Dog sniff search: A warrantless search that occurs by a police canine that is trained to respond if the animal smells contraband. Not considered a "search" for Fourth Amendment purposes.

Lawful arrest: An arrest that occurs with an arrest warrant or if a valid exception to the warrant requirement exists.

Search incident to lawful arrest: A warrantless search of a person or the immediate area that is within the wingspan of the person.

ADDITIONAL READINGS

Hessick, F. A., III. (2002). The federalization of airport security: Privacy implications. *Whittier Law Review, 24,* 43–69.

Hunter, D. (2002). Comment: Common scents: Establishing a presumption of reliability for detector dog teams used in airports in light of the current terrorist threat. *Dayton Law Review, 28,* 89.

Napolitano, J. (2010, November 14). Scanners are safe, pat-downs are discreet [op-ed]. *USA Today.* Retrieved from http://www.usatoday.com/news/opinion/forum/2010-11-15-column15_ST1_N.htm

Simonitsch, W. J. (2000). Comment: Visual body cavity searches incident to arrest: Validity under the Fourth Amendment. *University of Miami Law Review, 54,* 665.

Wells, H. (2007). *State v. Gant*: Departing from the bright-line *Belton* rule in automobile searches incident to arrest. *Arizona Law Review, 49,* 1033–1031.

CHAPTER 8

Searches of Houses and Real Property

KEY POINTS

- A person's residence cannot be searched without a warrant or one of the warrantless search exceptions that enable the police to search a home or seize items from a home.

- Among the most common reasons the police may enter a residence without a warrant is that they have lawful consent to enter the home.

- Officers may also enter a home, without consent or a warrant, if an emergency exists (exigent circumstances).

- Open fields are not subject to the Fourth Amendment because a person does not have any expectation of privacy in these areas.

FOURTH AMENDMENT AND SEARCHES OF HOMES

The extent to which the Fourth Amendment protects one's privacy rights in a residence or other dwelling place from warrantless searches depends on: (1) the nature of the property, (2) the authority one exerts over that piece of property, and (3) the specific warrantless exception that might recognize the reasonableness of the search or seizure. Persons have a heightened expectation that their residences and private property are protected from unreasonable searches and seizures under the Fourth Amendment. Whether officers can enter private space without a warrant depends on the circumstances surrounding the entry. For many years, the U.S. Supreme Court required officers to be legally present on private property for any warrantless seizure of criminal evidence to be admissible. The modern rule is a more flexible evaluation of the circumstances. For example, was there consent or exigent circumstances to justify the admission of an officer into a private dwelling or entry onto the private property? What is private space? Is public space that is owned by private individuals outside the protections of the Fourth Amendment? Common warrantless searches conducted on private real property are valid if consent is obtained or if an exigent circumstance exists. For other types of property, the Fourth Amendment does not apply at all, and the police do not need a warrant or some warrantless exception to enter the property.

CONSENT ENTRY SEARCHES

Many times, an officer gains entry into a home or residence by consent. A person opens a door and steps aside to allow the officers to step inside. Consent entry, however, requires that the officer show that a person who consented to the entry had "lawful authority" to consent to the entry, and that the consent to enter was given voluntarily and completely. A person has "lawful authority" to consent to a police search if he has sufficient *legal interest* in the property to waive the legitimate expectation of privacy in the dwelling or place to be searched. The "voluntariness" of consent depends upon the belief by a person that he or she *can* refuse the officer's request, but the officer is not required to tell a person that the individual can refuse the officer's request to enter the home.

Consent entry searches are problematic when the police arrive at a scene and have to quickly establish whether a person giving consent has the legal authority to provide it. Such authority might be limited depending on the type of premises and the extent of the property use rights of the individual. In *Stoner v. California,* 376 U.S. 483 (1964), the U.S. Supreme Court found that police entry into a hotel room, granted by a night clerk, was unlawful because the clerk did not have the authority to give consent to the police to enter the room. The court stated,

> It is important to bear in mind that it was the petitioner's constitutional right which was at stake here, and not the night clerk's nor the hotel's. It was a right, therefore, which only the petitioner could waive

by word or deed, either directly or through an agent. It is true that
the night clerk clearly and unambiguously consented to the search.
But there is nothing in the record to indicate that the police had any
basis whatsoever to believe that the night clerk had been authorized by
the petitioner to permit the police to search the petitioner's room.

A guest in a hotel room enjoys a reasonable expectation to privacy
from government intrusion in that room, and hotel staff, even those with
free access to the room, may not waive that right on behalf of the person
staying at the hotel.

In determining lawful authority to consent to enter a private place, officers will need to use good faith to ascertain if the person consenting can
legally give the consent. The officers can rely on statements by the person
granting entry and on other facts such as whether the person has a key or
has personal items kept in the place. Officers may also rely in good faith
upon a deceitful person's "apparent authority" (authority which appears
valid but actually is not) to give consent. Searches pursuant to aparrent
authority can be reasonable if the officers do not know about the person's
deception. The majority opinion, which drew some criticism from the dissent, examined the textual language of the Fourth Amendment and reiter-
ated that the standard for searches is "reasonableness," not consent. Thus,
the constitutional validity of a police determination of consent is not
whether the police were factually correct in their assessment, but whether,
based on the facts available to them at the moment, it was reasonable to
believe that the person consenting to a search had authority to do so.

ILLINOIS V. RODRIGUEZ, 497 U.S. 177 (1990)

Opinion by SCALIA.

Facts: The police gained entry to the defendant's apartment
with the consent and assistance of a woman, Fischer, who
had lived there with Rodriguez for several months. Fischer
was not a "usual resident" but rather an "infrequent visitor"
at the apartment. Her name was not on the lease, she did
not contribute to the rent, she was not allowed to invite
others to the apartment on her own, and she did not have

access to the apartment when Rodriguez was away. She did have some of her possessions in the apartment, but she did not have common authority over the apartment, and thus, her consent to the search was invalid. Rodriguez moved to suppress all evidence discovered during the search, and the motion was granted. The Illinois Supreme Court denied to hear the state's appeal, leaving intact the Circuit Court's decision to suppress the evidence, but granted permission to appeal to the U.S. Supreme Court.

Issue: Is a warrantless entry valid when based on the consent of a third party who the police, at the time of the entry, reasonably believe possesses common authority over the premises but who in fact does not?

Rationale and Decision: We see no reason to depart from this general rule with respect to facts bearing upon the authority to consent to a search. Whether the basis for such authority exists is the sort of recurring factual question to which law enforcement officials must be expected to apply their judgment, and all the Fourth Amendment requires is that they answer it reasonably. The Constitution is no more violated when officers enter without a warrant because they reasonably (though erroneously) believe that the person who has consented to their entry is a resident of the premises than it is violated when they enter without a warrant because they reasonably (though erroneously) believe they are in pursuit of a violent felon who is about to escape. . . .

But, as we have discussed, what is at issue when a claim of apparent consent is raised is not whether the right to be free of searches has been *waived,* but whether the right to be free of *unreasonable* searches has been *violated.* . . . As with other factual determinations bearing upon search and seizure, determination of consent to enter must "be judged against an objective standard: would the facts available to the officer at the moment . . . *warrant a man of reasonable caution in the belief*" that the consenting party had authority over the premises? . . . If not, then warrantless entry without* *further inquiry is unlawful unless authority actually exists. But if so, the search is valid.* . . . In the present case, the Appellate Court found it unnecessary to determine whether the officers reasonably believed that Fischer had the authority to consent, because it ruled as a matter of law that a reasonable belief could not validate the entry. . . . The judgment of the Illinois Appellate Court is reversed and remanded for further proceedings not inconsistent with this opinion.

So ordered.

EXIGENT ENTRY AND SEARCHES OF A HOME

When an emergency exists, officers can, without a warrant and without consent, enter a home or private dwelling place. Exigent circumstances create a situation where the need to complete the search of a home is immediate and sustain a legitimate reason why a person would not maintain the expectation of privacy in his or her home. Legitimate reasons include the protection of people's lives or property, and not the police officer's desire to do a search of the premises. Searches under this rule are directly tied to the legitimate reasons of the emergency that require immediate entry. A common basis for exigent entry is to provide emergency medical police assistance. If the police reasonably believe that someone inside the residence is in need of emergency assistance, then the officers can force a door open because the emergency requires the police to act immediately. Another exigent circumstance is destruction of evidence. In *Kentucky v. King*, 569 U.S. ___ (2011), the U.S. Supreme Court addressed exigent entry when officers followed a suspect who had sold drugs to an undercover informant into an apartment. When the officers arrived at the apartment building, they heard a door slam and assumed (wrongly) that the suspect had entered an apartment that smelled of marijuana. When they knocked and announced their presence, they heard noises consistent with the destruction of illegal substances and forcibly entered the apartment and seized drug paraphernalia. Justice

Alito stated: "We conclude that the exigent circumstances rule applies when the police do not gain entry to premises by means of an actual or threatened violation of the Fourth Amendment." In *King,* the evidence was deemed admissible by the Court because the officers arrived at the defendant's door and heard what sounded like evidence being destroyed. Potential destruction of evidence is an exigent circumstance that enables an officer to enter and search premises without first obtaining a warrant. In this situation, the officers were not the ones who created the exigency by announcing their presence. The occupants of the apartment were the ones who created the exigent circumstances by "choos[ing] not to stand on their constitutional rights but instead elect[ing] to attempt to destroy evidence [and have] only themselves to blame for the warrantless exigent circumstances that may ensue."

HOW AND WHEN CAN SEARCH WARRANTS BE EFFECTUATED?

A search warrant does not give officers free reign to search anyone at any time and in any place. A warrant is valid within the jurisdiction in which it is issued, and the searches performed pursuant to it must be reasonable. Such reasonableness involves the manner in which officers conduct the search; depending on where the search is conducted, courts might have concerns about the protection of a person's privacy during the search. In *Steagald v. United States,* 451 U.S. 204 (1981), officers searched the defendant's home without a search warrant pursuant to the arrest (with a valid warrant) of another person whom the police believed would be at the defendant's home. The police officers' valid warrant to arrest an associate of the defendant did not give them authority to search his home. The U.S. Supreme Court held that the search was not constitutional because the officers had time to get a search warrant for the defendant's home. The court stated:

> A search warrant requirement, under the circumstances of this case, will not significantly impede effective law enforcement efforts. . . . In any event, whatever practical problems there are in requiring a search warrant in cases such as this, they cannot outweigh the constitutional interest at stake in protecting the right of presumptively innocent people to be secure in their homes from unjustified forcible intrusions by the government.

Knock and Announce

To effectuate a search warrant, usually the police will be able to go to a person's home. The time of the effectuation is usually during the daylight hours for a misdemeanor or at any time of the day or night for a felony offense. In *Wilson v. Arkansas*, 514 U.S. 927 (1995), the Court held that the police must knock on the door, window, or other point of entry into a place when they seek entry into a home with a search warrant. If the resident does not answer the door, then officers can "force" entry. During a forced entry, the officers are expected to announce themselves and their purpose. Officers commonly avoid the "knock-and-announce rule" when there is a reason to fear that evidence sought inside the location will be destroyed. The U.S. Supreme Court acknowledges that it is very easy for persons to flush drugs down a toilet when officers appear at a residence.

Officers do not have to wait long at a person's door to effectuate a search warrant. In *United States v. Banks*, 540 U.S. 31 (2003), the Court held that the officers who waited only 20 seconds were acting reasonably when they entered the premises. The defendant was in the shower and contended that he did not hear the officers' loud knocking and that it would take longer than 20 seconds for him to answer his door. The Court rejected the defendant's claims because reasonableness does not depend on how long it would take a person to reach the front door, but how long it could take to destroy evidence. In *Hudson v. Michigan*, 547 U.S. 586 (2006), the Court held that the knock-and-announce rule is aimed at protecting a person's privacy, preventing violence, and preventing someone from destroying the evidence sought in a warrant. The Court was asked to consider whether the search and seizure of evidence from a person's home violated the Fourth Amendment when the officer executing a warrant waited just a few seconds, rather than the "expected" 20 seconds, before entering the residence. The Court determined that a knock-and-announce rule has no requirement that officers wait any stated amount of time; what matters is that the officers acted reasonably when they entered with a search warrant. Executing search warrants will require officers to enter into dangerous places, and they must act quickly to secure evidence. Because the knock-and-announce rule is not designed to protect citizens against unconstitutionally obtained evidence, but instead their privacy and dignity, evidence seized in violation of the knock-and-announce rule is not suppressed for this reason.

HUDSON V. MICHIGAN, 547 U.S. 586 (2006)

Opinion by SCALIA.

Facts: Officers executing a search warrant for illegal contraband knocked on Hudson's door. The officers waited only a few seconds before turning the doorknob, entering the apartment, and announcing their purpose. The search of the apartment turned up unlawful drugs and a firearm. Hudson claimed that the knock-and-announce rule was violated in the execution of the warrant because the officers did not wait at least 20 seconds to give him time to answer the door. The Michigan State Supreme Court declined review of the Court of Appeals' decision, which rejected the defendant's claim of a Fourth Amendment rights violation and affirmed his conviction.

Issue: Is the knock-and-announce rule pertaining to the execution of search warrants violated if the officers do not provide enough time for a person to answer the door?

Rationale and Decision: The interests protected by the knock-and-announce rule include human life and limb (because an unannounced entry may provoke violence from a surprised resident), property (because citizens presumably would open the door upon an announcement, whereas a forcible entry may destroy it), and privacy and dignity of the sort that can be offended by a sudden entrance. But the rule has never protected one's interest in preventing the government from seeing or taking evidence described in a warrant. Since the interests violated here have nothing to do with the seizure of the evidence, the exclusionary rule is inapplicable.

The value of deterrence [against police misconduct so as to exclude the evidence] depends on the strength of the incentive to commit the forbidden act. That incentive is minimal here, where ignoring knock-and-announce can realistically be expected to achieve nothing but the prevention of evidence destruction and avoidance of life-threatening resistance, dangers which suspend the requirement when there is "reasonable suspicion" that they exist. . . . Contrary to Hudson's argument that without suppression there will be no deterrence, many forms of police misconduct are deterred by civil-rights suits, and by the consequences of increasing professionalism of police forces, including a new emphasis on internal police discipline.

For the foregoing reasons we affirm the judgment of the Michigan Court of Appeals.

It is so ordered.

No-Knock Warrants

Under some circumstances, police officers may be given a "no-knock warrant." No-knock warrants allow officers to enter a residence to search for evidence (e.g., fruits of a crime or instrumentalities of crime) without first announcing that the police are at the residence and armed with a search warrant. The narrow circumstances for no-knock warrants focus on protecting officers in dangerous circumstances (residents might be armed) or protecting evidence such as drugs that could be easily destroyed. In 2002, the Chief Counsel for the Drug Enforcement Administration issued a memorandum that provided that federal law enforcement officers could make use of no-knock warrants, if reasonable. The memorandum stated:

> After giving full consideration to these submissions, and having reviewed the pertinent statutes and case law, we conclude that federal district court judges and magistrates may lawfully and constitutionally issue no-knock warrants—i.e., warrants authorizing officers to enter certain premises to execute a warrant without first knocking or otherwise announcing their presence where circumstances (such as a known risk of serious harm to the officers or the likelihood that evidence of crime will be destroyed) justify such an entry. . . . Even when authorized by such a no-knock warrant, however, a no-knock entry might nonetheless violate the Fourth Amendment if the officers have actual knowledge that the circumstances that justified the no-knock authorization no longer exist at the time the warrant is executed.

Thus, it is incumbent on officers to ensure that they are still acting within the reasonable expectation of individual liberty and privacy when seeking to enter a person's home with a warrant. The idea that officers can enter a residence without knocking was first addressed by the U.S. Supreme Court in *Richards v. Wisconsin*, 520 U.S. 385 (1997). In *Richards*, the magistrate refused to authorize a no-knock warrant. But when effectuating the warrant that was issued, the officers neither knocked nor announced themselves. Nonetheless, the court validated the search.

RICHARDS V. WISCONSIN, 520 U.S. 385 (1997)

Opinion by STEVENS.

Facts: On December 31, 1991, police officers obtained a warrant to search Richards' hotel room for drugs and related paraphernalia. The police requested a warrant that would have given advance authorization for a "no-knock" entry into the hotel room, but the magistrate explicitly deleted those portions of the warrant when issuing the order. The officers arrived at the hotel room at 3:40 a.m. One officer, Pharo, dressed as a maintenance man and led a team of several plainclothes officers and one uniformed officer. Pharo knocked on Richards' door and said that he was a maintenance man. With the chain still on the door, Richards cracked it open. Although there was some dispute as to what occurred next, Richards acknowledged that when he opened the door he saw the man in uniform standing behind Officer Pharo. . . . He quickly slammed the door closed and, after two or three seconds, the officers began kicking and ramming the door to gain entry to the locked room. When they finally did break into the room, the officers caught Richards trying to escape through the window. They also found cash and cocaine hidden in plastic bags above the bathroom ceiling tiles. The Wisconsin Supreme Court affirmed the defendant's conviction and held that the police officers did not have to knock and announce their presence when executing a search warrant in a felony drug investigation.

Issue: What is the test for determining knock-and-announce rules governing entrance into a person's residence under the Fourth Amendment?

Rationale and Decision: In *Wilson v. Arkansas*, 514 U.S. 927 (1995), we held that the Fourth Amendment incorporates the common law requirement that police officers entering a dwelling must knock on the door and announce their identity and purpose before attempting forcible entry. At the same time, we recognized that the "flexible requirement of reasonableness should not be read to mandate a rigid rule of announcement that ignores countervailing law enforcement interests," . . . and left "to the lower courts the task of determining the circumstances under which an unannounced entry is reasonable under the Fourth Amendment." In this case, the Wisconsin Supreme Court concluded that police officers are *never* required to knock and announce their presence when executing a search warrant in a felony drug investigation. In so doing, it reaffirmed a pre-*Wilson* holding and concluded that *Wilson* did not preclude this *per se* rule. We disagree with the court's conclusion that the Fourth Amendment permits a blanket exception to the knock and announce requirement for this entire category of criminal activity. But because the evidence presented to support the officers' actions in this case establishes that the decision not to knock and announce was a reasonable one under the circumstances, we affirm the judgment of the Wisconsin court. . . .

In order to justify a "no knock" entry, the police must have a reasonable suspicion that knocking and announcing their presence, under the particular circumstances, would be dangerous or futile, or that it would inhibit the effective investigation of the crime by, for example, allowing the destruction of evidence. This standard—as opposed to a probable cause requirement—strikes the appropriate balance between the legitimate law enforcement concerns at issue in the execution of search warrants and the individual privacy interests affected by no knock entries. . . .

> Although we reject the Wisconsin court's blanket exception
> to the knock and announce requirement, we conclude . . .
> that the officers had a reasonable suspicion that Richards
> might destroy evidence if given further opportunity to do so.
>
> . . . At the time the officers obtained the warrant, they did not
> have evidence sufficient, in the judgment of the magistrate,
> to justify a no knock warrant. Of course, the magistrate could
> not have anticipated in every particular the circumstances that
> would confront the officers when they arrived at Richards'
> hotel room. These actual circumstances—petitioner's appar-
> ent recognition of the officers combined with the easily dis-
> posable nature of the drugs—justified the officers' ultimate
> decision to enter without first announcing their presence
> and authority. Accordingly, although we reject the blanket
> exception to the knock and announce requirement for felony
> drug investigations, the judgment of the Wisconsin Supreme
> Court is affirmed.
>
> *It is so ordered.*

OPEN FIELDS RULE

According to the U.S. Supreme Court in *Hester v. United States*, 265
U.S. 57 (1924), the scope of the Fourth Amendment extends to "the
people in their 'persons, houses, papers and effects' [and] is not extended
to the open fields. The distinction between the latter and the house is as
old as the common law." An open field (such as farmland) is subject to
entry by officers without a warrant because it cannot be construed as a
person, house, paper, or effect, and thus does not implicate the Fourth
Amendment. But the curtilage of home (i.e., the yard, the driveway) is
protected by the Fourth Amendment because it is a part of the home and
private sphere. Curtilage harbors the intimate activity of one's home, but
generally ends at fencing or cars parked outside. Where does curtilage
end? Farmland may have "curtilage" that extends for miles, but the U.S.
Supreme Court considered open fields and farms in *Oliver v. United
States*, 466 U.S. 170 (1984). The open fields doctrine expressed by *Oliver*

described the outer boundaries for curtalige on large, privately owned properties. The Fourth Amendment protects unreasonable searches and seizures on properties associated with the home, but no expectations of privacy (and thus no protection by the Fourth Amendment) extend to areas that are distant and not within the immediate area of the home. Police may even trespass on open fields without tainting the evidence.

OLIVER V. UNITED STATES, 466 U.S. 170 (1984)

Opinion by POWELL.

Facts: Police received an anonymous tip that marijuana was being grown in the woods behind respondent Thornton's residence. Two officers entered the woods by using a path that existed between his residence and a neighboring house. The officers followed the path and found two marijuana patches fenced with chicken wire. After determining that patches were on Oliver's property, a warrant to search the property was obtained, and the officers seized the marijuana. The Maine Supreme Judicial Court affirmed the trial court's decision to suppress the evidence and held that the open fields doctrine did not apply in this situation.

Issue: Does the Fourth Amendment permit police officers to enter and search an open field without a warrant?

Rationale and Decision: We conclude, from the text of the Fourth Amendment and from the historical and contemporary understanding of its purposes, that an individual has no legitimate expectation that open fields will remain free from warrantless intrusion by government officers. . . . Initially, we reject the suggestion that steps taken to protect privacy establish that expectations of privacy in an open field are legitimate. It is true, of course, that petitioner Oliver and respondent Thornton, in order to conceal their criminal activities, planted the marihuana upon secluded land and erected fences and "No Trespassing" signs around the property. And it may be that, because of such precautions, few members of the public stumbled upon the marihuana crops seized by the police. Neither of these suppositions demonstrates, however, that the expectation of privacy was legitimate in the sense required by the Fourth Amendment. The test of legitimacy is not whether the individual chooses to conceal assertedly "private" activity. . . . Rather, the correct inquiry is whether the government's intrusion infringes upon the personal . . . and societal values protected by the Fourth Amendment. As we have explained, we find no basis for concluding that a police inspection of open fields accomplishes such an infringement.

Nor is the government's intrusion upon an open field a "search" in the constitutional sense because that intrusion is a trespass at common law. The existence of a property right is but one element in determining whether expectations of privacy are legitimate. . . . The law of trespass, however, forbids intrusions upon land that the Fourth Amendment would not proscribe. For trespass law extends to instances where the exercise of the right to exclude vindicates no legitimate privacy interest. . . . Thus, in the case of open fields, the rights of property protected by the common law of trespass have little or no relevance to the applicability of the Fourth. . . .

It is so ordered.

CONTEMPORARY ISSUES: PROTECTIVE SWEEPS OF A HOME

The police may go through a person's home upon lawful entry to see whether another person is in the home who may pose a threat to the officers; this action is called a protective sweep. Officers may not know when they enter a place whether other persons in the home could harm them while they are performing their official duties or making an arrest. To eliminate the risk of being harmed, the officers have a right to quickly check so as to determine whether anyone else is in the home if they have a reasonable suspicion for thinking that someone else might be there. If, during the sweep, the officers see evidence or fruits of a crime in plain view, this evidence may be seized under the plain view doctrine.

Protective sweeps are similar to a frisk of a person for weapons. The search of the home is limited in time and function to determine whether someone else is indeed in the home while the officers are present. In *Maryland v. Buie*, 494 U.S. 325 (1990), the U.S. Supreme Court discussed the constitutionality of protective sweeps. In *Buie*, the officers were investigating an armed robbery, and when they were inside the home, the defendant came up from the basement area. An officer went to the basement and found evidence associated with the bank robbery in plain view. The defendant claimed that the officers did not have probable cause to seize the item or any reason to clearly fear for their safety that would justify their entry into the basement.

MARYLAND V. BUIE, 494 U.S. 325 (1990)

Opinion by WHITE.

Facts: Two men committed an armed robbery in which one of the men wore a red running suit. That same day, police obtained arrest warrants for Buie and his suspected accomplice in the robbery. When the officers verified that Buie was at home, six officers went to his home. Once inside, the officers fanned out through the first and second floors. With his service revolver drawn, one officer, Rozar, twice shouted into the basement and ordered anyone down there to come out. Buie announced that he was in the basement and would come up the stairs; he was then arrested, searched, and handcuffed by Rozar. Thereafter, another officer entered the basement "in case there was someone else" down there. He noticed a red running suit lying in plain view on a stack of clothing and seized it. The Court of Appeals of Maryland held that the Fourth Amendment protects the "sanctity" of the home and that the search was unlawful without probable cause.

Issue: Can officers performing a protective sweep of a home seize evidence used in a crime that is found in plain view?

Rationale and Decision: It is not disputed that until the point of Buie's arrest the police had the right, based on the authority of the arrest warrant, to search anywhere in the house that Buie might have been found, including the basement. . . . It goes without saying that the Fourth Amendment bars only unreasonable searches and seizures. . . . That Buie had an expectation of privacy in those remaining areas of his house, however, does not mean such rooms were immune from entry. . . . In the instant case, there is an analogous interest of the officers in taking steps to assure themselves that the house in which a suspect is being or has just been arrested is not harboring other persons who are dangerous and who could unexpectedly launch an attack. The risk of danger in the context of an arrest in the home is as great as, if not greater than, it is in an on-the-street or roadside investigatory encounter. . . .

We should emphasize that such a protective sweep, aimed at protecting the arresting officers, if justified by the circumstances, is nevertheless not a full search of the premises, but may extend only to a cursory inspection of those spaces where a person may be found. The sweep lasts no longer than is necessary to dispel the reasonable suspicion of danger and in any event no longer than it takes to complete the arrest and depart the premises.

. . . The Fourth Amendment permits a properly limited protective sweep in conjunction with an in-home arrest when the searching officer possesses a reasonable belief based on specific and articulable facts that the area to be swept harbors an individual posing a danger to those on the arrest scene. We therefore vacate the judgment below and remand this case to the Court of Appeals of Maryland for further proceedings not inconsistent with this opinion.

It is so ordered.

Under *Terry v. Ohio*, officers who fear for their safety can frisk a person who was lawfully stopped or search the immediate area for weapons, although such a protective measure is limited in scope and duration (the person stopped or the immediate area). Under *Buie,* the protective sweep exception to a warrant allows officers to quickly enter other rooms of a house where a person is arrested to search for dangerous persons under the reasonable suspicion standard of *Terry.* As with other types of pretext searches, the police cannot just use the "protective sweep" to conduct a search for evidence by going from room to room. The officers need to articulate why they believe other persons might be in other rooms, and once a reasonable fear for the officers' safety has been abated, the justification for a sweep has been eliminated. The officers cannot use their mere presence in a home as an opportunity to violate the Fourth Amendment and conduct warrantless searches. Similarly, officers cannot arrest a person outside his or her home and justify nonconsensual their entry into that home to do a protective sweep without articulable reasonable suspicion to fear for their safety.

SUMMARY

The Fourth Amendment protects a person's home from unreasonable searches by the police. Officers cannot enter a private dwelling and conduct a search without cause. Entry into a dwelling requires that the officers secure a warrant or have a legitimate reason to enter the residence without the warrant. Often, a warrantless entry occurs when a resident provides consent to the officer to enter the abode. Officers may also enter if there is an emergency that would require their immediate entry into the residence: a person is severely ill, the officers are in "hot pursuit" or some other exigent circumstance. Entry, either with an arrest warrant or a search warrant, must be done reasonably. If officers are lawfully present in a home, the Fourth Amendment imposes additional requirements on them for the seizure of items.

GLOSSARY

Consent entry: The voluntary waiver of one's Fourth Amendment rights against police entry into a home or other property by a person with lawful authority to give consent. The burden is on the state to show that such waiver was not made under duress.

Exigent circumstances: Circumstances that create a need for an exception to the warrant requirement; these are rare instances in which the police or other state officials must enter a home or other place to respond to an emergency for the protection of someone's life or personal safety, or a risk of the destruction of evidence.

Open fields doctrine: Doctrine that the police may search a property outside its owners' curtilage because it is outside the scope of Fourth Amendment protections; entry to the property requires neither a warrant nor consent.

Protective sweep doctrine: Allows a police officer who is executing a warrant to arrest a person in his or her dwelling to search other rooms of the dwelling if there is reasonable belief that another person might be there and might pose a threat to the officer's safety.

ADDITIONAL READINGS

Leonetti, C. (2004–2005). Open fields in the inner city: Application of the curtilage doctrine to urban and suburban areas. *George Mason University Civil Rights Law Journal, 15,* 297.

O'Brien, L. A. (2007). Finding a reasonable approach to the extension of the protective sweep doctrine in non-arrest situations. *NYU Law Review, 82,* 1139–1173.

Sifferlen, M. J. (1991). Fourth Amendment: Protective sweep doctrine: When does the Fourth Amendment allow police officers to search the home incident to a lawful arrest? *Journal of Criminal Law and Criminology, 81,* 862–882.

Simmons, R. (2004). Not "voluntary" but still reasonable: A new paradigm for understanding the consent searches doctrine. *Indiana Law Journal, 80,* 773–824.

CHAPTER 9

Warrantless Searches and Privacy of Personal Effects

KEY POINTS

- Most searches of a person's personal effects by the police are completed without a warrant.

- If an officer is legally present and the officer observes illegal conduct or finds evidence of a crime, then a warrantless search and seizure of items in plain view is constitutional.

- If an officer stops a vehicle, it does not automatically justify a search of the vehicle.

- Searches of automobiles may be conducted if an officer stops a vehicle on the public highway and has probable cause to believe that evidence of a crime exists in the car.

- An officer can use a traffic law violation to pretextually stop a vehicle, but subsequent searches of an automobile must follow *Terry* stop or other constitutional guidelines if evidence found in the vehicle is to be legally admissible against a defendant.

WARRANTLESS SEARCHES OF PEOPLE'S PERSONAL EFFECTS

Most searches of people, their homes, and personal effects occur without a warrant. The legality of the search and any seizure of items will depend on whether probable cause existed before a police search. The police cannot use their authority to intimidate people and engage in "fishing expeditions." For personal effects to be searched and then seized, the police must have probable cause to believe that the search will uncover evidence associated with a particular crime. Whether an item is found is *not* relevant to determining if the search was legal. Again, the important consideration for determining a legal search is whether there was probable cause to precipitate the search in the first place. When warrantless searches occur, the need to establish probable cause is heightened because if probable cause does not exist, then the item could be excluded at trial under the exclusionary rule. If the search results in finding items, then the seizure of the items also needs to be connected to the legality of the search. If officers exceed the parameters of a lawful search or arrest, then the items seized could be excluded at trial. There are usually three types of items that may be seized: the fruit of a crime (e.g., stolen property), a criminal instrumentality (e.g., weapon), or an illegal substance (e.g., illegal drugs).

PLAIN VIEW

The plain view doctrine is a long-established exception to the requirement that officers need a warrant to seize items. Because police work requires officers to be on call 24/7, officers do not have to turn their backs on items they inadvertently discover. Items lying in plain view may be seized by officers, but the plain view doctrine has certain requirements that must be met if the evidence will later be admissible in court. First, the officer must become aware of the item by sight and have immediate access to it. Second, the officer must be legally present at the time he sees the item to be seized. Third, the officer must be able to readily identify the item as illegal or as the evidence of a crime. All three requirements must be met; otherwise, the plain view doctrine will not apply.

The first part of the plain view test is awareness: the officer must become aware of the item through sight, not smell or hearing. The second part of the plain view test is whether the officer was legally present. That is, the officer's presence at the location must not be unconstitutional in order for plain view doctrine to apply. The officer's legal presence in a place can be established by any number of factors, some discussed in the preceding chapters. An officer may be legally present if he or she is executing a valid arrest or search warrant, is making a legal arrest for a crime committed in the officer's presence, is in a private area if given consent to enter the place, or if she or he had to enter for an exigent circumstance (e.g., hot pursuit, to determine if someone is hurt in a home). How might officers gain lawful presence to be able to see evidence of crime in plain view? In *California v. Ciraolo*, 476 U.S. 207 (1986), the U.S. Supreme Court discussed the ability of officers to fly a plane over a private residence in order to see marijuana growing. The basis of the flight and recognition of marijuana helped the officers secure a search warrant for the property. The Court determined that the flight at 1,000 feet was legal because anyone could see the item in lawful airspace.

CALIFORNIA V. CIRAOLO, 476 U.S. 207 (1986)

Opinion by BURGER.

Facts: Police received an anonymous telephone tip that marijuana was growing in the backyard of the respondent, Ciraolo. Ciraolo's yard had a six-foot outer fence and a ten-foot inner fence completely enclosing the yard. Because the police could not see into the yard from the street due to the fence, two officers assigned to investigate the tip secured a private plane and flew over the yard at an altitude of 1,000 feet. The height of the plane was within navigable airspace. Both officers were trained in marijuana identification and from the plane were able to identify marijuana plants eight feet to ten feet high growing in a 15- by 25-foot plot in Ciraolo's yard; they photographed the area with a standard 35 mm camera. They then obtained a search warrant on the basis of an affidavit describing the anonymous tip and their observations. A photograph of Ciraolo's house, the backyard, and neighboring homes was attached to the affidavit. The warrant was executed the next day, and 73 marijuana plants were seized. The California Court of Appeals found that the aerial search was unlawful and reversed the defendant's conviction.

Issue: Does the Fourth Amendment prohibit officers to fly over a home at an altitude of 1,000 feet without a warrant to look in a fenced-in backyard within the curtilage of a home?

Rationale and Decision: The touchstone of Fourth Amendment analysis is whether a person has a "constitutionally protected reasonable expectation of privacy." . . . Clearly—and understandably—respondent has met the test of manifesting his own subjective intent and desire to maintain privacy as to his unlawful agricultural pursuits. . . . It can reasonably be assumed that the 10-foot fence was placed to conceal the marijuana crop from at least street-level views. So far as the normal sidewalk traffic was concerned, this fence served that purpose, because respondent "took normal precautions to maintain his privacy." . . . Yet a 10-foot fence might not shield these plants from the eyes of a citizen or a policeman perched on the top of a truck or a two-level bus. Whether respondent therefore manifested a subjective expectation of privacy from *all* observations of his backyard, or whether instead he manifested merely a hope that no one would observe his unlawful gardening pursuits, is not entirely clear in these circumstances. Respondent appears to challenge the authority of government to observe his activity from any vantage point or place if the viewing is motivated by a law enforcement purpose, and not the result of a casual, accidental observation.

We turn, therefore, to . . . whether that expectation is reasonable. In pursuing this inquiry, we must keep in mind that "[t]he test of legitimacy is not whether the individual chooses to conceal assertedly *private activity,*" but instead *"whether the government's intrusion infringes upon the personal and societal values protected by the Fourth Amendment."* . . . Respondent argues that, because his yard was in the curtilage of his home, no governmental aerial observation is permissible under the Fourth Amendment without a warrant. The history and genesis of the curtilage doctrine are instructive. "At common law, the curtilage is the area to which extends the intimate activity associated with the 'sanctity of a man's home and the privacies of life.'" . . . The protection afforded the curtilage is essentially a protection of families and personal privacy in an area intimately linked to the home, both physically and psychologically, where privacy expectations are most heightened. The claimed area here was immediately adjacent to a suburban home, surrounded by high double fences. This close nexus to the home would appear to encompass this small area within the curtilage. Accepting, as the State does, that this yard and its crop fall within the curtilage, the question remains whether naked-eye observation of the curtilage by police from an aircraft lawfully operating at an altitude of 1,000 feet violates an expectation of privacy that is reasonable.

That the area is within the curtilage does not itself bar all police observation. The Fourth Amendment protection of the home has never been extended to require law enforcement officers to shield their eyes when passing by a home on public thoroughfares. Nor does the mere fact that an individual has taken measures to restrict some views of his activities preclude an officer's observations from a public vantage point where he has a right to be and which renders the activities clearly visible. . . .

The observations by Officers Shutz and Rodriguez in this case took place within public navigable airspace, . . . in a physically nonintrusive manner; from this point, they were able to observe plants readily discernible to the naked eye as marijuana. That the observation from aircraft was directed at identifying the plants and the officers were trained to recognize marijuana is irrelevant. Such observation is precisely what a judicial officer needs to provide a basis for a warrant. Any member of the public flying in this airspace who glanced down could have seen everything that these officers observed. On this record, we readily conclude that respondent's expectation that his garden was protected from such observation is unreasonable, and is not an expectation that society is prepared to honor. . . . In an age where private and commercial flight in the public airways is routine, it is unreasonable for respondent to expect that his marijuana plants were constitutionally protected from being observed with the naked eye from an altitude of 1,000 feet. The Fourth Amendment simply does not require the police traveling in the public airways at this altitude to obtain a warrant in order to observe what is visible to the naked eye.

Reversed.

If legal presence is established, then courts will determine if the last part of the plain view test is established: inadvertent discovery. The officers cannot use their mere presence in a place to conduct warrantless searches. The item seized has to be in a place where the officers did not expect to find it. Once it has been inadvertently discovered, the officers may secure the evidence of a crime or seize illegal contraband. Under no circumstances should the officers use this warrantless search exception to violate a person's expectations of privacy. The Court has been clear that searches without a warrant are limited in scope. In a fractured decision in which several justices joined in part and dissented in part, the Court in *Coolidge v. New Hampshire*, 403 U.S. 443 (1971) found that no valid reason existed for the police to seize an automobile and subject it to three subsequent warrantless searches, two of which occurred one year after the seizure. The Court suppressed the automobile and items found in it (including contents from a vacuuming of the car's interior) because they were not seized incident to arrest, were not seized or searched under a valid warrant (the state's Attorney General, a member of the executive branch, had signed off on the warrant, which meant it had not been ordered by an impartial judicial magistrate), and were not inadvertently discovered. Although the automobile was in plain sight, sitting in the defendant's driveway, the officers anticipated finding the vehicle and the fibers in it that were thought to be the instrumentality of the crime (a murder). The Court stated: "[I]t is important to keep in mind that, in the vast majority of cases, any evidence seized by the police will be in plain view, at least at the moment of seizure. The problem with the 'plain view' doctrine has been to identify the circumstances in which plain view has legal significance, rather than being simply the normal concomitant of any search, legal or illegal." However, in *Horton v. California*, 496 U.S. 128 (1990), the Court backtracked on the *inadvertent* aspect of the "inadvertent discovery rule" when the officers seized weapons that the officers knew were used in a crime. The Court found that the officers secured a search warrant for some items because they had probable cause; they only suspected that other evidence existed at the scene, so the items were not part of the warrant. If in executing a valid search warrant, the officers see other items associated with a crime in plain view and it is immediately apparent that the items are incriminating evidence, the officers are able to secure them with a seizure. In practical effect, the *Horton* item means that most plain view cases will be the result of inadvertent discovery, but they no longer have to be. Inadvertance is no longer a necessary requirement for seizure, only that the officer immediately identify the object as evidence. For example, an officer may use the "plain view" doctrine to seize evidence without a warrant that he knows will be there in the following manner: if an officer knows that he is likely to find the gun used in a robbery as well as the proceeds somewhere, he may procure a warrant to search for the proceeds of the robbery, and may then lawfully seize the gun under "plain view" doctrine if he happens upon it while searching for the proceeds, even if he knew it would be there the whole time. An officer authorized to search for one thing may seize other evidence that he knows will be there, without in any way expanding the scope of his search.

AUTOMOBILE SEARCHES

Searches of automobiles have generated a tremendous amount of analysis by the Supreme Court. An automobile search is a specialized area of legal inquiry under the Fourth Amendment because searches of cars are viewed differently from searches of people and their homes. Because automobiles can leave a police jurisdiction quickly, police may need to respond quickly to a situation and search cars before the "evidence" sought is moved, destroyed, or generally outside the ability of the police to seize.

In addition, automobiles, unlike homes, are subject to public view. Cars can be found in public spaces, and passersby can easily look into cars through the windows and see all sorts of items lying about and subject to their inspection. Since a vehicle is subject to public view or inspection, it carries a lower expectation of privacy under the Fourth Amendment.

The U.S. Supreme Court first articulated the legal rules pertaining to searches of automobiles in *Carroll v. United States*, 267 U.S. 132 (1925). During the Prohibition Era, federal officers were charged with enforcing the Volstead Act (National Prohibition Act). In *Carroll*, the federal officers were not investigating or following any leads pertaining to the particular defendants, George Carroll and John Kiro. Rather, the officers saw a car that they suspected of carrying illegal alcohol and gave chase. The officers stopped the car on a public highway and immediately searched it. When they were looking through the small car, the officers noted that one seat seemed to be unusually heavy. One officer took a knife and tore open the seat and discovered bottles of illegal liquor. The officers had no probable cause to arrest either defendant at the time of the automobile stop, and the officers lacked a search warrant for the car. The officers acted upon probable cause to believe that there was illegal liquor in the car and conducted the search on that singular basis, arguing that if they had taken the time to obtain a search warrant, the car would have disappeared. In a ruling known as the *Carroll* doctrine, the Court held that cars that are located in a public space can be searched if there is probable cause where "it is not practicable to secure a warrant." If probable cause did not exist, then the officers would have been "acting on their peril" and because the warrantless search would be illegal. Warrantless searches based on probable cause are still upheld as reasonable and thus valid, but reasonable suspicion (which is required to *stop* a vehicle) is not enough to search it.

For years subsequent to *Carroll*, the general rule was that a vehicle on a public highway could be searched upon probable cause, without a warrant, but that the search was limited to the interior of the vehicle. The interior of the vehicle included any part of the car's interior: under the seats, in the glove compartment, in items within the vehicle that might contain the items sought, and so on. The search did not extend to the car's trunk space or items in the trunk until *United States v. Ross*, 456 U.S. 798 (1982). In *Ross*, the Court was directly asked to consider whether probable cause to believe that contraband is in the trunk of a car would enable officers to search the car trunk without consent, a warrant, or other noted exception to the Fourth Amendment. Relying on the *Carroll* Doctrine, the Court decided to extend the rule to the locked trunk of an automobile.

UNITED STATES V. ROSS, 456 U.S. 798 (1982)

Opinion by STEVENS.

Facts: An informant who had previously given reliable information telephoned a detective and told him that a person called "Bandit" was selling narcotics, which he kept in the trunk of a car parked at a particular address. The informant described the vehicle, and a subsequent license plate check indicated that the car was registered to Ross. In two passes through the neighborhood, the officers did not observe anyone matching the informant's description of "Bandit." To avoid alerting persons on the street, they left the area. The officers returned five minutes later and observed the car leaving the street. They pulled alongside the car, noticed that the driver matched the informant's description, and stopped the car. They ordered Ross out of the vehicle and searched him. The officers also searched the interior of the car and discovered a bullet on the car's front seat and a pistol in the glove compartment. Ross then was arrested and handcuffed. One of the officers took Ross's keys and opened the trunk, where a closed brown paper bag was found. The officer then opened the bag and discovered a number of glassine bags containing a white powder. Cassidy replaced the bag, closed the trunk, and drove the car to headquarters. At the police station, Cassidy thoroughly searched the car. In addition to the "lunch-type" brown paper bag, Cassidy found in the trunk a zippered red leather pouch. He unzipped the pouch and discovered $3,200 in cash. The police laboratory later determined that the powder in the paper bag was heroin. No warrant was obtained. The Court of Appeals held that the officers should not have looked in the defendant's car trunk without a warrant.

Issue: Can police conduct a warrantless search of an automobile's trunk under the Fourth Amendment if they have probable cause to believe there is criminal evidence in it?

Rationale and Decision: We begin with a review of the decision in *Carroll* itself. . . . No contraband was visible in the front seat of the Oldsmobile, and the rear portion of the roadster was closed. One of the agents raised the rumble seat but found no liquor. He raised the seat cushion and again found nothing. The officer then struck at the "lazyback" of the seat and noticed that it was "harder than upholstery ordinarily is in those backs." He tore open the seat cushion and discovered 68 bottles of gin and whiskey concealed inside. No warrant had been obtained for the search. . . . In an extensive opinion written by Chief Justice Taft, the Court held: "On reason and authority, the true rule is that, if the search and seizure without a warrant are made upon probable cause, that is, upon a belief, reasonably arising out of circumstances known to the seizing officer, that an automobile or other vehicle contains that which by law is subject to seizure and destruction, the search and seizure are valid. The Fourth Amendment is to be construed in the light of what was deemed an unreasonable search and seizure when it was adopted, and in a manner which will conserve public interests, as well as the interests and rights of individual citizens." . . . The Court explained at length the basis for this rule. The Court noted that, historically, warrantless searches of vessels, wagons, and carriages—as opposed to fixed premises such as a home or other building— had been considered reasonable by Congress. . . . Given the nature of an automobile in transit, the Court recognized that an immediate intrusion is necessary if police officers are to secure the illicit substance. . . .

The rationale justifying a warrantless search of an automobile that is believed to be transporting contraband arguably applies with equal force to any movable container that is believed to be carrying an illicit substance. . . . A lawful search of fixed premises generally extends to the entire area in which the object of the search may be found, and is not limited by the possibility that separate acts of entry or opening may be required to complete the search. Thus, a warrant that authorizes an officer to search a home for illegal weapons also provides authority to open closets, chests, drawers, and containers in which the weapon might be found. A warrant to open a footlocker to search for marihuana would also authorize the opening of packages found inside. A warrant to search a vehicle would support a search of every part of the vehicle that might contain the object of the search. When a legitimate search is under way, and when its purpose and its limits have been precisely defined, nice distinctions between closets, drawers, and containers, in the case of a home, or between glove compartments, upholstered seats, trunks, and wrapped packages, in the case of a vehicle, must give way to the interest in the prompt and efficient completion of the task at hand. . . .

But the protection afforded by the Amendment varies in different settings. The luggage carried by a traveler entering the country may be searched at random by a customs officer; the luggage may be searched no matter how great the traveler's desire to conceal the contents may be. A container carried at the time of arrest often may be searched without a warrant and even without any specific suspicion concerning its contents. A container that may conceal the object of a search authorized by a warrant may be opened immediately; the individual's interest in privacy must give way to the magistrate's official determination of probable cause.

In the same manner, an individual's expectation of privacy in a vehicle and its contents may not survive if probable cause is given to believe that the vehicle is transporting contraband. Certainly the privacy interests in a car's trunk or glove compartment may be no less than those in a movable container. An individual undoubtedly has a significant interest that the upholstery of his automobile will not be ripped or a hidden compartment within it opened. These interests must yield to the authority of a search, however, which—in light of *Carroll*—does not itself require the prior approval of a magistrate. The scope of a warrantless search based on probable cause is no narrower—and no broader—than the scope of a search authorized by a warrant supported by probable cause. Only the prior approval of the magistrate is waived; the search otherwise is as the magistrate could authorize.

The scope of a warrantless search of an automobile thus is not defined by the nature of the container in which the contraband is secreted. Rather, it is defined by the object of the search and the places in which there is probable cause to believe that it may be found. Just as probable cause to believe that a stolen lawnmower may be found in a garage will not support a warrant to search an upstairs bedroom, probable cause to believe that undocumented aliens are being transported in a van will not justify a warrantless search of a suitcase. Probable cause to believe that a container placed in the trunk of a taxi contains contraband or evidence does not justify a search of the entire cab.

. . . The exception recognized in *Carroll* is unquestionably one that is "specifically established and well delineated." We hold that the scope of the warrantless search authorized by that exception is no broader and no narrower than a magistrate could legitimately authorize by warrant. If probable cause justifies the search of a lawfully stopped vehicle, it justifies the search of every part of the vehicle and its contents that may conceal the object of the search.

The judgment of the Court of Appeals is reversed. The case is remanded for further proceedings consistent with this opinion.

It is so ordered.

After *Ross,* officers could open a car's glovebox and trunk and search any packages or luggage found within that could reasonably be thought to contain the probable cause items. *Locked* glove compartments or trunks, however, generally cannot be forcibly opened without a search warrant.

Does the search need to occur at the same time as the highway stop, or could it happen at a different time or location? In *United States v. Johns,* 469 U.S. 478 (1985), the Court determined that the search did not have to be contemporaneous with the vehicle stop. Unlike a search incident to an arrest, the probable cause to search a mobile vehicle is the sine qua non principle to legalize a warrantless search. The search only needs to take place within a reasonable time. The Court determined that exigent circumstances do not need to be established beyond the finding of probable cause to search a car, and the items within it, in a public place. In *Pennsylvania v. LaBron,* 518 U.S. 938 (1996), the Court found that the probable cause to believe that the vehicles contained illegal drugs was enough to validate a warrantless search under the automobile exception to the Fourth Amendment's warrant requirement. If probable cause does not exist to enable the search of a vehicle's trunk, the items seized will be inadmissible. As noted in *Ross,* "If probable cause justifies the search of a lawfully stopped vehicle, it justifies the search of every part of the vehicle and its contents that may conceal the object of the search."

Any item found in a car (locked or unlocked, baggage or brown paper bag) can be searched and then seized upon probable cause. In *California v. Acevedo,* 500 U.S. 565 (1991), the Court opined that it was time to provide one rule that pertained to all automobile searches. If officers have probable cause, they may search the automobile and all containers in it where they believe contraband or evidence may be obtained.

CALIFORNIA V. ACEVEDO, 500 U.S. 565 (1991)

Opinion by BLACKMUN.

Facts: Officers in California received a call from Hawaii drug enforcement agents that a package contained marijuana was being delivered. In order to determine who was to receive the package in California, officers watched the package as it was delivered and followed a suspect to an apartment. When Acevedo showed up at the apartment and left a short time later with a package that was similar to the one delivered from Hawaii, the officers observed Acevedo place it in the trunk of his car. When the defendant began to drive away, the officers stopped him, opened the trunk and the bag, and found marijuana. The California Supreme Court denied review; the California Court of Appeals held that the search of the bag taken from a car without a warrant was unconstitutional.

Issue: Does the "automobile exception" to the warrant requirement of the Fourth Amendment apply to searches of a closed container found in the trunk of a car?

Rationale and Decision: Contemporaneously with the adoption of the Fourth Amendment, the First Congress, and, later, the Second and Fourth Congresses distinguished between the need for a warrant to search for contraband concealed in "a dwelling house or similar place" and the need for a warrant to search for contraband concealed in a movable vessel. . . . In *Carroll,* this Court established an exception to the warrant requirement for moving vehicles, for it recognized "a necessary difference between a search of a store, dwelling house or other structure in respect of which a proper official warrant readily may be obtained, and a search of a ship, motor boat, wagon or automobile, for contraband goods, where it is not practicable to secure a warrant because the vehicle can be quickly moved out of the locality or jurisdiction in which the warrant must be sought." . . . In *United States v. Ross,* . . . we held that a warrantless search of an automobile under the *Carroll* doctrine could include a search of a container or package found inside the car when such a search was supported by probable cause. The warrantless search of Ross' car occurred after an informant told the police that he had seen Ross complete a drug transaction using drugs stored in the trunk of his car. . . . In *Ross,* therefore, we clarified the scope of the *Carroll* doctrine as properly including a "probing search" of compartments and containers within the automobile so long as the search is supported by probable cause.

In addition to this clarification, *Ross* distinguished the *Carroll* doctrine from the separate rule that governed the search of closed containers. . . . The Court had announced this separate rule, unique to luggage and other closed packages, bags, and containers, in *United States v. Chadwick,* 433 U. S. 1 (1977). In *Chadwick,* federal narcotics agents had probable cause to believe that a 200-pound double-locked footlocker contained marijuana. The agents tracked the locker as the defendants removed it from a train and carried it through the station to a waiting car. As soon as the defendants lifted the locker into the trunk of the car, the agents arrested them, seized the locker, and searched it. In this Court, the United States did not contend that the locker's brief contact with the automobile's trunk sufficed to make the *Carroll* doctrine applicable. Rather, the United States urged that the search of movable luggage could be considered analogous to the search of an automobile. . . . The Court rejected this argument because, it reasoned, a person expects more privacy in his luggage and personal effects than he does in his automobile. . . . Moreover, it concluded that, as "may often not be the case when automobiles are seized," secure storage facilities are usually available when the police seize luggage. . . .

. . . The facts in this case closely resemble the facts in *Ross.* In *Ross,* the police had probable cause to believe that drugs were stored in the trunk of a particular car. . . . This Court in *Ross* rejected *Chadwick's* distinction between containers and cars. It concluded that the expectation of privacy in one's vehicle is equal to one's expectation of privacy in the container, and noted that "the privacy interests in a car's trunk or glove compartment may be no less than those in a movable container." . . . It also recognized that it was arguable that the same exigent circumstances that permit a warrantless search of an automobile would justify the warrantless search of a movable container. . . . We now must decide the question deferred in *Ross:* whether the Fourth Amendment requires the police to obtain a warrant to open the sack in a movable vehicle simply because they lack probable cause to search the entire car. We conclude that it does not.

. . . We cannot see the benefit of a rule that requires law enforcement officers to conduct a more intrusive search in order to justify a less intrusive search. . . . Finally, the search of a paper bag intrudes far less on individual privacy than does the incursion sanctioned long ago in *Carroll.* In that case, prohibition agents slashed the upholstery of the automobile. This Court nonetheless found their search to be reasonable under the Fourth Amendment. If destroying the interior of an automobile is not unreasonable, we cannot conclude that looking inside a closed container is. In light of the minimal protection to privacy afforded by the *Chadwick-Sanders* rule, and our serious doubt whether that rule substantially serves privacy interests, we now hold that the Fourth Amendment does not compel separate treatment for an automobile search that extends only to a container within the vehicle.

The *Chadwick-Sanders* rule not only has failed to protect privacy, but it has also confused courts and police officers and impeded effective law enforcement. . . . We conclude that it is better to adopt one clear-cut rule to govern automobile searches and eliminate the warrant requirement for closed containers set forth in *Sanders.*

The interpretation of the *Carroll* doctrine set forth in *Ross* now applies to all searches of containers found in an automobile. In other words, the police may search without a warrant if their search is supported by probable cause. . . . In the case before us, the police had probable cause to believe that the paper bag in the automobile's trunk contained marijuana. That probable cause now allows a warrantless search of the paper bag. The facts in the record reveal that the police did not have probable cause to believe that contraband was hidden in any other part of the automobile and a search of the entire vehicle would have been without probable cause and unreasonable under the Fourth Amendment.

Our holding today neither extends the *Carroll* doctrine nor broadens the scope of the permissible automobile search delineated in *Carroll, Chambers,* and *Ross.* . . . Until today, this Court has drawn a curious line between the search of an automobile that coincidentally turns up a container and the search of a container that coincidentally turns up in an automobile. The protections of the Fourth Amendment must not turn on such coincidences. We therefore interpret *Carroll* as providing one rule to govern all automobile searches. The police may search an automobile and the containers within it where they have probable cause to believe contraband or evidence is contained.

The judgment of the California Court of Appeal is reversed, and the case is remanded to that court for further proceedings not inconsistent with this opinion.

It is so ordered.

Is It a Search Incident to an Arrest or an Automobile Search?

The ability to search a vehicle creates two divergent lines of inquiry. If the search is incident to an arrest, then the law promoting the search limits the search to the arrestee's wingspan and the search is to be contemporaneous with the arrest. Immediately after the arrest, police used to be able to perform sweeping searches of vehicles' inventories, opening containers if permitted by department policy (*Florida v. Wells,* 495 U.S. 1 [1990]). A search based upon probable cause is limited to the reasonable belief that criminal evidence will be found in the vehicle. These two confounding warrantless search exceptions are discussed in *Arizona v. Gant,* 556 U.S. ___ (2009). In *Gant,* the police had reasonable grounds to believe that Gant was driving on a suspended license. The officers had talked with Gant at a home that could have been the site of drug sales earlier in the day and had run a background check on him. At the time of Gant's arrest, they saw him drive up the driveway of a home and park the vehicle. The officers approached Gant and placed him under arrest for the driving offense. He was placed in a patrol car in handcuffs and then his vehicle was searched. The search turned up illicit drugs. The U.S. Supreme Court determined that the officers did not have probable cause to believe there would be drugs in the car because the arrest was not drug related. The search could not be constitutional under a *Carroll–Ross* analysis. The Court also held that the search could not be constitutional under the *Belton* rule pertaining to a search of containers in a car incident to a lawful arrest. The Court held that the privacy interests in a car are less than in one's person or home, but nonetheless worthy of constitutional protection. Because the officers did not need to protect their safety or secure evidence of the crime for which the person was arrested, the privacy interests of the car remain. The Court admonished the state that unconstitutional police practices are not to be continued. Police stops and arrests will no longer be used as a pretext to search the entire vehicle by law enforcement officials. If a person is not able to reach into a vehicle, then the police do not have the right to search the vehicle incident to a lawful arrest. Other warrantless search exceptions will need to be established to allow for the admissibility of evidence secured from a vehicle.

ABANDONMENT OF PROPERTY

Property that a person has no intention to keep ownership or possessory interest in is deemed to be abandoned. If a person puts items into a public trash bin or if his or her trash cans are placed on the street for pickup, then the items are no longer the personal property of the individual and can be seized without a warrant by the police. If an item is still within a home, then it is still under the control of a person who might later retrieve and keep it. Knowing whether a piece of property has been abandoned is important because seizure of the item and its admissibility in court hinges on whether a person maintains expectations of privacy. Officers cannot violate a person's right of privacy in order to search a person's trash bins inside a home. As with other constitutional principles guiding the Fourth Amendment, officers cannot enter a person's home without consent or a warrant, search a trash container, and seize its items. However, if an officer is lawfully present (e.g., on public ground) and finds abandoned property, it can be seized and used against a defendant in court.

Abandoned property can be seized without a warrant by the police because the person has shown that he or she no longer has intent to keep or safeguard it. By abandoning the property, the person has relinquished any expectation of privacy that the person might otherwise have had to keep it secure from state intrusion (search and seizure). Critical to the admissibility of such evidence is whether there is a clear indication that the person has given up the property and does not have any expectation that their property interests would be retained.

What if the police leave a tracking device on a person's car? Can the person remove and throw away the tracking device under a claim that the police have abandoned it by leaving it on a vehicle? This issue was raised in 2010 when a 20-year-old man in California found such a device when his car was was being serviced at an auto garage. The device was removed, and the FBI later showed up at the man's home and demanded that he return the device, under threat of arrest. The individual returned the device, but the question of whether it was abandoned was discussed on the web (see http://cyb3rcrim3.blogspot.com/2010/10/tracking-devices-abandoned-property-and.html). Arguably, it would seem that the state did not abandon the property because they did not have the intention of giving up their interest in the tracking device. Rather, the state expected to retrieve it at some point in time or continue to use it to ascertain if criminal activity was occurring. It should be noted that the Ninth Circuit has upheld the warrantless use of tracking devices, so long as they have been attached to cars while they were parked outside the home, but not if they were parked behind a fence.

CONTEMPORARY ISSUES: ROADSIDE CAR SEARCHES OF AFRICAN AMERICANS

The ability to stop an automobile on a public highway is lawful if there is a legitimate reason to stop a person. If a person has violated a traffic law or regulation, then an officer can stop the person (e.g., if the person runs a red light). Similarly, if there is a reasonable suspicion to believe that the person has violated the law, then an officer can stop the person (e.g., if the person is swerving on the road, giving the officer reason to believe that the person might be driving while intoxicated). In this context, research has shown that most officers have a legitimate reason to stop a vehicle. Some research has also shown that many officers do not know the race or ethnicity of a driver prior to the stop. Some reasons why the officer might not know the race or ethnicity is that some cars have dark, tinted windows or the officer was approaching a vehicle that has violated a rule of the road from the rear and could not see the driver. Thus, it is difficult to find a statistical connection between police stops and race.

A common method of searching a vehicle is for the police to obtain consent to the search. An automobile cannot be searched just because a driver has stopped it on a public highway, but it can be searched without consent if there is evidence of a crime in it. In *Whren v. United States*, 517 U.S. 806 (1996), the U.S. Supreme Court determined that police officers who are suspicious about a car in a high drug crime area can legally stop a car when it violates a minor traffic offense. In *Whren,* the officers were suspicious that the occupants of the vehicle might be engaged in illegal activity because of the manner in which the car was being driven and its location. Although pretextual, the lawful stop was based on a legitimate violation of traffic laws that the officer witnessed. Consequently, the subsequent seizure of cocaine from the car was constitutional even though the officer's stop was not motivated solely by the traffic violation. If an officer stops a motorist for a valid reason (such as failing to signal or running a stop sign), then the stop is constitutional even if the officer would not have stopped the driver but for the driver's race.

WHREN V. UNITED STATES, 517 U.S. 806 (1996)

Opinion by SCALIA.

Facts: Plainclothes vice squad officers were patrolling a "high drug area" of the city in an unmarked car. Their suspicions were aroused by the conduct of the youthful driver in a Nissan Pathfinder. When the police car executed a U-turn in order to head back toward the truck, the Pathfinder turned suddenly to its right, without signaling, and sped off at an "unreasonable" speed. The officers followed and were able to catch up with the vehicle at a light. One of the officers got out of his car and identified himself. As he approached the driver's window, he immediately observed two large plastic bags of what appeared to be crack cocaine in Whren's hands. Whren argued that the stop had not been justified by probable cause to believe, or even reasonable suspicion, that the petitioners were engaged in illegal drug-dealing activity. The Court of Appeals affirmed a denial of a motion to suppress.

Issue: Does the Fourth Amendment allow officers to stop a vehicle on a public highway for a traffic violation on the pretext that the occupants might be involved in other criminal activity?

Rationale and Decision: The Fourth Amendment guarantees "[t]he right of the people to be secure in their persons, houses, papers, and effects, against unreasonable searches and seizures." Temporary detention of individuals during the stop of an automobile by the police, even if only for a brief period and for a limited purpose, constitutes a "seizure" of "persons" within the meaning of this provision. . . . An automobile stop is thus subject to the constitutional imperative that it not be "unreasonable" under the circumstances. As a general matter, the decision to stop an automobile is reasonable where the police have probable cause to believe that a traffic violation has occurred. . . .

Recognizing that we have been unwilling to entertain Fourth Amendment challenges based on the actual motivations of individual officers, petitioners disavow any intention to make the individual officer's subjective good faith the touchstone of "reasonableness." . . . Instead of asking whether the individual officer had the proper state of mind, the petitioners would have us ask, in effect, whether (based on general police practices) it is plausible to believe that the officer had the proper state of mind. . . . Why one would frame a test designed to combat pretext in such fashion that the court cannot take into account *actual and admitted pretext* is a curiosity that can only be explained by the fact that our cases have foreclosed the more sensible option. If those cases were based only upon the evidentiary difficulty of establishing subjective intent, petitioners' attempt to root out subjective vices through objective means might make sense. But they were not based only upon that, or indeed even principally upon that. Their principal basis—which applies equally to attempts to reach subjective intent through ostensibly objective means—is simply that the Fourth Amendment's concern with "reasonableness" allows certain actions to be taken in certain circumstances, *whatever* the subjective intent. . . . While police manuals and standard procedures may sometimes provide objective assistance, ordinarily one would be reduced to speculating about the hypothetical reaction of a hypothetical constable—an exercise that might be called virtual subjectivity.

Moreover, police enforcement practices, even if they could be practicably assessed by a judge, vary from place to place and from time to time. We cannot accept that the search and seizure protections of the Fourth Amendment are so variable. . . . The difficulty is illustrated by petitioners' arguments in this case. Their claim that a reasonable officer would not have made this stop is based largely on District of Columbia police regulations which permit plainclothes officers in unmarked vehicles to enforce traffic laws "only in the case of a violation that is so grave as to pose an *immediate threat* to the safety of others." . . . This basis of invalidation would not apply in jurisdictions that had a different practice. And it would not have applied even in the District of Columbia, if Officer Soto had been wearing a uniform or patrolling in a marked police cruiser.

. . . It is of course true that in principle every Fourth Amendment case, since it turns upon a "reasonableness" determination, involves a balancing of all relevant factors. With rare exceptions not applicable here, however, the result of that balancing is not in doubt where the search or seizure is based upon probable cause. . . . Where probable cause has existed, the only cases in which we have found it necessary actually to perform the "balancing" analysis involved searches or seizures conducted in an extraordinary manner, unusually harmful to an individual's privacy or even physical interests—such as, for example, seizure by means of deadly force . . . , unannounced entry into a home,

. . . entry into a home without a warrant, . . . or physical penetration of the body, . . . The making of a traffic stop out of uniform does not remotely qualify as such an extreme practice, and so is governed by the usual rule that probable cause to believe the law has been broken "outbalances" private interest in avoiding police contact.

Petitioners urge as an extraordinary factor in this case that the "multitude of applicable traffic and equipment regulations" is so large and so difficult to obey perfectly that virtually everyone is guilty of violation, permitting the police to single out almost whomever they wish for a stop. But we are aware of no principle that would allow us to decide at what point a code of law becomes so expansive and so commonly violated that infraction itself can no longer be the ordinary measure of the lawfulness of enforcement. And even if we could identify such exorbitant codes, we do not know by what standard (or what right) we would decide, as petitioners would have us do, which particular provisions are sufficiently important to merit enforcement. . . . Here the District Court found that the officers had probable cause to believe that petitioners had violated the traffic code. That rendered the stop reasonable under the Fourth Amendment, the evidence thereby discovered admissible, and the upholding of the convictions by the Court of Appeals for the District of Columbia Circuit correct.

Judgment affirmed.

Some research indicates that African American drivers have their cars searched more often than Caucasian drivers. Arguing that racism is at the root of such stops and searches, African American defendants subject to the searches and seizures of drugs in their cars maintain that the state is unlawfully using traffic laws as a pretext to detain and arrest black persons. The claim of racism was specifically raised in *Whitehead v. Maryland*, 698 A.2d 1115 (1997). The defendant was stopped on a public highway, and the officer had him sit in the police vehicle while the officer checked to see if the driver had a valid license or any outstanding warrants. The defendant would not consent to a search of his vehicle by the officer, and the officer had no basis for thinking that the defendant was violating any drug law on the mere basis of the stop. Basing its decision on *Whren,* the Court of Special Appeals for Maryland determined that the subsequent search was unlawful. The Maryland Court stated:

> We are not condemning Trooper Donovan's motivation. We are mindful of the Supreme Court's opinion in *Whren* that put an officer's motivation for stopping a motor vehicle beyond attack for purposes of suppressing the fruits of a search. *Whren* would seem to hold that the actual motivation of the individual officer, in choosing a particular traffic violator, cannot be subject to constitutional inquiry or challenge. *Whren,* a 9–0 decision, without concurring opinions, did not provide guidance as to just how far the police may go in detaining and interrogating someone who has been stopped on the pretext of the enforcement of the traffic laws. The detention in *Whren* that the Supreme Court approved was brief, and the arrest for violation of the narcotics laws instantaneously followed the stop. We think it would be a mistake to read *Whren* as allowing law enforcement officers to detain on the pretext of issuing a traffic citation or warning, and then deliberately to engage in activities not related to the enforcement of the traffic code in order to determine whether there are sufficient indicia of some illegal activity. Stopping a car for speeding does not confer the right to abandon or never begin to take action related to the traffic laws and, instead, to attempt to secure a waiver of Fourth Amendment rights from a citizen whose only offense to that point is to have been selected from among many who have been detected violating a traffic regulation. . . . *Whren* . . . requires the police to issue the citation or warning efficiently and expeditiously with a minimum of intrusion, only that which is required to carry forth the legitimate, although pretextual, purpose for the stop. We are condemning not the stop itself, but the detention after the pretextual stop that was for the purpose of determining whether the trooper could acquire sufficient probable cause or a waiver that would permit him to search the car for illegal narcotics.

The officer in *Whitehead* decided to use a K-9 dog to sniff the vehicle for drugs, and the dog indicated that drugs were present near the driver's side of the vehicle. Because the dog sniff was not done pursuant to the reason for the defendant's stop, the court found the subsequent search was not constitutional. The court did not discuss the allegations of racism associated with the search. *Whitehead* indicates the uncertain state of the law, and given the controversy the issue has raised, either Congress or the Supreme Court will likely change the legal landscape soon. For now, pretextual stops are judicially disfavored but not clearly banned.

The perception that police tend to target African Americans more often than white drivers for traffic stops has led to the term "driving while black." Black drivers often believe that they are stopped and searched due to racist attitudes of police. More research needs to be completed to determine whether officers use pretext stops to unlawfully or lawfully search vehicles in particular communities. Some state and local departments have entered into consent decrees when their roadside stops and searches have been challenged on the basis of racism; they have agreed to monitor all stops and to collect data on the race and ethnicity of drivers, the reason for the stop, and the basis for any subsequent searches. When agreeing to these consent decrees, the department does not accept the allegations of racism but acknowledges that it is important to ensure that race is not used as a pretext to further intrusions into a person's privacy. Race is but one of the totality of factors an officer must use when determining whether probable cause exists.

SUMMARY

There are many reasons why the state may lawfully search and seize a person's personal items. Most of these searches and seizures occur without a warrant. One obvious reason to justify a warrantless search of personal property is that a person voluntarily consented to the search. However, a warrantless search and seizure of property might also be constitutional if a person has no reasonable expectation of privacy in the item. A person does not have a reasonable expectation of privacy, for example, if he or she abandons the property. A person may lose the expectation of privacy, likewise, if an officer is legally present and sees evidence of a crime in plain view. The plain view doctrine affirms the idea that officers should not be required to leave illegal items or items that are evidence of a crime if they, without searching for it, find it while they are lawfully doing their jobs. In this manner, the officers have to show that they came across the items inadvertently. Inadvertent discovery of criminal evidence or fruits of a crime enables the officer to seize the items to secure them; because the officer is legally present, the officer has not intruded on the person's privacy interests.

Automobiles can also be searched under various exceptions to the warrant requirement under the Fourth Amendment. Some searches of vehicles occur incident to arrest, others occur if a person voluntarily consents to a search, and others may occur during a frisk of the vehicle for weapons. Another primary exception to the need to have a warrant is the *Carroll* exception, a search of an automobile on the public highway in which probable cause exists for the officer to believe that evidence or fruits of a crime are in the vehicle. Car searches and seizures of evidence provoke debate on whether the police are using legitimate car stops as a pretext to search cars. Pretext searches are usually deemed unreasonable because the officers have exceeded a person's right of privacy under the Fourth Amendment. A stop does not automatically allow a car search or a car frisk. Car stops should be "short" in duration, and any searches or seizures must be justified under the particular warrantless exception raised by the state (e.g., probable cause, plain view, consent).

GLOSSARY

Automobile search: An automobile stop is a form of seizure that occurs every time a motor vehicle is stopped. Officers must have reasonable suspicion to stop a car, as they are seizing the vehicle, its driver, and its passengers. In order to search the car, they must have probable cause or make the search incident to an arrest.

Carroll **doctrine**: Allows the warrantless search of an automobile if there is probable cause to believe there is evidence or fruit of a crime within the vehicle.

"Driving while black": A phrase expressing the belief that the police are more likely to stop a person who is African American than Caucasian.

Plain view doctrine: Allows the warrantless search and seizure of items found by the police if the officer is lawfully present at a location and makes an inadvertent discovery of evidence of a crime.

Racial profiling: The use by the police of a person's race or ethnicity in the decision to make a stop or make an arrest of that person.

ADDITIONAL READINGS

Brennan, S. (2010, October 10). CYB3Crim3: Tracking devices, abandoned property and bailments. Available at http://cyb3rcrim3.blogspot.com/2010/10/tracking-devices-abandoned-property-and.html

Crutchfield, R. D., Fernandes, A., & Martinez, J. (2010). Racial and ethnic disparity and criminal justice: How much is too much? *Journal of Criminal Law and Criminology, 100,* 903–932.

Harris, D. A. (1997). "Driving while black" and other traffic offenses: The Supreme Court and pretextual traffic stops. *Journal of Criminal Law and Criminology, 87,* 544.

Lundman, R. J., & Kaufman, R. L. (2002). Driving while black: Effects of race, ethnicity, and gender on citizen self-reports of traffic stops and police actions. *Criminology, 41,* 195–220.

CHAPTER 10

Right to Counsel in Pretrial Stages

KEY POINTS

- The right to counsel exists at critical stages in the criminal justice process.

- A person who cannot afford counsel and who has been charged with a crime may have counsel appointed to represent him or her.

- The essence of a fair trial requires that a person have adequate legal representation.

- A person may have the right to have counsel at post-indictment lineups.

- If a person is not charged with any criminal offenses but is held indefinitely as an enemy combatant of the United States, the person has the right to have counsel.

THE SIXTH AMENDMENT'S RIGHT TO COUNSEL

Many people misunderstand the extent to which the right to counsel applies in a criminal case. The Sixth Amendment to the U.S. Constitution provides that (emphasis added):

> In all criminal prosecutions, the accused shall enjoy the right to a speedy and public trial, by an impartial jury of the State and district wherein the crime shall have been committed, which district shall

have been previously ascertained by law, and to be informed of the nature and cause of the accusation; to be confronted with the witnesses against him; to have compulsory process for obtaining witnesses in his favor, *and to have the Assistance of Counsel for his defence.*

While it is generally believed that the right to counsel attaches at all stages in the criminal processes, this is a mistaken belief. Criminal defendants have the right to counsel at the trial stage and during the direct appeal after their criminal conviction because it is part of the "criminal prosecution" of the accused. Depending on the state and federal law, the right to counsel might extend to some other pre- and post-trial proceedings. Knowing when the right to counsel applies to various criminal proceedings is important because a violation of the right to counsel could prevent the admission of materials, including witness or victim identifications, at a criminal trial. Under the Sixth Amendment, the right to counsel does not extend to criminal investigations when a person becomes a *suspect*, even if he or she is the primary suspect of a crime. It does not extend to *pre-indictment* lineups, but it does apply to persons who are subjected to *post-indictment* lineups (because after an indictment, the person is subject to criminal prosecution). The right to counsel aims to ensure that an accused will have a fair trial at "all critical stages" in the criminal prosecution.

One critical stage is when suspects are held for interrogation by officers. *Miranda v. Arizona, 384* U.S. 436 (1966), provides for right to counsel during custodial interrogations because suspects may not fully understand the nature of their rights or of the criminal processes that might await them. In order to ensure a voluntary confession, individuals need to be informed that they have a right to remain silent *and* also a right to counsel.

MIRANDA V. ARIZONA, 384 U.S. 436 (1966)

Opinion by WARREN.

Facts: Several cases dealing with the rights of persons arrested and subjected to custodial interrogation were consolidated for appeal to the U.S. Supreme Court. The first named case was *Miranda v. Arizona* (discussed in Chapter 5). The various defendants were not provided with counsel during their interrogations, and their subsequent confessions were admitted against them in their trials.

Issue: Does the Sixth Amendment's right to counsel protect persons during custodial interrogations?

Rationale and Decision: The cases before us raise questions which go to the roots of our concepts of American criminal jurisprudence: the restraints society must observe consistent with the Federal Constitution in prosecuting individuals for crime. . . . We granted certiorari in these cases . . . in order further to explore some facets of the problems thus exposed of applying the privilege against self-incrimination to in-custody interrogation, and to give concrete constitutional guidelines for law enforcement agencies and courts to follow.

We start here, . . . with the premise that that "the accused shall . . . have the Assistance of Counsel." . . . The presence of counsel at the interrogation may serve several significant subsidiary functions. . . . If the accused decides to talk to his interrogators, the assistance of counsel can mitigate the dangers of untrustworthiness. With a lawyer present, the likelihood that the police will practice coercion is reduced, and, if coercion is nevertheless exercised, the lawyer can testify to it in court. The presence of a lawyer can also help to guarantee that the accused gives a fully accurate statement to the police, and that the statement is rightly reported by the prosecution at trial. . . .

An individual need not make a pre-interrogation request for a lawyer. While such request affirmatively secures his right to have one, his failure to ask for a lawyer does not constitute a waiver. No effective waiver of the right to counsel during interrogation can be recognized unless specifically made after the warnings we here delineate have been given. The accused who does not know his rights and therefore does not make a request may be the person who most needs counsel. . . .

Accordingly, we hold that an individual held for interrogation must be clearly informed that he has the right to consult with a lawyer and to have the lawyer with him during interrogation under the system for protecting the privilege we delineate today. As with the warnings of the right to remain silent and that anything stated can be used in evidence against him, this warning is an absolute prerequisite to interrogation. No amount of circumstantial evidence that the person may have been aware of this right will suffice to stand in its stead. Only through such a warning is there ascertainable assurance that the accused was aware of this right.

If an individual indicates that he wishes the assistance of counsel before any interrogation occurs, the authorities cannot rationally ignore or deny his request on the basis that the individual does not have or cannot afford a retained attorney. The financial ability of the individual has no relationship to the scope of the rights involved here. The privilege against self-incrimination secured by the Constitution applies to all individuals. The need for counsel in order to protect the privilege exists for the indigent as well as the affluent. In fact, were we to limit these constitutional rights to those who can retain an attorney, our decisions today would be of little significance. The cases before us, as well as the vast majority of confession cases with which we have dealt in the past, involve those unable to retain counsel. While authorities are not required to relieve the accused of his poverty, they have the obligation not to take advantage of indigence in the administration of justice. Denial of counsel to the indigent at the time of interrogation while allowing an attorney to those who can afford one would be no more supportable by reason or logic than the similar situation at trial and on appeal struck. . . .

In order fully to apprise a person interrogated of the extent of his rights under this system, then, it is necessary to warn him not only that he has the right to consult with an attorney, but also that, if he is indigent, a lawyer will be appointed to represent him. Without this additional warning, the admonition of the right to consult with counsel would often be understood as meaning only that he can consult with a lawyer if he has one or has the funds to obtain one. The warning of a right to counsel would be hollow if not couched in terms that would convey to the indigent—the person most often subjected to interrogation—the knowledge that he too has a right to have counsel present. As with the warnings of the right to remain silent and of the general right to counsel, only by effective and express explanation to the indigent of this right can there be assurance that he was truly in a position to exercise it. . . .

After such warnings have been given, and such opportunity afforded him, the individual may knowingly and intelligently waive these rights and agree to answer questions or make a statement. But unless and until such warnings and waiver are demonstrated by the prosecution at trial, no evidence obtained as a result of interrogation can be used against him.

. . . Therefore, in accordance with the foregoing, the judgments of the Supreme Court of Arizona in No. 759, of the New York Court of Appeals in No. 760, and of the Court of Appeals for the Ninth Circuit in No. 761, are reversed. The judgment of the Supreme Court of California in No. 584 is affirmed.

It is so ordered.

Sixth Amendment Right to Effective Trial Counsel

When a person has counsel, the attorney must provide "effective" assistance to the client. Effective assistance requires an attorney to engage in reasonable practices within the ethical rules of professional conduct for attorneys. The history concerning the need for effective assistance in criminal cases dates to 1931 when eight illiterate young black males were convicted of raping two white females on a train. Each man was sentenced to death after a hasty trial in which they did not have a lawyer to represent them. In *Powell v. Alabama,* 287 U.S. 45 (1932), the U.S. Supreme Court determined that when criminal defendants are charged with a capital crime, they are entitled to legal representation. The defendants' trials started six days after the indictment. The charges, trial, and verdict were the subject of intense scrutiny over racism and subsequent findings that the girls lied about the rapes. The court stated the important need for counsel during a capital trial:

> The right to be heard would be, in many cases, of little avail if it did not comprehend the right to be heard by counsel. Even the intelligent and educated layman has small and sometimes no skill in the science of law. If charged with crimes, he is incapable, generally, of determining for himself whether the indictment is good or bad. He is unfamiliar with the rules of evidence. Left without the aid of counsel he may be put on trial without a proper charge, and convicted upon incompetent evidence, or evidence irrelevant to the issue or otherwise inadmissible. He lacks both the skill and knowledge adequately to prepare his defense, even though he have a perfect one. He requires the guiding hand of counsel at every step in the proceedings against him. Without it, though he be not guilty, he faces the danger of conviction because he does not know how to establish his innocence.

The court held that when a defendant is subject to the death penalty, is indigent, and cannot make his own defense, the state must provide counsel for him regardless of whether it was requested by the defendant or not.

The right to counsel has subsequently been extended to other criminal trials. Special circumstances (e.g., illiteracy) making it hard or impossible for a defendant to represent himself or herself in a criminal proceeding do not need to be established by a person seeking to have the court appoint counsel (*Gideon v. Wainwright,* 372 U.S. 33 [1963]). Rather, the right to counsel is to be afforded to a defendant who faces a deprivation of life or liberty where imprisonment of six months could be imposed. In *Argersinger v. Hamlin,* 407 U.S. 25 (1972), the court ruled that:

> The Sixth Amendment thus extended the right to counsel beyond its common-law dimensions. But there is nothing in the language of the Amendment, its history, or in the decisions of this Court, to indicate that it was intended to embody a retraction of the right in petty offenses wherein the common law previously did require that counsel be provided. . . . We reject, therefore, the premise that since prosecutions for crimes punishable by imprisonment for less than six months may be tried without a jury, they may also be tried without a lawyer. . . . Under the rule we announce today, every judge will know

when the trial of a misdemeanor starts that no imprisonment may be imposed, even though local law permits it, unless the accused is represented by counsel. He will have a measure of the seriousness and gravity of the offense and therefore know when to name a lawyer to represent the accused before the trial starts. The run of misdemeanors will not be affected by today's ruling. But in those that end up in the actual deprivation of a person's liberty, the accused will receive the benefit of "the guiding hand of counsel" so necessary when one's liberty is in jeopardy.

Convicted defendants often claim that they suffered "ineffective assistance of counsel," which is to say that one's attorney was so poor that it effectively deprived the defendant of their Sixth Amendment right to counsel. Although frequently raised, this claim is nearly impossible to prove, as the standard is not merely whether the outcome would have been different with competent counsel, but whether the counsel was so poor that the entire proceeding was unfair. A lawyer who is outrageously poor is not ineffective, and stratagems that turn out poorly are not ineffective. Successful claims involve attorneys sleeping through trial or neglecting to examine basic evidence.

In *Premo v. Moore*, 562 U.S. ___ (2011), the U.S. Supreme Court was asked to consider if a convicted felon is entitled to habeas corpus relief when he pled guilty to charges of felony murder while relying on the ineffective assistance of counsel. His attorney did not challenge the potentially invalid admission of a confession prior to his plea deal. As the Court notes, to show that an individual was denied effective assistance of counsel, the person must establish both (1) that the lawyer was deficient in performing legal duties and (2) that the deficiency prejudiced the defendant. Federal courts will not "second guess" legal advice or the reasons why a person might accept a plea deal when determining whether to grant habeas relief.

ARRESTS AND THE RIGHT TO COUNSEL

Other instances in which counsel is needed occur when a suspect has been arrested and is being transported by the police without his or her retained counsel present. In *Brewer v. Williams,* 430 U.S. 387 (1977), the defendant was subject to a "Christian burial" speech by officers in the vehicle transporting him back to Des Moines, Iowa, from Davenport.

The defendant had retained counsel who repeatedly told the transporting officers that his client wished to assert his *Miranda* rights. The officers had been asked to respect the defendant's rights and not question him during the 160-mile trip. The Court, in determining that the defendant's *Miranda* rights were violated by the officers who played on his weak psychological state of mind and strong religious beliefs, held that the right to counsel is essential to the retention of the right to remain silent.

BREWER V. WILLIAMS, 430 U.S. 387 (1977)

Opinion by STEWART.

Facts: Williams was convicted of killing a girl, and the U.S. Supreme Court held that the police violated his *Miranda* rights and that statements made to the police while they were transporting him from Davenport to Des Moines, Iowa, were to be suppressed. In a retrial, evidence found at the scene was admitted against Williams even though it had been found by the police as a result of the defendant's statements. The transporting officers were informed by counsel that they were not to talk with the defendant. The Court of Appeals affirmed the District Court's finding that the evidence should not have been admitted at the defendant's trial.

Issue: Did the police violate *Miranda*?

Rationale and Decision: This right, guaranteed by the Sixth and Fourteenth Amendments, is indispensable to the fair administration of our adversary system of criminal justice. Its vital need at the pretrial stage has perhaps nowhere been more succinctly explained than in Mr. Justice Sutherland's memorable words for the Court 44 years ago in *Powell v. Alabama* . . . : "[D]uring perhaps the most critical period of the proceedings against these defendants, that is to say, from the time of their arraignment until the beginning of their trial, when consultation, thorough-going investigation, and preparation were vitally important, the defendants did not have the aid of counsel in any real sense,

although they were as much entitled to such aid during that
period as at the trial itself. . . ."

There can be no doubt in the present case that judicial
proceedings had been initiated against Williams before
the start of the automobile ride from Davenport to Des
Moines. A warrant had been issued for his arrest, he
had been arraigned on that warrant before a judge in a
Davenport courtroom, and he had been committed by the
court to confinement in jail. . . . [T]he State has produced
no affirmative evidence whatsoever to support its claim of
waiver, and, *a fortiori,* it cannot be said that the State has
met its "heavy burden" of showing a knowing and intelligent waiver of . . . Sixth Amendment rights. . . .

Despite Williams' express and implicit assertions of his
right to counsel, Detective Leaming proceeded to elicit
incriminating statements from Williams. Leaming did not
preface this effort by telling Williams that he had a right to
the presence of a lawyer, and made no effort at all to ascertain whether Williams wished to relinquish that right. The
circumstances of record in this case thus provide no reasonable basis for finding that Williams waived his right to the
assistance of counsel. . . . The crime of which Williams was
convicted was senseless and brutal, calling for swift and
energetic action by the police to apprehend the perpetrator
and gather evidence with which he could be convicted. No
mission of law enforcement officials is more important. Yet
"[d]isinterested zeal for the public good does not assure
either wisdom or right in the methods it pursues." . . . The
pressures on state executive and judicial officers charged
with the administration of the criminal law are great,
especially when the crime is murder and the victim a small
child. But it is precisely the predictability of those pressures
that makes imperative a resolute loyalty to the guarantees
that the Constitution extends to us all.

The judgment of the Court of Appeals is affirmed.

It is so ordered.

The extent to which the right to counsel applies to deportation cases is still unclear. In January 2009, the Attorney General in the Bush administration, Michael Mukasey, issued an opinion that immigrants do not have the right to challenge their deportation on the grounds of ineffective assistance of counsel. In June 2009, that opinion was nullified by the Obama administration's Attorney General, Eric Holder, who issued a three-page opinion restating the previous rules regarding assistance of counsel in deportation hearings (see http://www.abajournal.com/ news/immigrants_can_reopen_deportation_cases_if_effective_counsel_ is_denied_ag_h/). In short, ineffective assistance of counsel can impact the decision to deport a person (deportation is a government deprivation, which implicates the Fifth Amendment), and it is a fundamental part of American court processes that people have the opportunity to litigate their claims with effective counsel.

SIXTH AMENDMENT AND PRE- AND POST-INDICTMENT LINEUPS, SHOWUPS, AND PHOTO ARRAYS

When a crime occurs, the police need to determine who might have committed it and whether they have enough information to formalize an arrest. If they do not have clear information to formulate probable cause, then the police will need to continue to investigate to determine who may be charged within the statute of limitations. Time is of the essence in determining who may have committed a crime; the less serious the offense, the less time the police have to make an arrest. For felony offenses, the statute of limitations to bring charges will be several years (depending on state law, although the crime of murder may not have any time limitations). Nonetheless, the longer a crime investigation continues, the greater the likelihood that the crime investigation will go cold and an arrest will not occur. When an unknown individual commits a crime and a victim or witness promptly reports the offense and gives a particularized description of the offender, the police may scan a community to look for the individual who fits the description. The individual can be stopped and detained for investigative purposes. If further investigation leads to probable cause for the officer to believe that the person is the one who is sought, then the person can be arrested.

One method to determine if a person is the one sought pursuant to the call for assistance about a crime is through a lineup. In a lineup, a suspect is asked to join other persons in a line at police headquarters. The victim or witness will view the lineup through a privacy window or see-through mirror and try to identify the person who committed the offense. The lineup does not have to occur on the date of the crime incident, but when the lineup occurs will determine if a suspect has the right to counsel during the lineup. In *Kirby v. Illinois*, 406 U.S. 682 (1972), the court analyzed the right to counsel in regard to pre-indictment lineups.

KIRBY V. ILLINOIS, 406 U.S. 682 (1972)

Opinion by STEWART.

Facts: Two officers stopped Kirby and his companion and asked for their identification. Kirby produced a Social Security card and traveler's checks in the name of Willie Shard. After taking Kirby to the stationhouse, the officers learned that Shard had been robbed. A police car was then dispatched to Shard's place of employment, where it picked up Shard and brought him to the police station. Immediately upon entering the room in the police station where the petitioner and Bean were seated at a table, Shard positively identified them as the men who had robbed him two days earlier. No lawyer was present in the room, and neither Kirby nor his companion had asked for legal assistance or been advised of any right to the presence of counsel. More than six weeks later, the petitioner and Bean were indicted for the robbery of Willie Shard. Upon arraignment, counsel was appointed to represent them, and they pleaded not guilty. At a pretrial hearing a motion to suppress Shard's identification testimony was denied, and at the trial, Shard testified as a witness for the prosecution. He was cross-examined at length regarding the circumstances of his identification of the two defendants and picked out Kirby during the trial as one of the persons who robbed him. The Illinois Supreme Court affirmed the defendant's conviction on appeal.

Issue: Does an individual have the right to counsel during a lineup/showup prior to formal charges being filed (at the pre-indictment stage)?

Rationale and Decision: In *United States v. Wade,* 388 U.S. 218, and *Gilbert v. California,* 388 U.S. 263, this Court held "that a post-indictment pretrial lineup at which the accused is exhibited to identifying witnesses is a critical stage of the criminal prosecution; that police conduct of such a lineup without notice to and in the absence of his counsel denies the accused his Sixth [and Fourteenth] Amendment right to counsel and calls in question the admissibility at trial of the in-court identifications of the accused by witnesses who attended the lineup." . . . Those cases further held that no "in-court identifications" are admissible in evidence if their "source" is a lineup conducted in violation of this constitutional standard. "Only a *per se* exclusionary rule as to such testimony can be an effective sanction," the Court said, "to assure that law enforcement authorities will respect the accused's constitutional right to the presence of his counsel at the critical lineup." . . . In the present case, we are asked to extend the *Wade-Gilbert per se* exclusionary rule to identification testimony based upon a police station showup that took place before the defendant had been indicted or otherwise formally charged with any criminal offense.

We note at the outset that the constitutional privilege against compulsory self-incrimination is in no way implicated here. The *Wade-Gilbert* exclusionary rule . . . stems from a quite different constitutional guarantee—the guarantee of the right to counsel contained in the Sixth and Fourteenth Amendments. Unless all semblance of principled constitutional adjudication is to be abandoned, therefore, it is to the decisions construing that guarantee that we must look in determining the present controversy.

The initiation of judicial criminal proceedings is far from a mere formalism. It is the starting point of our whole system of adversary criminal justice. For it is only then that the government has committed itself to prosecute, and only then that the adverse positions of government and defendant have solidified. It is then that a defendant finds himself faced with the prosecutorial forces of organized society, and immersed in the intricacies of substantive and procedural criminal law. It is this point, therefore, that marks the commencement of the "criminal prosecutions" to which alone the explicit guarantees of the Sixth Amendment are applicable.

In this case, we are asked to import into a routine police investigation an absolute constitutional guarantee historically and rationally applicable only after the onset of formal prosecutorial proceedings. We decline to do so.

What has been said is not to suggest that there may not be occasions during the course of a criminal investigation when the police do abuse identification procedures. Such abuses are not beyond the reach of the Constitution. As the Court pointed out in *Wade* itself, it is always necessary to "scrutinize any pretrial confrontation. . . ." The Due Process Clause of the Fifth and Fourteenth Amendments forbids a lineup that is unnecessarily suggestive and conducive to irreparable mistaken identification. . . .

The judgment is affirmed.

Various critical stages in addition to custodial interrogations include indictment (*United States v. Wade,* 388 U.S. 218 [1967]) and post-indictment interrogation (*Massiah v. United States,* 377 U.S. 201 [1964]), arraignment (*Hamilton v. Alabama,* 368 U.S. 52 [1961]), preliminary hearings (*Coleman v. Alabama,* 399 U.S. 1 [1970]), during trial, and direct appeal from a criminal conviction. A defendant may not have the right to counsel when appearing before a court for a bail or bond hearing the first time; this right depends solely on state law. The ability to be released pending a trial is arguably a critical stage in the criminal justice system because an unrepresented accused might spend a considerable amount of time in jail (see Colbert, 1998).

Problems with Lineups, Showups, and Photo Arrays

Usually officers who are conducting a lineup, showup, or photo array know who the suspect is. Consequently, some researchers argue that the police might inadvertently point out the suspect to the victim or witness. This can be done if the lineup is suggestive (e.g., the suspect is several inches taller than the other persons in the array), if the officer does something during the showing of a photo array (e.g., taps the suspect's photo), or if the officer does a subsequent showing with only the suspect being a repeat face in the photo array or repeat person in the lineup. Eyewitnesses are notoriously inaccurate. The presence of an attorney during a lineup or showup can ensure that officers are not overtly or inadvertently suggesting to witnesses who should be selected. Photo arrays may also be suggestive if a witness has been shown one photo more than once: is the witness selecting the offender, or just remembering the person from a previous viewing? To limit the suggestibility of identification procedures, some police departments are using double-blind processes in which the officers conducting the lineups or showups do not have any connection with the investigation and therefore cannot influence the selection of any particular suspect.

Attorneys Not Required

Officers are not constitutionally required to advise suspects of their right to counsel during criminal investigation; arrest, unless they interrogate the suspect; grand jury proceedings; habeas corpus; or parole or probation proceedings. Be aware that state or federal laws may provide the right to an attorney during one or more of these periods; however, failure to provide counsel will not be a constitutional violation. Officers must *Mirandize* defendants of their right to counsel before interrogation, lineups after filing formal charges, preliminary examination, or arraignment.

Dogs have a stronger sense of smell than humans and have been used in police work for investigative purposes. Dog sniff tests have been used by the police to trace a suspect's movements from a crime scene or after an escape, and to indicate the presence of illicit substances such as explosives and drugs. In recent years, dogs have also been used by some police agencies to identify suspects from trace elements left at crime scenes. In recent years, dog sniff lineups have been called into serious question because of problems associated with handlers who have used questionable tactics in police investigative processes. In Arizona, the Arizona State Supreme Court held one dog handler to be a charlatan. In Texas, the Innocence Project has documented numerous instances in which a dog handler has used inappropriate methods to select a suspect who had been the subject of police suspicion. In some investigations, identification of a suspect by a dog was later found to be flawed after another individual came forward and was subsequently convicted of the crime (Innocence Project, 2009). Currently, the target of an investigation does not have the right to counsel during a dog sniff lineup; indeed, the suspect might not even be present.

CONTEMPORARY ISSUES: GUANTANAMO BAY AND MILITARY TRIBUNALS

In 2002, President Bush established a detention center at Guantanamo Bay to hold "enemy combatants" captured during the War in Afghanistan and Iraq. These detainees have claimed that they should not be tried by military tribunals and should have the right to a fair trial and the right to counsel. In one of the first U.S. Supreme Court cases to be heard on the constitutional rights of Guantanamo detainees (*Hamdi v. Rumsfeld,* 542 U.S. 507 [2004]), the Court held that a detainee could not be held indefinitely without having access to an attorney. In one case, the Bush administration claimed that Yaser Esam Hamdi, an American citizen, was an enemy combatant (and thus could be denied access to counsel), but Hamdi claimed that he was only Osama bin Laden's driver.

HAMDI ET AL. V. RUMSFELD, SECRETARY OF DEFENSE, ET AL., 542 U.S. 507 (2004)

Opinion by O'CONNOR.

Facts: Hamdi was arrested as an enemy combatant (see Chapter 4). He was not specifically charged with a crime and was denied access to legal counsel. The Court of Appeals found that the executive branch should oversee the detention of enemy combatants during wartime.

Issue: Do enemy combatants have a Sixth Amendment right to counsel?

Rationale and Decision: At this difficult time in our Nation's history, we are called upon to consider the legality of the Government's detention of a United States citizen on United States soil as an "enemy combatant" and to address the process that is constitutionally owed to one who seeks to challenge his classification as such. . . . In June 2002, Hamdi's father, Esam Fouad Hamdi, filed the present petition for a writ of habeas corpus under 28 U.S.C. §2241 in the Eastern District of Virginia, naming as petitioners his son and himself as next friend. The elder Hamdi alleges in the petition that he has had no contact with his son since the Government took custody of him in 2001, and that the Government has held his son "without access to legal counsel or notice of any charges pending against him. . . . The habeas petition asks that the court, among other things, (1) appoint counsel for Hamdi. . . . Hamdi asks us to hold that the Fourth Circuit also erred by denying him immediate access to counsel upon his detention and by disposing of the case without permitting him to meet with an attorney. Since our grant of certiorari in this case, Hamdi has been appointed counsel, with whom he has met for consultation purposes on several occasions, and with whom he is now being granted unmonitored meetings. He unquestionably has the right to access to counsel in connection with the proceedings on remand. No further consideration of this issue is necessary at this stage of the case.

The judgment of the United States Court of Appeals for the Fourth Circuit is vacated, and the case is remanded for further proceedings.

It is so ordered.

In *Hamdan v. Rumsfeld*, 548 U.S. 557 (2006), the U.S. Supreme Court also determined that the Bush administration could not create independent military tribunals to try the detainees. The right of defendants to a fair trial in the judicial system is closely tied to the right to counsel. At the time of this printing, at least one detainee has been found guilty in federal court after an open trial.

SUMMARY

In general, a person has a right to counsel in order to ensure that his or her constitutional rights are protected. Counsel is able to assist persons charged with crimes or those detained and waiting to be charged by making sure that their liberty interests are not violated. Counsel can help arrestees by ensuring that their arrests are valid and their rights to a fair trial are protected. The extent of this right has been debated in recent years with the indefinite detainment of persons deemed to be enemy combatants in overseas military detention facilities. The right to counsel does not exist at all stages of a criminal process: A criminal defendant has the right to counsel only at critical stages in the criminal justice process. Critical stages include times when the police have a person in custody and wish to interrogate him or her, when the person is going to be placed in a post-indictment lineup, and when the person is at trial. In addition, the right extends to persons detained indefinitely without formal criminal charges under the assumption that they are enemy combatants.

GLOSSARY

Critical stage in criminal justice process: Critical stages during the criminal justice processes include custodial interrogation, post-indictment lineup, and court processes.

Ineffective assistance of counsel: The claim that one's attorney was so poor that it effectively deprived the defendant of their Sixth Amendment right to counsel. Although frequently raised, this claim is nearly impossible to prove, as the standard is not merely whether the outcome would have been different with competent counsel, but whether the counsel was so poor that the entire proceeding was unfair.

Lineup: A law enforcement method in which a suspect appears in a line along with a number of other individuals to determine whether a witness or victim can identify him or her as the person who committed the crime.

Photo array: Refers to a number of photographs that might have a perpetrator's picture among them; a witness or victim attempts to identify the person who committed the crime by looking at these photographs.

Post-indictment lineup: A police lineup that occurs after a person has been formally charged with a felony.

Pre-indictment lineup: A police lineup that occurs prior to the indictment of a suspect.

Right to counsel: A Sixth Amendment right of an accused to have legal representation at all critical stages during the criminal justice process.

Showup: A method of offender identification in which the witness or victim "informally" sees a suspect close in time to the commission of the offense.

ADDITIONAL READINGS

Colbert, D. (1998). Thirty-five years after Gideon: The illusory right to counsel. *University of Illinois Law Review 1998, 1.*

Engler, R. (2010). Connecting self-representation to civil Gideon: What existing data reveal about when counsel is most needed. *Fordham Law Journal, 37, 37.*

Innocence Project. (2009). "Wrongful Convictions Involving Unvalidated or Improper Forensic Science that Were Later Overturned through DNA Testing." Retrieved on September 20, 2011 at http://www.innocenceproject.org/docs/DNA_Exonerations_Forensic_Science.pdf

Marcus, P. (2009). Why the United States Supreme Court got some (but not a lot) of the Sixth Amendment right to counsel analysis right. *St. Thomas Law Review, 21, 142.*

Raban, O. (2010). On suggestive and necessary identification procedures. *American Journal of Criminal Law, 37.* Available at http://beta.law.uoregon.edu/faculty/ofer/necessaryandsuggestive.pdf

Tinmouth, L. (2009). Note: The fairness of a fair trial: Not guilty pleas and the right to effective assistance of counsel. *Boston College Law Review, 50, 1607.*

Index